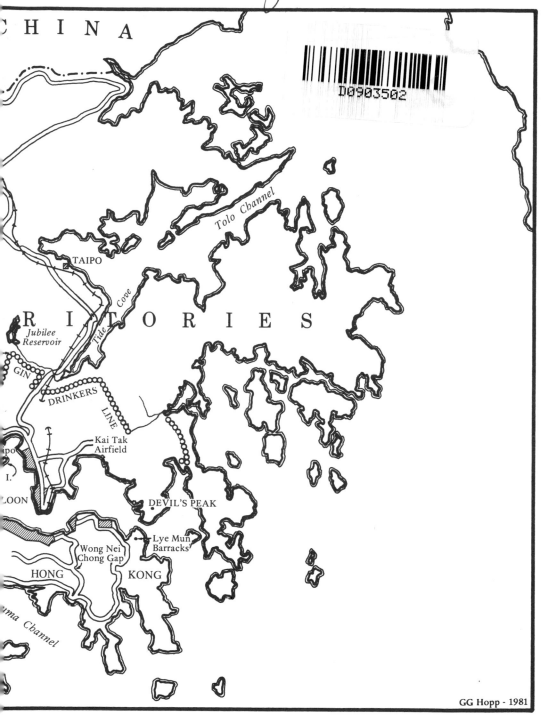

CHINA

Tolo Channel

TAIPO

Tide Cove

RITORIES

Jubilee
Reservoir

GIN

DRINKERS

LINE

Kai Tak
Airfield

ipo

I.

LOON

DEVIL'S PEAK

Lye Mun
Barracks'

Wong Nei
Chong Gap

HONG

KONG

ma Channel

GG Hopp - 1981

No Reason Why

No Reason Why

The Canadian Hong Kong Tragedy
— an examination

by Carl Vincent

Canadian Cataloguing in Publication Data

Vincent, Carl, 1939-
No reason why

Bibliography: p.
Includes index.
ISBN 0-920002-12-9

1. Hong Kong—Siege, 1941. 2. World War,
1939-1945—Hong Kong. 3. World War, 1939-
1945—Canada. 4. Canada—Military policy.
I. Title.
D767.3V54   940.54'25   C81-090137-4

© Canada's Wings, Inc. 1981
Box 393, Stittsville, Ontario
Canada K0A 3G0

Cover art by Don Connolly
Printed by The Intelligencer, Belleville, Ontario

Contents

Foreword

In the very early hours of Boxing Day, 1941, a few hundred exhausted Canadian and British soldiers pulled themselves up from their position amongst the scrub and rocks of Stanley Peninsula on the island of Hong Kong, and stumbled back into that tiny segment of land that was the only part of the Crown Colony not yet in Japanese hands to await their captors.

These Canadians were all that was left of the 1st Battalion, Royal Rifles of Canada. The previous afternoon the remnants of the 1st Battalion, Winnipeg Grenadiers had become captives of the Japanese when the rest of the garrison had capitulated. Despite the hopelessness of the situation, however, the British Brigadier commanding the forces on Stanley had demanded a copy of the surrender order in writing before he would agree to give in. One company of the Royal Rifles had celebrated their Christmas Day by suffering 70% casualties in the counter-attack that, for idiotic futility, ranks with the Charge of the Light Brigade.

By the time the last Royal Rifleman had passed into Japanese hands, 290 Canadians had already died in Hong Kong. A further 267 were to die in the course of an incredibly brutal captivity. Of the 1418 remaining members of the force who lived to return to Canada there were few who had not suffered physically and mentally from their ordeal. The survivors still bear the scars.

What were these soldiers doing there? Why were almost two thousand men, most of them either from Quebec City and the towns and farms of Eastern Quebec or from the city and suburbs of Winnipeg, fighting and dying thousands of miles from home in the hopeless and unsung defence of an unfamiliar island off the Chinese coast?

On the surface the story is simple. The British government, in the face of a possible war with Japan, wished to strengthen the garrison of the colony of Hong Kong and asked Canada to send two battalions. Canada agreed and these troops arrived shortly before the Japanese attack. With the rest of the garrison they participated in a gallant but hopeless defence until Hong Kong surrendered on 25 December 1941. Their despatch to Hong Kong had attracted little attention, and the fall of the colony was just one more disaster in the black months after Japan entered the war.

The survivors had not endured their captivity long, however, before the first rumbling occurred on the home front. Led by the prominent Ontario Progressive Conservative George Drew, accusations began to be levelled at the government that the men who fought at Hong Kong had been poorly trained and equipped. This was the kindling spark, and as the prisoners of war started to drop like flies in the Japanese camps, the politicians back in Canada commenced to jockey for position, the Opposition seeking to make political capital out of the government's presumed negligence and the government attempting to deny or belittle the charges. The only positive reaction by the government to these accusations was the appointment of a Royal Commission in February 1942 to investigate the matter. The Commissioner was the Chief Justice of Canada, Sir Lyman Duff. An enormous quantity of evidence was heard by the Royal Commission between 2 March and 31 March 1942. Duff's findings, tabled in June 1942, did not censure the government to any degree and hence pleased nobody but the Liberals. There was a minor furore but the government simply stood fast and allowed the commotion to die down. The question was raised again in 1948 after the British report on Hong Kong operations had been released but interest soon dissipated.

The controversy has flared up periodically, particularly when the surviving veterans have made attempts to have their compensation increased as a result of the excessive hardships to which they had been subjected. In addition to domestic aspersions cast at their training and fighting ability, the men of the Canadian Hong Kong Force have suffered at the hands of British official reports of the fighting and British "popular" historians, some of whom either imply or directly state that the Canadians' poor training and low morale rendered them worse than useless on the battlefield and a hindrance rather than an asset to the defence.

There has never been an attempt to create a detailed and coherent account of the Canadian involvement with the defence of Hong Kong. It was as a reaction to the melange of myth, rumour, unfounded accusations, one-sided accounts, and official whitewash that currently exists that I was impelled to write this book. The number of questions it seeks to answer is legion. Did Britain and/or Canada realize that the defence of Hong Kong was hopeless? Why did Canada agree to send troops? Was there any deceit involved? Why were these particular battalions chosen? Were they as badly trained as has been insinuated? How did the Canadians *really* do in battle? Have they simply been used as scapegoats by the British? Have they been given all that rough a deal since the war? The questions multiply.

This book is based to a great extent on primary sources. I believe that in this particular case the large numbers of contemporary documents provide a better basis for a complete and accurate narrative than any recollection of events that took place forty years ago. I have made the account as logical, consecutive, and clear as I could and have indicated my sources as fully as possible.

In preparing this book it has been impossible to avoid becoming emotionally involved with the narrative, and if, on occasion, I have let my feelings show, I can only crave the reader's indulgence.

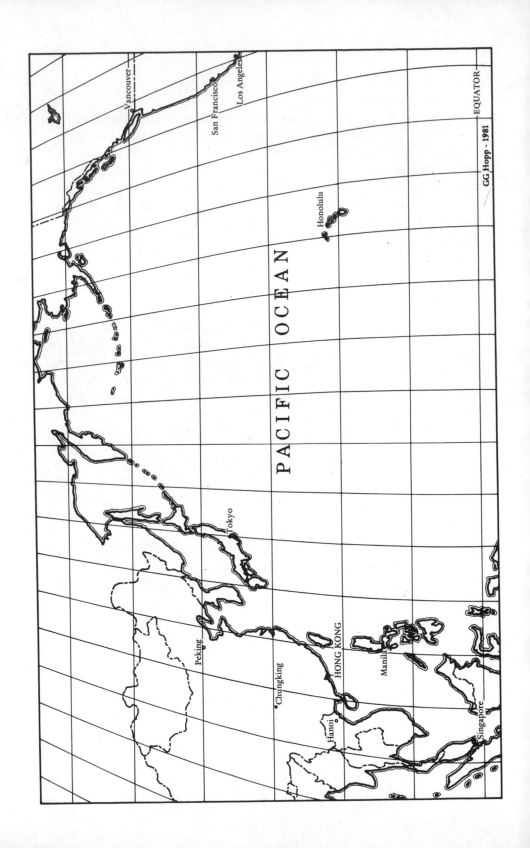

PACIFIC OCEAN

Vancouver

San Francisco

Los Angeles

Honolulu

Tokyo

Peking

Chungking

HONG KONG

Hanoi

Manila

Singapore

EQUATOR

GG Hopp - 1981

Naval Base to Outpost
——defence policy for Hong Kong

The colony of Hong Kong was, in 1941, one of the smallest but most valuable jewels in the British Empire's crown. The actual island of Hong Kong had been ceded to the United Kingdom by China in 1842 as part of the spoils of the Opium War, and it is ironic that exactly one century later it was to return, albeit temporarily, to Asiatic hands. When it first came into British possession it was practically uninhabited and of little obvious value. It was, however, in a very strategic location for trade with all of southern China. Under British rule and law Hong Kong rapidly developed as a trading port in its own right and as a base for the commercial and military exploitation of one of the richest areas in China. In 1860 the closest portion of the mainland, the Kowloon Peninsula, and its adjacent islands were ceded to the British, and in 1898 some 360 square miles of territory inland from Kowloon, which became known as the New Territories, was leased from the Chinese government for ninety-nine years, that is, until 1997.

During the palmy years of the *Pax Britannica,* Hong Kong was the headquarters and main base of the China Station of the Royal Navy. Even when there was no real military threat there were abundant British political and commercial interests in East Asia that frequently required protection or reinforcement. Hong Kong was therefore maintained in a reasonably high state of defensive preparedness, while troops from its garrison could be conveyed where they were most needed by the long arm of the Royal Navy.

This state of affairs was to last until the end of the First World

War. With the added protection to British interests in the Far East afforded by the Anglo-Japanese Alliance of 1904, the Royal Navy was able, during the 1914-18 conflict, to reduce its China Squadron to a minimum. However, by the end of the "War to End Wars", Great Britain was becoming a little embarrassed by her aggressive *protegé* and was establishing stronger ties with the United States. In the face of the increasing likelihood that the Anglo-Japanese Alliance would shortly be terminated, a 1921 War Office study concluded that "there was no chance of making Hong Kong sufficiently secure against attack."[1] Therefore Britain turned to Singapore, where, through the 1920's and 1930's, they constructed a massive and well-protected naval base, in fits and starts due to periodic economic problems, changes in government, and disarmament conferences. The Washington naval treaties of 1922 which, among other provisions, prevented the signatories from upgrading their existing bases in the Northwest Pacific, further reinforced the naval importance of Singapore, and diminished that of Hong Kong.

Despite this the Royal Navy still maintained a moderately strong presence at Hong Kong. Normally stationed there were an aircraft carrier, a cruiser squadron, and destroyer and submarine flotillas. The colony's fixed defences were still formidable though they could not be expanded or modernized, while its infantry garrison usually consisted of four battalions. In 1936 the Hong Kong defence scheme stated that, despite the gloomy prognostication of the 1921 study, "Hong Kong is . . . a strategic point vital to the conduct of our Fleet, Army, and Air Force."[2]

The first attempt to examine Hong Kong in light of the need for defence against a possible Japanese attack appears to have been made in 1935. The Inspector of Fixed Defences, General Barron, made a personal inspection of the defences and submitted a report. Barron stated that the defence of Hong Kong posed a different problem from other British defended ports abroad for several reasons. It was open to attack from the rear either across the frontier or by a landing in the Leased Territories. Its great distance from the United Kingdom meant an exceptionally long period before relief could be expected to arrive. Barron described the Hong Kong defences as "deplorable" and stated that the island of Hong Kong would be "easy prey . . . and that in the face of a determined attack by land or sea the fortress could not hold out even for the arbitrary period before relief." Barron considered that because of the irregular coastline the only practical defence line on the mainland was one just three miles from Kowloon which stretched from Junk Bay on the right via Razor Hill to Tide Cove, and from there along the Shing Mun River to Smugglers Ridge and Gin Drinkers Bay. The defence line eventually established along the evocatively named terrain was to become known as the Inner Line or, more familiarly, the Gin Drinkers Line after the bay on its left flank. General Barron recommended an extensive modernization program for the fixed defences, the construction of a system of pill-boxes and splinter-proof dugouts along the Gin Drinkers Line, and an increase in the garrison from four to six infantry battalions.[3] His plan was adopted, with some modification, by the Committee of Imperial Defence in January 1936. The Committee noted, in passing, that three of the main problems in defending Hong Kong were the presence of large numbers of Chinese, the reliance on imported food, and the fact that approximately half of the island's water supply was piped from the mainland.[4]

With the start of the Sino-Japanese war in 1937 the defence of Hong Kong came under increasingly close scrutiny. The Chiefs of Staff made an appreciation of the situation in June 1937 and came to the conclusion that "the retention of Hong Kong is *not* essential for the security of Singapore, ie it should be treated as a valuable outpost only."[5]

In view of the lapsing of the Washington Treaty and the resulting need to strengthen the Hong Kong base the General Officer Commanding, China (in charge of British troops in Hong Kong and other detachments actually in China at Shanghai and Tientsin), General A.W. Bartholomew, had prepared a report on the defence of Hong Kong, which he submitted in July 1937. In this "Report on the 'Unrestricted' Defence of Hong Kong . . ." he argued that 15-inch coast defence guns, a division of infantry, and an air garrison of five squadrons would be necessary. General Bartholomew, who seems to have been the only realistic Hong Kong Commander in the years immediately before the Japanese attack, believed that at least a division was necessary to hold any portion of the mainland, and he queried the wisdom of making any resistance at all to a mass attack.[6] He was subsequently to state that with his current garrison "the chances, however, of effecting a prolonged resistance seem slight."[7]

Through 1937 and 1938 the defence of Hong Kong was being considered by the Chiefs of Staff. With the feeling in 1937 being that it would be useless to lock up eight or nine battalions in Hong Kong, the suggestion was made that the garrison be reduced to two battalions, which should be sufficient for symbolic prestige and adequate to maintain law and order.[8] This reduction was never carried out, however, because in the face of the subsequent Japanese aggression it was felt that such a move would be seen as weakness on the part of the United Kingdom. In July 1938 a sub-committee of the Chiefs of Staff prepared a policy draft on Hong Kong defence which was to form the basis for defence plans until just before the Japanese assault on the colony. After reviewing the pros and cons of evacuation this draft noted that the defence of Hong Kong presented serious problems, including the absence of an adequate airfield and the lack of a suitable position for a defence line. Also, the Japanese occupation of southern China would render the possibility of a successful defence even more unlikely. When it was considered that Japanese artillery near the Gin Drinkers Line could bring the harbour under fire, and that the scale of air attack was likely to be high, it was not recommended that Hong Kong be held as either a major or minor naval base. The defence of Hong Kong should therefore concern itself solely with denying the use of the harbour to the Japanese. Four battalions would be adequate for this. They could fight a rear guard action from the frontier to the Gin Drinkers Line, conduct a limited defence of the line, and then retire to the island, accepting the loss of a great deal of naval equipment and facilities as inevitable. A stand was not to be made on the Gin Drinkers Line because, in view of its length (10½ miles), a division would be required to hold it. For this reason and because of expense, work on it was to stop immediately. The garrison was to remain at four battalions instead of the six authorized in 1936.[9]

British policy regarding Hong Kong had by this time evolved to the point where the colony was treated as an outpost—that is, a fortress whose function was to delay the enemy—and it continued to be regarded officially as an outpost right up to the time of Japanese attack.

When Canadian-born Major General A.E. Grasett succeeded Bartholomew as General Officer Commanding, China in November 1938, he was fully briefed on the new defence policy and warned to keep the decision not to make a stand on the Gin Drinkers Line a secret.[10] Grasett had a low opinion of the fighting quality of the Japanese Army. This opinion led him to consider the War Office decision not to make a stand on the Gin Drinkers Line an error.

Accordingly, he attempted throughout his Hong Kong appointment to obtain one or two extra battalions for the Hong Kong garrison, and his perseverance in this crusade after his appointment had ceased was responsible for the involvement of Canadians in the battle for Hong Kong. His first attempt was made in a report dated 1 May 1939 when he stated that if reinforcements could be made available through the evacuation of troops from North China or elsewhere, the additional battalions would be employed on the mainland to stiffen resistance on the Inner Line of defence. However somebody at the War Office was obviously not convinced. On the bottom of this report was written in ink: "We have cabled him [Grasett] to say that this extra battalion, even if available, should not be allowed to change his mind as to policy, ie, no undue holding of mainland."11

There were no major changes in either policy or actual military presence at Hong Kong until June 1940 when France capitulated, Italy entered the war and Britain and the Commonwealth stood alone. Britain would now have to maintain a large Mediterranean fleet, and ships of the Royal Navy from all around the world were recalled to provide it. Almost every unit on the China Station sailed west, and the once-proud China Squadron was a pale shadow of its former self. The altered war situation meant that naval, air, and military reinforcements for the Far East would become much more difficult to provide and their passage east would not be particularly easy. In addition, Japan had begun to flex her muscles, a fact that was not lost on British planners. In late October 1940 the Chiefs of Staff Committee on the Far East submitted a very interesting document which translated the political situation into military terms. After noting that Japan's long-term aim was to exclude Western powers from the Far East, the Committee predicted that her immediate aim was "likely to be the exclusion of British influence from China and Hong Kong." The Committee then stated that the British garrisons in North China (Tientsin and Shanghai), being strategically useless and in a tactically hopeless position, should be withdrawn. Turning to Hong Kong, the Committee reported:

> Hong Kong is not a vital interest and the garrison could not long withstand Japanese attack. Even if we had a strong fleet in the Far East it is doubtful whether Hong Kong could be held now that the Japanese are firmly established on the mainland of China, and we could not use it as an advanced naval base.

After repeating that Hong Kong was an outpost, the Committee recommended that if a general settlement became possible with Japan, Hong Kong should be demilitarized for a suitable *quid pro quo.* In any case, "we do not recommend that our garrisons in North China or Hong Kong should be reinforced in any circumstances."[12]

The precarious position of Hong Kong was also recognized by the Admiralty. In the standing orders for the British merchant fleet in case of war with Japan the Admiralty advised: "Ships between Singapore and Japan proceed Singapore if possible, otherwise to Philippine Islands. Ships not to proceed Hong Kong or ports in British Borneo unless no other course open to them."[13]

To counteract this grimly realistic viewpoint, a curious redirection with regard to Hong Kong was occurring in British military circles actually in the Far East. The new Commander-in-Chief the Far East, Air Chief Marshal Sir Robert Brooke-Popham, had arrived in Malaya in October 1940, and at once had begun to take a more optimistic view of the British position in the area. In late December or early January he had visited Hong Kong, where the General Officer Commanding, Major General Grasett, also was optimistic about the possibility of successfully resisting a Japanese attack.

Grasett does not appear to have convinced Brooke-Popham of the ultimate defencibility of Hong Kong, but he did make the point that reinforcing the garrison would improve the defence capabilities of the colony and would have a desirable political effect. Brooke-Popham wrote to his superiors in early January 1941. His first paragraph stated: "Policy for defence of Hong Kong in event of war must remain unchanged viz defence of island for longest period *in hope that situation may so develop that relief may be effected* [author's italics]." Brooke-Popham then listed the main arguments against reinforcement: the need for troops in Malaya was greater, the stronger the Hong Kong garrison the greater the loss if it fell, and finally that "we have *no good reason for basing plans on probability of relief* [author's italics]." Following this he pointed out the arguments for sending reinforcements: the repercussions from an early fall would be great, reinforcement would boost Chinese morale, and it would be in line with the policy of firmness toward Japan. Because of these factors, stated Brooke-Popham, "I propose to increase the garrison from four regular infantry battalions to first five and then six battalions, as soon as I judge one or two battalions can be released from Malaya by additional battalions from India though these might be of lower standard of training."[14]

This proposal was sent by the Chiefs of Staff to General Ismay, who was Winston Churchill's personal Chief of Staff and Military Secretary, and who passed it on to the Prime Minister. Churchill's reply to Ismay showed, in no uncertain terms, that he wholeheartedly agreed with the policy his Chiefs of Staff had maintained till that date:

> This is all wrong. If Japan goes to war with us there is not the slightest chance of holding Hong Kong or relieving it. It is most unwise to increase the loss we shall suffer there. Instead of increasing the garrison it ought to be reduced to a symbolical scale. Any trouble arising there must be dealt with at the Peace conference after the war. We must avoid frittering away our resources on untenable positions. Japan will think long before declaring war on the British Empire, and whether there are two or six battalions at Hong Kong will make no difference to her choice. I wish we had fewer troops there, but to move any would be noticeable and dangerous.[15]

At the next Chiefs of Staff meeting on 8 January 1941 Brooke-Popham's proposal was considered, along with Churchill's memo. On 10 January the Chief of the Imperial General Staff recommended that Hong Kong should not be reinforced, but that the official "period before relief" be increased from 90 to 130 days. This did not mean that it was expected to relieve the fortress after this time but simply that its reserves of food and ammunition should be increased. The Chiefs of Staff also re-examined the air attack scale predicted for Hong Kong. In 1938 this had been assessed by the Committee for Imperial Defence as frequent heavy and medium attacks by land-based aircraft. Since then the Japanese had obtained at least two more airfields within 100 miles of Hong Kong and probably more. It was now estimated that "the scale of air attack on Hong Kong would be something like the heaviest imaginable."[16]

When the Chiefs of Staff communicated their reply to the Commander-in-Chief Far East on 14 January 1941, they minced no words. No reinforcements were to be allowed:

> We view Hong Kong as an undesirable military committment but demilitarization is not now possible [due to the political effect on China and Japan] . . . . an increase of the regular infantry garrison from four to six regular battalions would unlikely influence . . . the Japanese and could not affect the ultimate result. It would, however, increase the loss should the fortress fall. As you say, we have no good reason for basing plans on a relief of the garrison being possible.[17]

Brooke-Popham was not easily rebuffed. On 19 January he reiterated his pleas. This time he reasoned that military operations might be hampered in the event of an attack because of the probable necessity of using troops to aid the police in dealing with the large Chinese population. One battalion was now allotted to the mainland, but if this allocation was raised to three battalions the time factor of the delaying action would be increased by six. The two extra battalions would, in addition, allow reserves for relief of the soldiers in the pill-boxes who were now suffering from malaria. Turning to strategy, Brooke-Popham stated that now that the Australians were reinforcing Singapore it was not a question of cutting losses, but of retaining places for future *offensive* operations![18]

The Chiefs of Staff examined this second request. They concluded that:

1. admittedly the 3600 police then in Hong Kong could not control the Chinese, but an additional two battalions would not markedly improve the situation;

2. the Japanese would soon learn the exact scale of reinforcements and plan accordingly; and

3. as far as keeping bases was concerned the Committee did not consider that Hong Kong could hold out for 130 days. It would be undesirable and unreasonable to expect the United States Navy to relieve it, and it was unlikely that the British Fleet could relieve it within 130 days.[19]

On 25 January 1941 the Air Ministry passed on this negative response to Brooke-Popham's request.[20] The subject was to lie dormant for another eight months. Unfortunately for Canada, it was then resurrected.

Yellow Peril
—awareness of the Japanese menace

In a study of any aspect of the war in the Pacific, one question that constantly arises is, how much of Japan's intentions did the Western powers know, and how much ought they to have known? This is especially pertinent given the fact that the first 100 days in the East were ones of unrelieved disaster for the Allies, and the subsequent course of the war was determined by the need to fight back from a long range.

In the case of the fall of Hong Kong, the question of how much the Canadian government knew or ought to have known in September 1941 was one of the major points examined in the hearings of the 1942 Royal Commission set up to investigate the sending of Canadian troops to Hong Kong. It also became a major issue when the Hong Kong controversy was re-opened in 1948. It is an important point, for the government leaders testified that the apparent unlikelihood of imminent war was a major factor in their decision to send troops to reinforce the colony. One may go on from this to ask whether the Canadian government should have realised that war with Japan, whether imminent or not, was a strong possibility, and given this, whether or not it was wise to reinforce Hong Kong.

The sources of information available to the Canadian government were varied. The major source for most members of the government was probably the public actions of Japan herself, as reported by the press. Canada had a legation in Tokyo which, of course, sent many reports back to the Department of External Affairs. There were also sources of information from returning businessmen, missionaries, and officers, which perhaps were not studied as closely as they might have been. Finally the Canadian government had access to almost all of the information available to the government of the United Kingdom. Military Intelligence was exchanged between the War Office and the Canadian Department of National Defence, while the British Secretary of State for the Dominions kept the Secretary of State for External Affairs informed on high level diplomatic developments. A connection with the United States prior to December 1941, via the Joint Board of Defence, does not seem to have been a route for information regarding Japan. United States Intelligence about the Far East reaching Canada invariably came via London.

When the decision to reinforce Hong Kong was taken by the Canadian government, Japan had been a major industrial power for over three decades. A closed society prior to 1857, Japan had since become the most modernized country in the Far East. In her foreign policy, however, she soon began to show a willingness to resort to force which disconcerted those who had earlier applauded her drive for prosperity. Shortly after the First World War Japan began to make ominous noises to China, demanding concessions in trade and even territorial rights. These external developments were matched by an increasing internal domination of Japan by the Army.

The long range plans of the Japanese were most succinctly presented in the famous "Tanaka memorial" of 1927. Supposedly written by the Japanese Prime Minister, Baron Tanaka, in 1927 and presented to the Emperor, this paper has often been called a forgery. Nevertheless, with hindsight, it can certainly be seen to have been very accurate. The memorial began with the proposition that Japan must expand or die, because without the raw materials she needed to feed her industry, Japan would be slowly strangled by the other Great Powers. The key to this expansion was seen to be China. With China bent to Japanese will, the whole Far East would eventually fall under the hegemony of Japan, which would thus be guaranteed the resources she needed. The other powers could be excluded from the region and further advances into India, Russia, and Australia could be taken at opportune times.

Such a document might, with reason, have been dismissed as nonsense in 1927, but in 1931 Japan began to put her plans into effect, starting with Manchuria. A minor incident on the Manchurian Railway was the excuse for Japan to intervene, and the puppet regime of Manchoukou was set up, in contravention of the censure of the

League of Nations. The Sino-Japanese war began in earnest in 1937, when another minor incident (this time in Peking) triggered a Japanese invasion of North China. Hostilities soon spread to Central China, and both Shanghai and Nanking were occupied in late 1937. The latter, then the capital of Chiang Kai Shek's government, was the scene of an incredibly barbaric occupation by Japanese troops, which did much to alienate public opinion outside Japan, especially in the United States.

Even after this China refused to negotiate and the Chinese government retired to Chungking to continue the fight. The Japanese began to realise that they might have bitten off more than they could chew, as Chinese troops, beaten in almost every encounter, simply retired further into the vast interior and lived to fight another day.

The next stage of the war occurred when Japanese troops landed at Bias Bay on the coast of South China in October of 1938 and quickly took Canton. With this campaign the Japanese came into possession of the whole coastline of China, a situation which they felt would force China to the bargaining table. Another effect of this campaign was to place Japanese troops within 20 miles of Kowloon and Hong Kong Island.

Paralleling these military ventures were developments inside Japan. A constant stream of propaganda flowed from the government-controlled Japanese press, emphasizing the need for Japan to break the power of the West in the Pacific area. It was stressed that the Japanese people had a sacred mission to restore Asia to the Asians and to establish a "Greater East Asia Co-Prosperity Sphere" where the Asiatic races could develop their economies in harmony, free from the domination of the Western powers. Japanese society became more and more rigid, and those sections of the population concentrated in capital and labour who argued for a *rapprochement* with the West were gradually silenced. The military, and particularly the Army, gained an ascendency over Japanese political life which precluded any possibility of liberalization. It was soon accepted as axiomatic that Japan must assert her "rights" in Asia, with force if necessary. "With very few and trifling exceptions the whole nation is behind the present ideas of expansion."[1]

The Japanese attempt to impose a new order on Asia was, of course, contrary to American and British interests. For many years both countries had affirmed an "open door" policy toward China which they were desirous of maintaining. In addition, Japanese naval control of the Pacific was a prospect which Britain at least could not afford to ignore, as it would imperil not only New Zealand and Australia, but India as well, and hence the life's-blood of the Empire. Shortly after the First World War the United Kingdom began to take a closer look at defence requirements in the Far East. It was at this time that it was realised that Hong Kong could not be successfully defended, and the decision was taken to make Singapore the military and naval cornerstone of British power in the Far East.

While the Singapore base was nearing completion and the state of Hong Kong defence was still being discussed, Japan continued her southward thrusts. In March 1939 Japan seized the Spratley Islands, southwest of Indo-China, in the middle of a minor dispute over them in which Britain and France were also involved. These islands had little military value, but the action reiterated Japan's methods of diplomacy. When, in June 1939, Japan acquired the large island of Hainan, 300 miles south of Hong Kong, "The isolation of the Colony was well-nigh complete".[2] Japan was definitely seen as the enemy by this time, and the British Chiefs of Staff concluded that possibly "The first intimation that we should receive that Japan has joined Germany and Italy against us would be an attack on Hong Kong."[3]

Japan had already joined Germany and Italy on the philosophical level. Japan was not strictly Fascist in the European model, but many of the ingredients were there—nationalism, militarism, a strong contingent of secret police, and, especially, a virulent hatred of communism. In 1936 Japan, Germany, and Italy signed the Anti-Comintern Pact, an essentially toothless treaty, but one which nevertheless affirmed ties of kindred feeling between the three countries. This is not to say they were all good friends—they were not—but on their basic approach to foreign affairs, the German ideas of *lebensraum* were similar to Japan's "Co-Prosperity Sphere", and they could look on each other's ambitions with sympathy, particularly as their different "spheres" were very far apart.

The beginnings of the Second World War in many ways increased the tension in the Far East. It became much more likely that Japan would attack, yet the basic British defence policy did not change. All through the so-called phony war "the cornerstone of our strategy [was] the despatch to the Far East of a fleet of sufficient strength to bring Japanese Fleet to action."[4] The United Kingdom could still envisage this as long as she could rely on France safeguarding the Mediterranean with her fleet.

The big change came about with the fall of France and the entry of Italy into the war. The immediate military effect was that Britain now had to maintain naval control of the Mediterranean as well as the Atlantic, and thus had no fleet for the Pacific. The "cornerstone of our strategy" was no longer applicable. The immediate political effect was that Japan began to make aggressive noises. On 20 June, 1940, the Canadian *Chargé d'Affaires* in Tokyo warned the government that Japan might take advantage of the European situation.[5] This was confirmed on 29 June 1940 by the statement of Mr. Arita, the Japanese Foreign Minister which redirected pressure toward French Indo-China. In Japan, however, Arita's statement was construed by some Japanese being too soft on Britain and the Netherlands' East Indies and was considerably criticized. The Japanese were hardly being soft on the British—by late June they were pressing for the withdrawal of the Shanghai garrison, the closing of the Burma Road to China, and the closing of the Hong Kong border. Extremists and younger Army officers were clamouring for active collaboration with the Germans.

These extremists soon forced a showdown with the Yonai government whose fall in mid-July showed the power of both the German Ambassador (rumoured to have a big finger in the pie) and the Army. The more pro-Axis Konoye government took over. On 26 July the Chief of the Canadian General Staff warned the War Committee that "Japanese expansionist ideas were to the south."[6]

Canada became embroiled in a minor way with Japan in September, when the Canadian Pacific ship *Empress of Asia* was bombed by a Japanese patrol, who claimed they thought it was the target ship on which they were practising. Four Chinese servants were injured, two seriously. As the *Empress* was the largest ship in Japanese waters at the time and was flying the Union Jack, and as visibility that day was exceptional (over 50 km) few believed it an accident. The Japanese stuck to their story, though they apologized and offered compensation. In view of the incredible record of airmen of all nations throughout the Second World War bombing friendly ships despite distinctive appearance, adequate identification markings and perfect visibility, it may well have been a genuine mistake.

September also saw major developments on the diplomatic and military fronts. Japan applied pressure to the hapless and helpless Vichy French colony of Indo-China and obtained permission to build and man airbases in the north. The Japanese Director of Military

Intelligence told the British Military Attache at the time that "it was a matter of pure indifference to the Japanese Army whether or not we re-opened the Burma Road, since if we re-opened it the Japanese would bomb it out of existence."[7]

In early September the Foreign Ministry of Japan was also shaken up, with 5 ambassadors and 19 ministers being recalled. The Vice-Minister of Foreign Affairs announced that this reflected a new policy of "government by real he-men . . . we intend to build up an iron Foreign Staff."[8] The Canadian *Chargé d'Affaires* reported that "the shake-up was brought about by Army influence", and was designed to force "the gradual disappearance of those with liberal ideology".[9] Perhaps the most ominous of the new appointments was that of Lieutenant General Tatekawa to the USSR. He believed in strengthening Tokyo/Berlin/Rome ties while becoming friendly toward the Soviet Union.

The new policy was soon put into concrete form. On 27 September 1940, Japan, Italy, and Germany signed the Tripartite Pact. The Pact was designed, among other things, to keep the United States out of war but its actual effect was to make public opinion in that country even more hostile to the Axis. Nevertheless, Japan had signed a definite defensive treaty with the two enemies of the West. On his way home Foreign Minister Matsuoka stopped off in Moscow and, with Hitler's knowledge, signed a Non-Aggression Pact with the USSR. The stage was now set for the Foreign Minister to "press on with just as much of a southern expansion policy as he thought he could get away with."[10] In October 1940 the Japanese Ambassador to the USSR was given wide powers to negotiate with the Russians on many topics which had proved to be stumbling blocks in the past. The stronger Russo-Japanese relations grew, the greater the danger to the south.

The United States finally began to react to the threat. The Secretary of State, Cordell Hull, made it plain to the British Ambassador in October that from then on the United States would take a very tough stand with Japan.[11] The Commonwealth countries also began to work out a comprehensive policy involving sanctions against Japan.

On December 24, 1940 the Dominions Office sent a telegram to External Affairs containing an appreciation of the situation in Japan. It noted two main currents within Japanese politics. The radical nationalists, the group presently on top, were totalitarian, pro-Axis, and in favour of an arrangement with the Soviets. The second faction, reactionary nationalists, were more anti-Russian. Although they were anti-West as well, they were more willing to compromise for the time being. (A useful terminology is to call them the "Strike South" and "Strike North" factions.) The Strike North group were represented in their clearest form in the Kwantung (Manchurian) Army. According to this appreciation of the situation, Japan appeared to be cooperating more and more with Germany, possibly because she wanted Germany's help "when and if the time comes for further developments in the south."[12] In the meantime Japan was slowly infiltrating into the south. In late November it had been reported to the War Committee of the Canadian Cabinet that Japanese forces were in virtual control of Indo-China. The naval and air strategical advantages accruing to them from this position would be hard to overestimate. The British stopped all trade to Japan in retaliation.[13]

In late January 1941, Canada and the United Kingdom began to make arrangements with Argentina to act as their "protecting power" in the event of war with Japan. It was also reported to the Canadian Government that the United States and United Kingdom were to hold talks regarding a common defence policy in the Far East, to which the Dominions and the Dutch were to be invited.[14]

Relations between the United Kingdom and Japan became even further strained in January over the use of the Japanese flag by German raiders and the Japanese provisioning of German ships sheltering in Japanese waters. It was finally being recognized that a crisis could be expected in the Far East. According to notes made for Prime Minister Mackenzie King in February 1941, the "possible first move would be Japanese demand for the surrender of Hong Kong."[15] The danger in the area was repeated in several long memoranda sent from London to Ottawa. One of 7 February 1941 said that the British and Americans were now closely involved in talks regarding the Japanese menace and the means of dealing with it. Both governments agreed that a tough stance was necessary.[16] Another 10 days later noted that Japan was moving south on the diplomatic front. Militarily, their occupation of Indo-China and their influence in Thailand posed a grave threat to both Singapore and Malaya.[17]

Throughout most of 1941 Japan blew hot and cold and played a war of nerves. The embargo imposed by the Commonwealth and United States had gone into effect. On 23 April 1941 it was reported to the Canadian Government that the export of copper, nickel, zinc, lead, antimony, cadmium, iron, and steel to Japan had been stopped.

The Japanese ambassador to Canada was said to be indignant.[18]

At a meeting of the War Committee of the Canadian Cabinet on 13 May, it was stated that Japan was "unshaken in her determination to stand with the Axis Powers". At this session there was also a discussion of Canada's war role so far. Canadian troops had not yet fired a shot, morale was slipping, and public interest was slackening.[19]

In an appreciation of the situation sent from London to Ottawa for the perusal of the Prime Minister, it was stated that the United States attitude was something of a deterrant to Japan, but that the threat of attack was still great.[20] The British were evidently undecided though, because a new set of telegrams read to the War Committee on 3 June 1941 stated that an early war with Japan was now unlikely.[21]

The opening of hostilities between Russia and Germany on 22 June 1941 made the prediction of Japan's actions even more difficult. The well-known Japanese hatred of Russia made war between those countries likely, yet this would be an aberration from Japan's long-standing southward-oriented policy. A memo prepared on 23 June 1941 by Dr. H.L. Keenleyside for the Under Secretary of External Affairs, Norman Robertson, discussed the position. Keenleyside concluded that, all things considered, a Japanese attack on Russia was unlikely, despite the potential prizes. ". . . it would seem rather more reasonable to expect that Japan would take advantage of Russian preoccupation with Germany to hold her continental boundaries with a minimum strength and to direct all her energies to increasing the tempo of southern advance."[22]

Reasonably enough, British opinion on Japanese intentions was affected by the outbreak of war between Germany and Russia. The British government informed the Canadian government in July that they believed that "Japan's early entry into war could now be expected. The United States was of the same opinion . . ."[23] The Prime Minister also received a memo from the Department of External Affairs warning of imminent war with Japan. The direction was unknown, but the best guess was southwest through Siam and Indo-China.[24] During the summer and fall of 1941 the War Committee of the Canadian Cabinet was kept constantly informed of the diplomatic and military situation in the Far East.

At this time the various governments with interests in the Pacific area were holding discussions of the situation in relation to Japan. The attitude of the American and British governments toward Japan was becoming more strict. At the end of the summer the United

States warned Japan that any further aggression would lead to hostilities. In Canada the War Committee of the cabinet was discussing plans for the evacuation of Canadian nationals from Japan. The solid front displayed against Japan seemed to be having enough effect to produce a guarded optimism among Western governments but the British government warned the Canadian Department of External Affairs that if the situation became favourable to the Japanese it was "unlikely that extremest elements could be restrained".[25] British, Canadian, and other Dominions' diplomatic and consular personnel in the Far East were being instructed when and how to send any information which pointed to the threat of war.

Besides all the information given to the government leaders, a steady stream of data was being passed to National Defence Headquarters from the British War Office. The Defence Schemes and appreciations mentioned earlier were also available a very short time after they were published or prepared. Hong Kong, in addition, was the site of a British Army Intelligence Unit, which published a monthly intelligence digest,[26] copies of which were forwarded to National Defence Headquarters.The troop dispositions of the Japanese, particularly in China, were recorded with some accuracy every month. The January 1941 issue of this digest noted that Japan was drifting into a position where she would have no option but to fight, while the February issue warned that "the showdown has been postponed rather than avoided". Japanese were moving into the south, and the landing undertaken at Bias Bay in South China effectively cut lines of communication between Canton and Hong Kong and resulted in two brigades being positioned very close to the Hong Kong border. The March report stated that the Japanese were cooling a little due to United States toughness, and two months later it was suggested that the signing of the Russo-Japanese neutrality pact would give an impetus to the southward expansion. This issue reported that both the Japanese Naval heavy bombers and the *Zero* fighters were of good quality. The June issue reported that troop dispositions in South China were sufficient only for garrison duty, but by the next month, troops were noted moving south.

In the following months a partial mobilization seemed to have occurred in Japan and submarines were noticed patrolling the Hong Kong approaches. Even so, the writers of the intelligence digest reported that the country was still sitting on the fence. In October 1941 the report again noted the vacillation but stated that internal elements in Japan might force the issue *particularly if there were a cabinet change.* (The October issue dealt with the month preceeding.) Junks in Hong Kong waters were being harassed, and Japanese planes continually violated Hong Kong airspace. By the end of September extra squadrons of heavy bombers had reinforced Canton from Formosa and 30,000 Japanese soldiers were in the Canton area.

A further source of information available to National Defence Headquarters was an extensive series of notes on Japan by Colonel Mullahy, the former United Kingdom Military Attaché in Japan. In early September 1941 he submitted a resume called the "History of Militarism in Japan 1931-41", which chronicled the escalating scale of Japanese aggression in Manchuria, China, and the Far East, as well as the increasing influences of the Army in Japanese life. On 27 September 1941 he noted: "it is increasingly obvious that the divergence of view is very wide [between United States and Japan] , and certain that the United States, backed 100% by the British Empire, will drive a very hard bargain with Japan." The Japanese were trying to appear conciliatory while at the same time tightening their grip on Indo-China. On 15 September 1941 Mullahy noted that a new Defence Headquarters set up in Japan appeared to give the Emperor, and hence, he thought, the saner elements, more control over the Army and Navy.[27] (In the light of recent research it now appears possible that Emperor Hirohito was actually very much involved with the planning and execution of all phases of Japanese expansion from 1921 onward.)

Not only was all of this information from British sources available at National Defence Headquarters, but a good many of the senior officers there had experience specifically with the Hong Kong problem, as the defence of the Colony was considered a "classic" staff college problem. Some officers, for instance Brigadier Macklin, the Director of Staff Duties, had even been to Hong Kong. When Lieutenant General Stuart, Chief of the General Staff, testified at the hearing of the Royal Commission, he stated that when he studied the problem in 1928 it was decided that Hong Kong could hold out for 60 days with a garrison of 6 battalions. (This was, of course, long before the Japanese squatted on the Hong Kong border.) It does not seem that the implications registered with him when he testified in the next breath that by 1941 it was agreed that relief could not be anticipated before 120 days—that is twice as long as Hong Kong was expected to hold out under the easier 1928 conditions.[28]

It is quite obvious that there was very little information regarding the Japanese menace in general and the defence of Hong Kong in particular that was not available to the Canadian government or its senior military officers at the time the decision was being taken to send Canadian troops to Hong Kong.

Japan was expanding aggressively, and the practically defenceless colony of Hong Kong was in its path. Yet with this knowledge readily available the decision was still made to reinforce Hong Kong with Canadian troops. The only real question after all is said and done is—why?

A Hitherto Unregarded Source...
—the British request

Of all possible theatres of employment for Canadian troops, the last to cross anyone's mind before the summer of 1941 would probably have been Hong Kong. Anyone, that is, except for one man, Major General A.E. Grasett, former General Officer Commanding at Hong Kong. The twin circumstances of his Canadian birth and his responsibility for the defence of Hong Kong between November 1938 and July 1941 can be held largely responsible for the chain of events culminating in the despatch of Canadian troops to the colony.

The defence of Hong Kong was something of an *ideé fixe* with Grasett. This is neither strange nor particularly reprehensible—the domination of an officer's military thinking by a single tactical problem for nearly three years is bound to make a lasting impression. Unfortunately, this fixation was accompanied by an exaggerated belief both in the defencibility of Hong Kong and in the Japanese soldier's lack of fighting quality. Grasett's compulsion to see his theories vindicated was to have a dire effect on almost 2,000 Canadians.

On 19 July 1941, Grasett handed over command at Hong Kong to Major General C.M. Maltby and left for England. Whether the route home which took him across Canada was selected for him or was his own choice is difficult to ascertain. Whichever the case, in August of that year Grasett was in Ottawa where he stopped off to have "long discussions" with the Chief of the Canadian General Staff, Major General H.D.G. Crerar. The two men had been contemporaries at Canada's Royal Military College in Kingston, although Crerar, starting out with the Royal Canadian Artillery, had spent his military career with the Canadian forces while Grasett upon graduation had joined the Royal Corps of Engineers and had spent his career in the British Army.

The exact nature and tone of these discussions is unknown, the only information being Crerar's recollections and his testimony at the 1942 Royal Commission investigating the despatch of Canadian troops to Hong Kong. It is certain, however, that one of the topics covered would have been the military situation in Hong Kong. Grasett believed that the defensive capability of the colony had been persistently underrated by his superiors and expressed the view, as Crerar remembered it, that the "addition of two or more battalions to the forces then at Hong Kong would render the garrison strong enough to withstand for an extensive period of siege an attack by such forces as the Japanese could bring to bear against it."[1]

This recollection of Crerar's is undoubtedly accurate. What remains and will probably continue to remain an enigma is to what degree Crerar encouraged Grasett in his hopes for Canadian participation. In his testimony concerning these discussions Crerar never mentioned any suggestion being made that Canada supply the troops Grasett wanted. It is nevertheless logical that the availability and disposition of Canadian battalions would come up in the course of the conversations without reference to Hong Kong. It would have been strange for Grasett to suggest to his superiors the probable willingness of Canada to supply troops for Hong Kong without at least a tacit commitment from the Canadian Chief of General Staff. The virtual rubber-stamp endorsement given by Crerar to the subsequent British request gives some indication that it came as no surprise to him. On the other hand, Grasett appears to have possessed an incredibly sanguine disposition and it is within the bounds of probability that any reaction on Crerar's part short of leaping to his feet and bellowing, "Never, no never!" might be interpreted as an affirmative reaction. We may never know.

Grasett was back in London by 3 September, when he reported to the War Office where he was present at a meeting of the Chiefs of Staff. In addition to briefing them on his view of the Hong Kong situation, he submitted his proposal that the garrison be increased by two battalions. For the first time, at least in writing, he made the suggestion that Canada might be willing to supply the troops.

Grasett does not appear to have gained unanimous acceptance of his point of view. What appears to be an extract from the content of the meeting states that:

1. Canada could probably find the troops
2. Any troops sent would be practically untrained
3. The political effect might be undesirable in that it might result in greater attention being given to the Japanese menace to the Canadian Western Seaboard, with the consequent locking up of troops in the Vancouver area.[2]

Major General J.N. Kennedy, Director of Military Operations and Plans, stated in a draft minute to the Chief of the Imperial General Staff, Sir John Dill,

I agree that in view of Mr. Mackenzie King's recent speech indicating the desire for Canadian troops to be placed in the front line of battle, and in view of the greater interest now being shown by the Canadian Government in the Pacific, it might now be possible to obtain small reinforcements from Canada for Hong Kong.

I suggest, however, that this factor should not be allowed to induce you to reverse your present policy of sending no reinforcements to Hong Kong. The Canadians might never be involved in a front line battle, and, if they are, it will merely mean more forces being locked up in a fortress which at the moment has very little chance of being relieved.[3]

This minute was never sent to the Chief of the Imperial General Staff, but was instead marked "CANCELLED". What prompted Kennedy's change of mind is unknown, but what he actually sent, dated 7 September 1941, was: "If you think General Grasett has made out a good case, the Chiefs of Staff may wish to submit it to the Prime Minister."[4]

The Chief of the Imperial General Staff must have decided that Grasett had made out a good case, for on that same day a note was drafted for submission to the Prime Minister by the Chiefs of Staff:

We have taken the opportunity of discussing the present situation in Hong Kong with Major General GRASETT, who was commanding the garrison in that colony until 19th July.

Major General Grasett brought up again the question of an infantry reinforcement of the garrison which he suggests the Canadian Government might be agreeable to provide. He considers that the garrison is insufficient to provide any reserve to meet eventualities. Three battalions man sectors on the island, while the fourth battalion has to be withdrawn from the mainland after effecting a programme of demolitions, and then becomes responsible for the defence of the southern beaches. To have reinforced a year ago would have been to throw good money after bad. The situation is now so changed that in 4½ months relief might be possible and such a reinforcement might well prolong resistance for a further considerable period.

The present policy is that Hong Kong is to be regarded as an outpost and held as long as possible (C.O.B. (40) 592 para. 37). Though it has been decided not to send reinforcements, in the event of war, it was never intended that the forces available to the commander should not be adequate for the task. We agree that, at present, the available forces are insufficient to implement the defence plan, which is to deny to the enemy the dry dock and harbour for 130 days.

A small reinforcement of one or two battalions would increase the strength of the garrison out of all proportion to its numbers, and would provide a strong psychological stimulus to the garrison and to the colony. It would show Chiang Kai Shek that, in spite of our wide commitments, we really intend to fight it out at Hong Kong, and would also have a salutary effect on the Japanese.

You will remember this policy was last reviewed in January, 1941 (Your minute No. D 9/1 of 7th January, 1941 to Major-General Ismay refers), when it was decided not to send any more reinforcements to Hong Kong. Since then, however, the position in the Far East has changed radically and Japan has shown a certain weakness latterly in her attitude towards Great Britain and the United States.

Recently the United States has displayed a greater interest in the Far East and have despatched small reinforcements to the garrison of the Philippines. Reinforcement of Hong Kong from Canada would thus be accepting a wider commitment in Imperial defence, similar to that which has been assumed by Australia in Malaya.

For these reasons, the Chief of Staff consider that a reinforcement of up to two battalions infantry should now be made to the garrison of Hong Kong. If the Prime Minister approves, we suggest that Mr. Mackenzie King should be approached with a view to obtaining this reinforcement.[5]

This draft note was discussed at the Chiefs of Staff meeting on 10 September. There is no record of the actual give-and-take of the meeting, but it is apparent that the statement "in 4½ months relief might be possible", vague though it might be, was too much for the Chief of Naval Staff to swallow. He drew attention to it and stated that he "considered this misleading".[6] The note eventually sent to Churchill and dated 10 September read:

PRIME MINISTER

On the 3rd September, the Chiefs of Staff heard an interesting account on the present situation in Hong Kong from General Grasett who had been General Officer Commanding there until July. From this, one important point arose.

2. The present defence policy at Hong Kong is that the Island is to be regarded as an outpost and held as long as possible. In describing the tasks of the force in Hong Kong General Grasett said that of the army garrison of four battalions, one was to be deployed on the mainland and charged with the task of withdrawing to the Island after carrying out extensive demolitions. This battalion was also needed for the defence of the Island. It was essential therefore that it should be safely extricated from the mainland. He pointed out the great advantages to be obtained from the addition of one or two battalions and suggested that these might be supplied by Canada.

3. The Chiefs of Staff have previously advised against the despatch of more reinforcements to Hong Kong because they considered that it would only have been to throw good money after bad, but the position in the Far East has now changed. Our defences in Malaya have been improved and Japan has latterly shown a certain weakness in her attitude towards Great Britain and the United States.

4. A small reinforcement of one or two battalions would increase the strength of the garrison out of all proportion to the actual numbers involved, and it would provide a strong stimulus to the garrison and to the Colony. Further, it would have a great moral effect in the whole of the Far East and it would show Chiang Kai Shek that we really intend to fight it out at Hong Kong.

5. The United States have recently despatched a small reinforcement to the Philippines and a similar move by Canada would be in line with the present United States Policy of greater interest in the Far East.

6. The Chiefs of Staff are in favour of the suggestion that Canada should be asked to send one or two battalions to Hong Kong, and submit this proposal for your approval. If you agree, the necessary approach would be made through the Dominions Office.[7]

It will be noted that the suggestion as to the possibility of relief after 4½ months has been completely eliminated from the minute, as has the reference to the possibility of the proposed reinforcements prolonging resistance.

Churchill was prepared to accept the recommendation of his Chiefs of Staff. On 15 September he noted: "It is a question of timing. There is no objection to the approach being made as proposed; but a further decision should be taken before the battalions actually sail."[8]

No time was wasted once the Prime Minister's approval had been obtained. On 19 September 1941 the following telegram was sent by the Dominions Office to the Canadian government via the Department of External Affairs:

No. 162 MOST SECRET

In consultation with late General Officer Commanding who has recently arrived in this country we have been considering the defences of Hong Kong. Approved policy has been that Hong Kong should be regarded as an out-post and held as long as possible in the event of war in the Far East. Existing army garrison consists of four battalions of infantry and although this force represents the bare minimum required for the task assigned to it we have thought hitherto that it would not ultimately serve any useful purpose to increase the garrison.

Position in the Far East has now, however, changed. Our defences in Malaya have been improved and there have been signs of a certain weakening in Japan's attitude towards us and the United States.

In these circumstances it is thought that a small re-inforcement of the garrison of Hong Kong, e.g. by one or two more battalions, would be very fully justified. It would increase the strength of the garrison out of all proportion to the actual numbers involved and it would provide a strong stimulus to the garrison and to the Colony, it would further have a very great moral effect in the whole of the Far East and would reassure Chiang Kai Shek as to the reality of our intention to hold the Island.

His Majesty's Government in Canada will be well aware of the difficulties we are at present experiencing in providing the forces which the situation in various parts of the world demands, despite the very great assistance which is being furnished by Dominions. *We should therefore be most grateful if the Canadian Government would consider whether one or two Canadian battalions could be provided from Canada for this purpose.* [underlined in original] It is thought that in view of their special purpose in the North Pacific the Canadian Government would in any case have wished to be informed of the need, as we see it, for the reinforcement of Hong Kong and the special value of such a measure, even though on a very limited scale, at the present time. It may also be mentioned that the United States have recently despatched a small re-inforcement to the Philippines. It would be of the greatest help if the Canadian Government would cooperate with us in the manner suggested and we much hope that they will feel able to do so.

If the Canadian Government agree in principle to send one or two battalions we should propose to communicate with you again as to the best time for their despatch having regard to the general political situation in the Far East. [underlined in original] [9]

The foregoing documents have been quoted in full in order to observe the evolution of the content of the request to Canada. It can be seen that the actual military requirement is progressively played down while the diplomatic and political aspect is correspondingly emphasized.

Perhaps the most significant difference between the telegram of 19 September and the previous notes is the reference to Hong Kong being viewed as an outpost. The notes say that the present policy *is* that Hong Kong should be regarded as an outpost, whereas the telegram says that the policy *has been*. In any event, it was on this telegram alone that the Canadian government's decision was based.

The Canadian Army Should
Take This On...
—the Canadian response

When the telegram carrying the British request arrived the Minister of National Defence, the Honorable J.L. Ralston, was absent in the United States and the Minister of National Defence for Air, the Honorable C.G. Power, was acting in his place. That morning Power met the Minister of National Defence for Naval Services on the street and they "discussed the matter at some length".[1] By the next meeting of the War Committee of the Cabinet they had decided to take on the commitment.

Before describing the actual authorization of Canadian participation in the defence of Hong Kong, it might be useful to examine what Canada's leaders thought her role should be in the Second World War. There is no doubt that these leaders, along with most Canadians, felt that the Dominion should do everything possible to help the United Kingdom win the war. This did not mean that Canada should be required to commit her troops and her armaments blindly. Unlike the case in the First World War, the defence of Canada was a factor which had to be considered. Prime Minister Mackenzie King wrote a memo on 5 September 1939 on the "Question of Canadian Overseas Forces", outlining his beliefs on the broad policy to be followed.

> The Government should have much clearer information than is yet available of the war operations planned or intended by the British and Allied governments. It is not enough to get simply suggestions from the British as to what Canadian action would be the most effective without at the same time having the information in question, so that the Canadian government can form their own judgement whether the Canadian action suggested would in reality be the most effective.[2]

Later that year Brigadier H.D.G. Crerar, the man who was to become Canada's top military officer and the man who was Chief of the General Staff at the time of the British request, wrote down his ideas of general policy:

> In view of the war effort they are making, Canada and the other Dominions have a right to be consulted on policy, and to be kept advised of the strategic position. Spasmodic issue of information will not be enough . . .
>
> When the Dominions are asked to furnish troops or air forces, they ought to be told how it is proposed to employ them, and this cannot be done once and for all, *but must be a continuous process* throughout the war. If we are to cooperate to the full, we must have full knowledge.
>
> . . . Some machinery, therefore, should be set up, preferably within the framework of the Committee of Imperial Defence, so that the Dominions, through their representatives on the staffs of the High Commissioners, may obtain full information on the current military situation, and the strategy designed to meet it.[3]

When the time came to put these policies into practice, however, the leaders of Canada proved to be remarkably uninquisitive. This is all the more surprising considering that the Canadian government *did* have enough information at their disposal to form their own opinions on the matter. Hong Kong defence schemes, intelligence reports, Japanese diplomatic intelligence, and similar relevant material were all in Canadian hands, and a brief glance at the first two in particular would have (or should have) given them pause.

C.G. Power, the Associate Minister of National Defence, stated at the hearings of the Royal Commission investigating the despatch of Canadian troops to Hong Kong: "I do not think there was ever any question really, or any discussion as between General Crerar and myself as to any reason why we should not take it on." Power recognized that Hong Kong was in a rather poor position, but "took it for granted that the military authorities had assessed all that." Power considered the Dominions Office argument sufficiently strong. The battalions could be spared, therefore the United Kingdom should have them.

Power had always felt that "if it were possible and we could spare the men, [we] should send men to other theatres of war . . ." On 24 September Power and Crerar had a long talk and concluded that two battalions could be taken away from home defence forces. Power did not ask, however, for any sort of military appreciation of the defencibility of Hong Kong.[4]

Judging by the minutes, the discussion of the subject at the Cabinet War Committee meeting of 23 September was very short. The telegram was read and agreement in principle was reached. Mackenzie King insisted on first gaining the assent of Ralston, the Minister of National Defence, and obtaining the advice of General McNaughton in England.[5]

Ralston was located at the Ambassador Hotel in Los Angeles and an officer at the Canadian Legation in Washington was sent out to contact him. The officer, who brought with him a copy of the 19 September telegram, was instructed to tell Ralston that the "War Committee are prepared to accept... CGS sees no military risk in despatching Canadian Battalions for this purpose."[6] When the copy of the telegram reached the Minister, he went over it very carefully. The message implied that time was of the essence, so by that night he had made his decision. His reasons for accepting the proposal were largely contained in the telegram itself. Two battalions would do more than such a force normally could. Japan was to be given a show of strength which might cause them to hesitate, and China would be reassured. All these elements "seemed to me to make... a decision in the affirmative almost inevitable unless there was some overriding factor that made that impossible or undesirable." Other circumstances also had their effect. Ralston was acutely conscious that the United States was not yet ready for war, and anything that prevented her and Japan from clashing was all to the good. Another, perhaps major, influence was that Ralston felt "it was Canada's turn to help. ... Australia had been doing a great deal in Libya and elsewhere; the New Zealanders had been in Crete; and the South Africans in Abyssinia."

The only doubt that Ralston had was on the matter of military feasibility. Ralston wanted to reassure himself on this point, as he could "remember Hong Kong being an outpost to be held as long as possible. I think that was generally understood."[7] He therefore telephoned Crerar that night to obtain confirmation. Crerar later testified that "I told him that I had definitely recommended that the Canadian Army should take this on."[8] Probably the last real chance the government had of going into the request in depth disappeared with these words. Ralston arranged for an answer approving in principle to be sent to Ottawa via Washington.

The Honorable Angus L. Macdonald, the Minister of National Defence for Naval Services, was to tell a similar story at the Commission. The reasons given in the cable seemed to make sense to him, and he knew that the naval strength in the Far East was in the process of being reinforced, (the *Prince of Wales* and the *Repulse*). Beyond this was a simple desire to help. Macdonald stated emphatically, "I do not think it was thinkable for this country to offer a negative answer to the request of the United Kingdom."[9]

At a further meeting of the War Committee on 20 October 1941, at which Ralston was present, the final decision was made to notify the British that Canadian troops would be made available to reinforce Hong Kong. Mackenzie King participated very little in the discussion, except to make it plain that "agreement in that particular did not later afford an argument for conscription."[10]

No Reason Why

—an analysis

The Canadian soldiers who fought at Hong Kong in December 1941 and either died in the hopeless struggle or else passed into a brutal and all too often fatal captivity are the possessors of a unique distinction. They are the only Canadian soldiers and possibly the only Commonwealth soldiers of the Second World War who were deliberately sent into a position where there was absolutely no hope of victory, evacuation, or relief. In all other disasters to British arms such as Norway, France in 1940, Greece, Crete, Singapore, and Arnhem, one or another of these possibilities existed. For example, more or less successful evacuations were achieved in the first four, reinforcements were reaching Singapore until a few days before its capitulation, while Arnhem was a calculated gamble which, if successful, offered the prospect of an early victory. Even the greatest debacle in which Canadians played a major role, the bloodstained tragedy that was the Dieppe raid, was, while open to criticism of its conception, planning, and execution, nevertheless designed to permit the evacuation of the raiding forces.

But what of Hong Kong? Admitted by most informed opinion (including the men who requested that Canadian troops be sent) to be incapable of a prolonged and successful defence, was there any reason why nearly two thousand Canadians should have been caught up in the bloody shambles that marked its fall?

Of the British actors in the drama, Major General A.E. Grasett was the only one who appears to have honestly believed that an additional two battalions would markedly upgrade Hong Kong's ability to resist assault. His belief was unfortunately based on a contempt for Japanese military ability, a fixed determination to "put up a good show", and remarkably poor powers of military appreciation. Even Brooke-Popham, who was willing to reinforce the colony by taking two battalions from Malaya, was impelled primarily by political and diplomatic reasoning rather than military logic.

It is difficult to avoid a grudging admiration for the British Chiefs of Staff and the War Office in the Hong Kong situation. However their judgement may be faulted in other respects, and whatever one may think of their actual motives for requesting Canadian reinforcements for the colony, they were one hundred percent correct in their opinion of the indefencibility of Hong Kong. They considered that there was no possibility of a successful defence until relief could be expected, they therefore had resolved to treat it as an outpost, they had held to this opinion for a number of years, and at no time changed their minds, even after the Canadians were on their way. Events were to prove them absolutely right.

There is abundant evidence to show that the despatch of the Canadians did not alter the policy of regarding Hong Kong as an outpost in the slightest. On 5 November, while the Canadians were still *en route,* the Chiefs of Staff became perturbed at indications that the Commander-in-Chief, Far East, considered that these reinforcements indicated a change in policy toward Hong Kong. They soon put him straight:

War Office
to
C in C Far East   6 November 1941
    1. Our policy regarding defence of Hong Kong remains unaltered. It must be regarded as an outpost and held as long as possible.[1]

Herein lies the mystery. Precisely what happened at the War Office between 3 and 9 September 1941 during Grasett's visit? It is obvious from Kennedy's cancelled draft memo to the Chief of the Imperial General Staff that they were all set to give his proposals as short shrift as they gave those made by his superior, Sir Robert Brooke-Popham, eight months earlier. Grasett failed to convince them of Hong Kong's defencibility, and all reasons subsequently given for requesting the despatch of reinforcements had been considered earlier and deemed insufficient. What new elements could Grasett have introduced to have made the Chiefs of Staff reverse their stand? The only possible one is Grasett's suggestion that the two battalions might be obtained from a "hitherto unregarded source"[2]—Canada.

The desirability of Canadian reinforcements was at first viewed a little sceptically (see page 26), especially as the War Office was well aware that any troops supplied by Canada would not be fully trained. It would appear that the political and morale advantages of the reinforcement, plus the fact that the United Kingdom did not have to supply the troops, won the day and prompted the cancellation of Kennedy's original memo.

Perhaps the most completely frank explanation is a War Office document dated 1 January 1942 which states:

> It was considered that this small reinforcement would:
> (a) Be in line with our more forward policy in the Far East.
> (b) Show the USA and Chiang Kai Shek that we intended to fight it out for Hong Kong.
> (c) Hearten the existing garrison.
> (d) Give Canada an opportunity to take a more active part in the defence of her Pacific interests.[3]

It was probably the first two reasons given that most influenced Winston Churchill in the reversal of the position he had taken so strongly in January 1941. He was most anxious to stand shoulder to shoulder with the United States in their confrontation with the Japanese, and this was one more way of showing Roosevelt that the Commonwealth was doing its part. Presumably Churchill, in his eagerness to do this, either forgot the risk to the garrison or considered it worth taking.

The telegram to Canada requesting the troops stated that the "approved policy had been that Hong Kong should be regarded as an outpost and held as long as possible in the event of war in the Far East." It may be regarded as nit-picking, but it appears important to this writer that this was phrased in the past tense—the sentence gives the impression that the outpost policy is no longer the official one. One cannot but wonder if the alteration was made with deliberate intent. In any event, the Canadians never thought to ask the British whether Hong Kong was still an outpost or whether the policy regarding it had been changed.

The telegram went on to say that the position in the Far East was changing and Malayan defences were improved. Also, "there have been signs of a certain weakening in Japan's attitude towards us and the United States." This was not what Foreign Minister Anthony

Eden thought, as a telegram received in Canada the next day (20 September) showed. The British Ambassador to Tokyo had written that Japan was moving away from the Axis and the moderates were gaining control. Eden replied that the Japanese loss of faith in the Tripartite Pact was merely the result of doubts of its being the best means to their established end—expansion. The "moderates" in Japan were those who questioned only the methods being used and not the final end in view. The United States and United Kingdom had to keep up a strong front, as it would be folly to give up anything in the expectation of a serious Japanese offer of a settlement of outstanding differences. Eden was very sceptical about any Japanese interest in making concessions in a search for peace.[4] In reality, then, there was no "weakening" in the Japanese attitude, and the United States and Japan were as far apart as ever in the Washington talks. The United Kingdom government was perfectly aware that the talks were going nowhere.

It was said that the two battalions would increase the strength of the garrison out of all proportion to the actual numbers involved. We have seen this phrase before. The reinforcement would "reassure Chiang Kai Shek as to the reality of our intention to hold the Island." A more accurate phrase might have been that used by the War Office in the memorandum of 1 January 1942 quoted earlier, "show Chiang Kai Shek", considering the long-standing desire of the Chinese to obtain possession of the Colony. Hong Kong had been something of a bone of contention between China and the United Kingdom since before the start of the Second World War. One of the main arguments against the earlier proposed demilitarization was that it would be hard for the United Kingdom to repossess the Colony after the war if it were given up without a fight. One may even go as far as to ask against whom the United Kingdom had the "intention of holding the Island", as all previous defence schemes made it plain that it was not expected that Hong Kong would be able to withstand a determined Japanese assault. It is probable that, as well as the immediate reasons for reinforcement, there was a very real determination on Britain's part to keep control of the Island on a long-term basis. If this is true, it is a pity that she used Commonwealth troops in her bid to accomplish this end.

Nevertheless, the politicians in Canada had the final word. They based their decision on two sources of information only—the statement of the United Kingdom that troops were required and it would be desirable that Canada supply them, and the advice of the Canadian Chief of the General Staff that it was militarily feasible to supply the battalions and that Canada should accept the commitment. These statements, and a strong and genuine desire that Canada play her part in the war, led to a practically unquestioning, positive response to the request.

The politicians had thus made their decision. What of the role of Major General Crerar, the Chief of the General Staff? His duties included "military policy and strategy" and "advice as to the conduct of operations of war and orders in regard to military operations,"[5] as well as intelligence. He had, in effect, "advised" the government when asked by Ralston and Power for his opinion. One may, however, question the adequacy of his attempt to consider all aspects of the decision. We have seen that he had had conversations with the ex-General Officer Commanding, Hong Kong a few months before, yet other than this Crerar made absolutely no attempt to inform himself on the situation at Hong Kong, preferring to rely, *in toto,* on the opinions of his old RMC comrade. The relevant material was available to the Canadian General Staff. Lieutenant Colonel William Murray, who was responsible for the collection and distribution of this type of information, was not asked for any summary of intelligence relating to Hong Kong. Brigadier Gibson, who as Director of Military Operations and Intelligence was Murray's immediate superior, also testified at the Royal Commission hearings that his Branch had not been asked for any information.[6] In other words, the military authorities displayed a noticeable indifference to the actual military situation in the colony.

Crerar did not concentrate on this aspect of the request in any event when he made his Royal Commission deposition. He felt that:

> the decision for or against the despatch . . . [was] necessarily required to be taken on the highest policy level. The proposed action, whatever the military risks of the enterprise, needed to be examined from the broad view as to its contributory value to the eventual winning of the war. [He then quoted the example of the British despatch of troops to Greece in 1940.] In the case of the despatch of Canadian troops to Hong Kong . . . political and moral principles were involved, rather than military ones, and on such a basis, the matter required to be considered and decided by the War Committee of the Cabinet.[7]

This evasion of responsibility would undoubtedly have caused Pontius Pilate to send out for a second washbasin. General Crerar was, of course, entitled to his own opinion, but he seems to have forgotten in this instance that his job was to give *military*, not political or moral advice. Once politicians know all the facts they make their decision, and often it is quite properly the moral and political factors which win out over the military, as was the case in the example of Greece. The difference lies in the fact that the British government was well aware of the dangers inherent in the Greek expedition but accepted the risk for political reasons. The Canadian government most definitely did *not* take into consideration the risks involved in sending troops to Hong Kong, because they neither asked nor were told about them. In effect, Crerar usurped their jobs by failing to make it plain to the politicians that the military risks were very real, even when Ralston specifically questioned him on this point. Despite Grasett's optimism, Crerar, with his wide experience, must have been well aware that Hong Kong, even if not in a hopeless position, could be expected to bear the brunt of a very heavy attack in the event of war, with no chance of relief for a considerable period. If he wished his memory refreshed, reasonably up-to-date information was available at National Defence Headquarters or from the British. Even Power and Ralston were vaguely aware that Hong Kong was in an exposed position, but in the absence of any definite information from the top military advisor to the government, they presumably assumed that the situation was not all that bad.

Crerar, moreover, in his written testimony sent to the Commission, went on to state that "the question posed in Telegram No. 162 [the request] . . . required from me a statement as to whether Canada could provide two battalions to assist in the defence of Hong Kong . . ."[8] This is a rather narrow contraction on Crerar's part of his responsibilities. In the light of the statement of his duties quoted earlier, the telegram required from him an effort to study the situation, work out the pros and cons, and outline these to the politicians so that they could make a decision based on all the relevant information. The Chief of the Canadian General Staff was surely expected to do more than just scout around for two extra battalions.

It is difficult, even in retrospect, to know what to make of Crerar's attitude. He had the reputation of being a man of integrity and a competent soldier. He was later to lead the First Canadian Army to victory in Northwest Europe. While there is little point in imputing motives from this distance in time, it is possible that even if he was suffering under the lash of his conscience for his negligence in the

Hong Kong affair, he felt that as he was doing a good job in other respects, there was no point in crying *mea culpa* and he should be permitted to get on with the war without raking up the dead bones of past sins of omission.

Lieutenant General Stuart, Crerar's successor as Chief of the General Staff, also testified at the Royal Commission. His testimony made it abundantly clear that the General Staff *did* have access to Hong Kong defence plans. He mentioned some aspects of them in considerable detail. He did not say, however, what the gist of these plans was except to say that the garrison would be "in for a hard time" in the event of war. According to Stuart, to defend "as long as possible" was just a standard army phrase—"there is no futility about the thing".[9]

General McNaughton, commanding the Canadian forces in England, was also informed about the sending of the troops to Hong Kong. Although he had no responsibility in the matter, he testified at the hearings. McNaughton "took for granted that the wording of the cable was something which could not be refused." He went on to explain later the situation in regard to such a proposal: "They [the War Office] were the only group, the only organization, able really to assess the situation, and, as we trusted their judgement, it was up to us either to reply in the affirmative, or to refuse."[10]

The final effect of the Canadian General Staff's attitude to the problem was therefore a failure to submit to the government for their consideration one of the primary pieces of information involved with the Hong Kong question—that "it has always been well-known in the Services that there would be considerable difficulties in defending Hong Kong, which presumably had obviously increased by the proximity of the Japanese forces before the war started."[11]

Both the British and United States governments had plenty of information at their disposal in September 1941 to show that war in the Far East was virtually inevitable sooner or later. Despite occasional "weakening" on Japan's part, she never once, after 1931, made any real concessions in her dealings with other Powers. The oft-stated aim of every Japanese government, whether "moderate" or otherwise, was expansion in the Pacific area, and after the mid-thirties this expansion began to take an increasingly southward direction. This was natural and obvious, for despite Japan's hatred and fear of Russia, her real economic interest lay in the oil, rubber, and tin of the south.

In regard to the position of Hong Kong, it had been recognized as early as 1921 that the colony would be in grave danger in the event of war with Japan. This was during a period when England had no military worries about Germany, when Japan had a much smaller navy, and when England still ruled the waves. The deterioration of the British position *vis-a-vis* Japan over the next two decades could only serve to reinforce this conclusion. When Japanese troops and air forces reached a position within a few miles of the Island it became difficult to see how the defensive position could get much worse. This was common knowledge in military circles throughout the Commonwealth, and, to do the British Chiefs of Staff justice, they were well aware of this and were at no time prey to any false illusions.

While there was therefore never any change in the military policy regarding Hong Kong, Britain was determined by September 1941 to present a solid front with the United States against Japan, and also to demonstrate to the Chinese that Britain was still a force to be reckoned with in Asian affairs. There was undoubtedly as well a notion that the current Hong Kong garrison was inadequate to put up the kind of resistance called for by the plans. None of these factors by themselves or in combination was sufficient to persuade the British to reinforce the colony, but they were powerful enough when it was suggested that two battalions could be made available from a "hitherto unregarded source" that the British government abandoned a long-standing military policy based on a succession of intelligent appreciations of the situation, and two Canadian battalions became the most exposed pieces in a giant game of bluff.

In Canada, the situation was even simpler. Neither the politicians, lulled by the probably deliberate ambiguous wording of the request, nor Crerar, who appears to have accepted Grasett's beliefs whole-heartedly, thought to obtain either from the British government or from their own sources of information (which were perfectly ade-quate in this case) the answer to the question: "If war comes, as it likely will, what will be the fate of Hong Kong and of our soldiers?" The only honest answer to such a query would have been, "All our appreciations of the situation, including the current one, indicate that Hong Kong almost certainly will fall before it can be relieved and the garrison will either be killed fighting or be taken prisoner." While it is remotely conceivable that a Canadian government under the Liberals and led by Mackenzie King would be willing to cold-bloodedly immolate 2,000 Canadians on the altar of either Imperial solidarity or Far Eastern defence, it does severely strain one's concept of the possible.

Once having received the request, the Canadian government seems to have assumed that, provided the battalions were available, an affirmative answer was the only one possible. To these busy and sincere men, with neither the knowledge needed nor the inclination to read between the lines or wonder about motivations, the telegram made sense, and unless there were sound military reasons for questioning the request, a yes was automatic. There *were* sound military reasons for questioning it, but the Chief of the General Staff did not pass these reasons on to the government.

There was no reason why Canadian troops should have been despatched to the doomed outpost of Hong Kong—but through a combination of British cynicism and Canadian thoughtlessness, they were sent anyway.

Units of Proven Efficiency. . .
—the force is selected

Although the final decision to agree to the request by the United Kingdom Government was not made until 20 October 1941, the Canadian General Staff had commenced preparations well before that date to select the two battalions that would be required in the event of a positive response.

The selection process was set in motion on 23 September by Colonel W.H.S. Macklin, Director of Staff Duties, who soon produced a memo on the subject. As one criterion that he considered vital in making the selection was that "units farthest advanced in training should be given preference",[1] he requested Colonel J.K. Lawson, Director of Military Training, to prepare a list of battalions within Canada in order of training level. Lawson duly produced the list the next day. There were 26 battalions currently serving in Canada and Newfoundland and these were divided into three categories. The first category, Class A, contained those furthest advanced in training and consisted of the nine battalions of the 4th Division, which was earmarked for transfer overseas in the next year, and one battalion in Newfoundland. Of the seven battalions in the intermediate Class B, four were in the newly-formed 6th Division and three were employed on Coast Defence duties. Class C was composed of nine battalions— "those units which, due either to recent employment or insufficient training, are not recommended by DMT to be available for operational consideration at the present time."[2]

Macklin, after examining the list, noted that if any of the Class A battalions from the 4th Division were selected to go to Hong Kong they "could be replaced, in most cases, by units from the same area". Macklin was referring to the policy of having major Canadian formations contain units representing a reasonable geographical cross-section of the country. He also suggested the General Officer Commanding 4th Division should be consulted before any steps were taken. Macklin proposed two alternatives for selecting the Hong Kong units. The first was to choose two battalions from the 4th Division: one from the East, one from the West. The second alternative included four battalions from Colonel Lawson's Class B, from which the two for Hong Kong could be chosen. Units from Class C were not mentioned at all.[3]

The first alternative was sent to Major General L.F. Page, General Officer Commanding 4th Division, for his comments. He replied in a memo strongly urging that the units not be taken from his Division. He argued that training would be disrupted at the Brigade level as one or more Brigades would have units of different levels of training. Moreover, taking two of his battalions would be very bad for morale, as his men would believe the Division was being broken up and would not go overseas at all. Class B battalions, he felt, would be just as well trained as any from the 4th Division. If, despite this, two 4th Division units were to go, Page reluctantly recommended that the British Columbia Regiment and either the Canadian Grenadier Guards or the Irish Regiment of Canada be chosen.[4]

An officer such as Page who has devoted a great deal of energy and planning to creating a fighting formation cannot be accused of rationalization when he resists any attempt to dismember it—he has excellent reasons. Whether these reasons should prevail against higher policy is not for him to judge. Certainly the arguments of the 4th Division's Commander must have carried some weight, as he was not required to give up any of his battalions. After Page's reply was received, the Winnipeg Grenadiers and the Royal Rifles of Canada were selected from Class C. In other words, Macklin's second alternative, the battalions in Class B, appears to have been completely ignored.

On 30 September 1941 Major General Crerar submitted his recommendation to the Minister of National Defence. Outlining his reasons for choosing the Royal Rifles and Winnipeg Grenadiers, he wrote, "As these units are going to a distant and important garrison where they will be detached from Canadian forces, a primary consideration is that they should be efficient, well-trained battalions capable of upholding the credit of the Dominion in any circumstances." It would be unsound, he said, to "disrupt" the 4th Division, and it seemed to him best to select units from among those on Coast Defence duty or from the 6th Division. In recommending the Royal Rifles and the Winnipeg Grenadiers, General Crerar wrote:

> 10. As you know, these units returned not long ago from duty in New-foundland and Jamaica respectively. The duties which they there carried out were not in many respects unlike the task which awaits the units to be sent to Hong Kong. The experience they have will therefore be of no small value to them in their new role. Both are units of proven efficiency.
>
> 11. In my opinion, the balance of argument favours the selection of these two battalions. I would be very reluctant to allot them indefinitely to a home defence role as the effect on their morale, following a period of "semi-overseas" responsibilities would be bound to be adverse. The selection represents both Eastern and Western Canada. In the case of the Royal Rifles, there is also the fact that this battalion, while nominally English-speaking, is actually drawn from a region overwhelmingly French-speaking in character and contains an important proportion of Canadians of French descent.[5]

Ralston approved his Chief of General Staff's recommendation on 9 October.

On the face of it the process of selection of these two battalions exhibits at least one startling inconsistency. Their inclusion in Class C was presumably because the Director of Military Training considered (and with good reason) that they "required a period of refresher training". Nevertheless, Crerar proposed sending them back into what he considered (at least in his recommendation to the Minister) a situation that was to be largely identical to the one from which they had just emerged and which had produced this need for training. This renders farcical the Director of Staff Duties' recommendations that the most well-trained units be given priority, the Director of Military Training's arrangement of units by training level, and the Chief of General Staff's own statement that the units should be "well-trained".

There is some evidence, however, that other factors may have been involved in the selection of the Royal Rifles of Canada as one of the two battalions for Hong Kong. They were a Quebec City regiment, and the Honorable C.G. Power, Associate Minister of National Defence, represented a Quebec City riding and had a son in the Regiment. Major John H. Price, the Royal Rifles' Second-in-Command, was an old friend of Power as were many of the other officers. On 13 September 1941, Price wrote to Power telling him that the unit was most anxious to get into a larger formation and participate in "advanced and collective training. . . . I hope that, with the interest you have in our welfare, you will be willing and able to convince the military authorities that it is bad policy to keep a unit like ours just killing time . . ." .

Power replied 22 September 1941 that he had "made inquiries" into the future of the unit as he knew the regiment would soon be fed up. "I have made certain representations and will continue to do so. . . . I have some hope that events overseas may soon develop to the point where it will be possible for your lot to have the opportunity it deserves."

Price was somewhat mollified, and writing back on 1 October 1941, said he realized, as did the rest of the battalion, that "there is a lack of battlefields at the moment. Our main problem is that of training and it would be of tremendous assistance if we could be sent to some area where advanced training is possible . . ."[6]

Did C.G. Power exert his influence when the battalions were being chosen? Mackenzie King, in his diary on 19 December 1941 when Hong Kong was under siege, wrote:

> Those who have been so keen to send our forces overseas realise the kind of reaction likely to follow in the country where losses occur, and the danger draws nearer to our own shores. It was Power himself who was keenest on having the Quebec Regiment go, he mentioning at the time that his own son was a member of it.[7]

It seems highly likely that soon after Power's reply to Price the Royal Rifles of Canada were earmarked for Hong Kong. In that event it would have been awkward to send a battalion from the 4th Division as the other half of the force. The Winnipeg Grenadiers, with similar experience in a garrison role, would most nearly match the Royal Rifles in its standard of training, and so was the battalion selected.

Both Eastern and Western Canada...

—the two battalions

When Canada went to war in 1939 the country's full-time army was a tiny Permanent Force totaling little more than 4000 all ranks. This small band of professional soldiers was backed up by the Non-Permanent Active Militia, units whose soldiers trained and served part-time. These units were distributed across Canada—there were 91 infantry battalions alone. On the outbreak of war, many of these Non-Permanent Active Militia battalions were mobilized to form a Canadian Active Service Force and filled their ranks through the recruiting of volunteers. As the war progressed and Canada's military requirements increased, others of these units were mobilized and brought up to their full wartime establishment. In almost every case the greater percentage of the initial officers and NCO's in any of the Active battalions had served with the Non-Permanent battalion.

The two battalions which were to form Canada's contribution to the defence of Hong Kong had been chosen to represent both Eastern and Western Canada. They were, in almost every way, typical of those from which, between 1939 and 1945, Canada created a remarkably successful and formidable army.

Both the Royal Rifles of Canada and the Winnipeg Grenadiers had, before the war, been regiments of the Non-Permanent Active Militia, that small but dedicated body of men who, on evenings, weekends, and the occasional summer camp, strove to keep Canada's army alive despite lack of equipment, pay, and government and public interest. As C.P. Stacey, probably Canada's most respected military historian, puts it:

It would be difficult, indeed, to over-estimate the debt of the wartime Army to the Non-Permanent Active Militia. It provided the foundation upon which the great new structure was built. It produced, to no small extent, the leaders who built and developed that structure. And it gave the Army a group of personnel, officers, and men, who continued to play dominant parts in it even when the great majority of the Army's members had come to be volunteers of no militia experience recruited from civil life. It is a notable fact that, at the end of hostilities with Germany in 1945, three of Canada's five fighting divisions were commanded by citizen soldiers who in 1939 had been captains or majors in the Non-Permanent Active Militia. And if further evidence of the Militia's contribution is required, one might rehearse the list of those who won the Commonwealth's highest awards for gallantry. Of the ten Victoria Crosses won by the Army during the Second World War, six were awarded to former members of the Active Militia—five from the Non-Permanent Active Militia and one from the Permanent Force. Of the three Canadian soldiers who won the George Cross, two had served in the Non-Permanent Active Militia.[1]

The Royal Rifles of Canada was a militia regiment of considerable seniority which could trace its ancestry back as far as 1862, when six independent companies were grouped in the Quebec City area at the time of the war scare during the early stages of the American Civil War. The regiment remained in existence throughout subsequent defence budgetary feasts and famines, surviving various militia reorganizations. Yet, unless one includes a short period on guard duty during the Fenian Raids, it had never gone into action as a unit until it fought at Hong Kong, although it supplied contingents that fought with considerable distinction in the 1885 Northwest Rebellion, the South African (Boer) War, and the First World War. In the 1914-1918 conflict no less than 24 battalions had Royal Riflemen on their strength, and these men were awarded no less than 1 Victoria Cross, 4 Distinguished Service Orders, and 22 Military Crosses, plus assorted other honours.

The Royal Rifles had not been one of the militia regiments selected for mobilization at the start of the Second World War. It must, however, have been regarded as a reasonably efficient unit as it was ordered to prepare for action in late June 1940. Although in most cases battalions were activated in groups to fill the establishment of a larger formation such as a new division, the Royal Rifles was the only battalion mobilized on this date. With the swift and surprising German triumph in Europe at this time the importance of Newfoundland, not then a part of Canada, to the security of Canada and to North Atlantic trade and communications became particularly apparent, and Canada undertook to assist in the air and land defence of the island. A battalion was detached from the 2nd Division for temporary service there (later to be replaced by another from the 3rd Division), but a unit which was not part of one of the divisions already formed for overseas service was needed for garrison duty in Newfoundland. The Royal Rifles of Canada was to form this new Active Battalion.

The Royal Rifles of Canada mobilized at Quebec City and moved to Valcartier Camp in September 1941. A local militia cavalry unit, the 7/11 Hussars, had been amalgamated with the Royal Rifles in June, providing a valuable increase in officers, NCO's, and trained or partially trained men at the commencement of mobilization.

Appointed to command the Active Battalion of the Royal Rifles was an officer of the pre-war Permanent Force, Lieutenant Colonel William J. Home, MC. Home, a veteran of the First World War, was, according to the testimony of witnesses at the 1942 Royal Commission, an excellent officer. General Foulkes did write to the Minister of National Defence in 1948 that, "There is some doubt about Home himself, he was removed from commanding a Company in the RCR as unfit to command in war, and later was appointed to the RRC."[2] There is no doubt, however, that in 1941, at least, he was regarded as competent and able. The Second-in-Command was Major John Herbert Price, MC, the son of Sir William Price, one of the most prominent businessmen of Quebec City. John Price, a graduate of the Royal Military College and a veteran of the First World War, was also highly regarded. No less than three lieutenant colonels had voluntarily reverted to the rank of major to join the new Active Battalion—Price, T.G. MacAuley, and C.A. Young. Indeed, Young had been Commanding Officer of the Royal Rifles immediately prior to the unit's mobilization. The rest of the officers were almost wholly drawn from the Royal Rifles or the 7/11 Hussars. A shortage of trained NCO's led to the selection of promising candidates from the ranks who had then to be trained for the purpose.

Recruiting up to full establishment commenced immediately with officers heading off into the townships around Quebec City, and it went very well. By autumn the battalion was up to full strength, and a Regimental Wing for the initial training of recruits was established in Quebec City.

The battalion was recruited from Eastern Quebec, primarily the

Quebec City area, but a considerable number of Gaspesians and men from northern New Brunswick also enlisted. It was an English-speaking unit but approximately 25% of its strength consisted of bilingual French-Canadians. The Inspector General's inspection reports indicate that the quality of the officers, NCO's, and men was quite high. In addition, most of the men were taller and huskier than average. Lieutenant Colonel Home appears to have made this one of the major criteria in the selection of recruits.

The Royal Rifles remained at Valcartier Camp until the early fall of 1940, when they went to Sussex, New Brunswick. At both Valcartier and Sussex the main activity was training. In November 1940 the battalion moved to Newfoundland. The primary task of the unit was to protect the major airfield complex on the island. Half the battalion was posted to Botwood, on the coast, the other half with Battalion Headquarters was stationed at Gander Airport, some miles inland and to the south of the large seaplane base at Botwood. Guard duties took up a good deal of the time, especially at Gander, but some training was carried out.

In May 1941 the battalion was reunited to form the infantry garrison of St. John's, Newfoundland. Poor weather seriously hampered training, but schemes up to battalion level were undertaken. In September 1941 the Royal Rifles were transferred back to Canada and posted to Saint John, New Brunswick, where they were just starting to take up Coast Defence duties when, on 10 October, they received the warning order for Hong Kong.

The Winnipeg Grenadiers were of more recent origin than the Royal Rifles but were also the possessers of a not undistinguished record. Formed as a militia unit in 1908, they had raised the 11th Battalion of the Canadian Expeditionary Force in the First World War, and later carried the battle honours won by this unit on their colours.

At the beginning of the Second World War the Winnipeg Grenadiers were one of the units that had been selected for almost immediate mobilization. Recruiting was most successful and by late October 1939 the battalion was up to strength.

The Commanding Officer of the Winnipeg Grenadiers was originally Lieutenant Colonel D.M.M. Kay. In June 1941 Kay was posted to National Defence Headquarters and was succeeded in command of the Grenadiers by Lieutenant Colonel J.L.R. Sutcliffe, an officer of the First World War who had seen service in France, Belgium, India,

Mesopotamia, Persia, Russia, and Turkey. The Second-in-Command was Major George Trist, another World War I veteran. Most of the officers and NCO's of the Active Battalion had worked together for years in the Militia unit. The battalion was regarded as an average one— not outstanding, but quite efficient, and well disciplined. The officers were seen as "useful and competent".[3]

The Winnipeg Grenadiers had been designated as a machine-gun battalion. They took their basic training through the winter and began range firing with the Vickers medium machine-gun as soon as the snow cleared in Spring. In May 1940 the unit was converted to a rifle battalion and, with the exception of one company which garrisoned Bermuda from June to August, was posted to Jamaica, where it relieved a British army battalion required elsewhere. In Jamaica the Grenadiers were committed to very onerous guard duties, with only one company at a time free to conduct training.

The Winnipeg Grenadiers were in Jamaica for over 16 months. During that period full-time training for each company was undertaken for only two weeks each, at Montpelier Camp. Most of the time was spent on guard duty and individual training. Not one shot was fired during the whole time the Grenadiers were in Jamaica. The battalion was further hampered by a heavy incidence of malaria and dengue fever among the troops. The Grenadiers were, moreover, on a reduced establishment during the stay in Jamaica, and this plus the sick rate further limited the opportunities for training.

The battalion was transferred back to Canada with the intention of making it part of the 6th Division, then in the initial stages of formation. It was moved in three stages, ending in early October 1941, and was almost immediately warned for service overseas.

The Standard Battalion

One of the greatest sources of controversy concerning the Canadian involvement in the defence of Hong Kong is the state of training and equipment of the two battalions of C Force, and there can be no question that the degree to which they fell short of an acceptable standard in these categories, or if they fell short at all, is of major importance.

A Canadian infantry battalion up to its full war establishment consisted, in August 1941, of 799 all ranks, made up, in theory, of 32 officers, 45 warrant officers, staff sergeants, and sergeants, 72 corporals and lance sergeants, and 650 privates and lance corporals. Under wartime conditions, however, this rank structure was far from universally observed. In addition each battalion had a medical officer, a paymaster, six men from the Royal Canadian Ordnance Corps (armourer, shoemaker, and four motor vehicle fitters), and, usually, a chaplain and his driver.

The battalion was broken down into Battalion Headquarters, Headquarters Company, and four rifle companies, normally designated as A, B, C, and D Companies.

Battalion Headquarters' strength was 55 all ranks. These included the battalion's Commanding Officer (usually a lieutenant colonel), the Second-in-Command (usually a major), the Adjutant, the Regimental Sergeant Major, and intelligence, military police, and medical personnel.

All companies were commanded by a major or captain and possessed a Company Sergeant Major. The Headquarters Company consisted of a small Company Headquarters (6 all ranks) and six specialist platoons. They were the Signal Platoon (36 all ranks), the Anti-Aircraft Platoon with four twin Bren guns (18 all ranks), the Mortar Platoon with six 3-inch mortars in Universal Carriers (46 all ranks), the Carrier Platoon with 13 Universal Carriers (64 all ranks), the Pioneer Platoon (22 all ranks), and the Administration Platoon with transport, ordnance stores, and technical personnel.

The four rifle companies were the backbone of the battalion. Each of these companies had a strength of 123 all ranks, made up of a 12-man Company Headquarters which included the Company Commander and the Company Second-in-Command (usually a captain), and three 37-man platoons. Each platoon was normally commanded by a lieutenant or second lieutenant. This Platoon Commander was assisted by the Platoon Sergeant.

There were three 10-man sections within the platoon. For battle, each section was tactically organized into an eight-man rifle group under the Section Commander (a corporal) and a two-man Bren group with a single Bren light machine-gun. The section, with its two mutually supporting groups, was the smallest tactical unit in the battalion.

The full war establishment of a battalion called for 31 bicycles and 102 motor vehicles. These latter consisted of 27 motorcycles, 2 station wagons, 1 light car, 37 fifteen-hundredweight trucks, 13 three-ton trucks, and 21 tracked Universal Carriers. By far the greater part of these vehicles were with the Battalion Headquarters or with Headquarters Company—at the lowest level each platoon had one fifteen-hundredweight truck. Most of the vehicles were devoted to material rather than men. It was still an army of footsloggers—when on the move, unless extra transport was provided from outside the battalion, the official establishment laid down that 308 men rode vehicles or bicycles while the other 491 walked!

In the quality of its weaponry, the Canadian infantry battalion was, with few exceptions, well up to the standard of any of its allies or opponents. The main personal weapon was the Lee-Enfield No.1 Mk.3 bolt-action rifle, of .303 calibre, the same weapon that had served through the First World War. In using a rifle of this vintage the Commonwealth forces were in no way at a disadvantage. All the major combatants saw out the Second World War largely armed with one version or another of their 1914-1918 rifles, with the exception of the United States, whose army converted in 1942 to a semi-automatic rifle that offered a slight increase in firepower at the sacrifice of simplicity and freedom from mechanical problems. The Lee-Enfield was a rugged and accurate weapon that, in well-trained hands, could deliver a surprising volume of fire for a bolt-action rifle.

The Bren .303 light machine-gun used by Canada was one of the British Army's more inspired acquisitions and was, arguably, the finest weapon of its class on either side during the Second World War. Though incapable of delivering the incredible stream of fire of the German MG34 and MG42 belt-fed weapons, in accuracy, ruggedness, and ease of maintenance it transcended all its contemporaries. There were three Brens in each rifle platoon, one per section, plus 13 in the Carrier Platoon. The Bren was a simple weapon to use, but considerable practice was required for the instinctive operation necessary in battle.

Submachine-guns were just beginning to be standard equipment in the Commonwealth forces, and 42 were found in the 1941 version of the Canadian infantry battalion. Most were in the rifle platoons where the corporal commanding each section carried one. They were Thompson .45-calibre weapons, the notorious "Tommy guns". Not particularly accurate, they were capable of delivering a heavy volume of fire and were effective weapons at close quarters.

Another personal weapon was the hand grenade. While it did not occupy the prominent position during the Second World War that it did in the earlier conflict with its trench warfare, the grenade was still an extremely useful weapon and the only effective way of reaching an enemy behind cover at close range. Of course, a great deal of practice was necessary to hurl these 1½-pound missiles with confidence and accuracy.

A weapon found at the platoon level was the 2-inch mortar. Each platoon had one and it served as the platoon commander's reserve of fire with which he could bring down explosive and smoke shells to support his attack or defence. This uncomplicated high-angle weapon was not difficult to operate, but much training and practice was requried to achieve any degree of accuracy with it.

Two other types of weapon were scattered through the battalion. One was the Boys .55-calibre anti-tank rifle, a shoulder-held weapon with a horrendous kick. Useless against most modern armoured vehicles, it was effective against older light tanks and armoured cars, but played little part in the fighting in Hong Kong. The other was the .38 revolver carried by the officers, who frequently discarded it in battle at the earliest opportunity in favour of something more lethal, preferably a Thompson gun.

The 3-inch mortars of the mortar platoon were the battalion commanders' main source of firepower and these useful and accurate weapons could blanket a substantial area with explosives or smoke in a surprisingly short time. However, the same stricture applied as with the smaller 2-inch version—simple to operate, their crews still required practice and training to attain accuracy. Because of the weight of these weapons (125 pounds), to say nothing of the weight of their ammunition (each round weighed 10 pounds), they were carried into action on Universal Carriers, although they could, if necessary, be broken down into three components to facilitate man-handling. They could be fired from the carriers as well as from ground positions.

The carriers were lightly-armoured, tracked vehicles, used, in the case of the Carrier Platoon, for reconnaissance and to bring a rapid reinforcement of personnel or firepower to any point. At this period they were armed with a single Bren, hence the common terminology of "Bren Carrier".

There were no medium or heavy machine-guns with the unit as these were concentrated in special machine-gun battalions. The twin Brens in the anti-aircraft platoon were not particularly effective against aircraft as their rate of fire was rather slow for that purpose, but, should they be brought to bear on enemy infantry, they could be devastating.

To employ this rather complicated organization or any portion thereof in the field with any degree of success required an enormous amount of practice and training. Even at the lowest tactical level, that of the ten or fewer men in the rifle section, the successful inter-locking employment of the rifles and Bren groups with mutual support and perfect co-ordination in so much as a simple "fire and movement" advance was far less simple than it might seem to the layman. It required a degree of instinctive reaction and confidence that could only be acquired through repetition under varied circum-stances. When one realizes the additional complications inherent in employing the three sections of a platoon, then the four platoons of a company, and then the entire battalion with its internal supporting weapons and equipment, all in the face of enemy opposition, to say nothing of the necessity of co-ordination with friendly troops and with what artillery, armour, and air support are available, the full dimensions of training start—but only just start—to become apparent.

We Were Appalled by Their Lack of Training. . .

—the force's training

Perhaps the greatest single amount of testimony given at the Royal Commission hearing dealt with the actual state of training of the Royal Rifles of Canada and the Winnipeg Grenadiers in October 1941. The evidence taken was varied, and conflicting opinions were expressed. It is hardly surprising that the Commissioner could have found considerable justification for his conclusion that both units were reasonably well trained. Much of the evidence, however, pointed to the contrary, and evidence available since the war has tended to confirm the latter view.

One of the difficulties associated with this topic is the lack of hard information. When a training report says that "Bren gun instruction was carried out", this may often apply only to one company, one platoon, or even one section. Perhaps the only solid evidence would be the percentage of men in each battalion that had carried out standard tests on the different weapons. This evidence is difficult to locate, and when it is available, it normally refers to TOET's—Tests of Elementary Training. This data is useful, but in a negative way, as these are the simplest tests of all and are carried out before a man so much as fires one shot with a particular weapon. If we find, as we do, that not all of the men in the battalions had even done TOET's on the rifle, let alone the Bren or mortars, it gives some idea as to the actual state of training. An even more serious handicap in the actual battle was the lack of training in the support weapons—mortars, anti-tank rifles, Brens, et cetera—as well as the lack of experience in tactical manoeuvres. This last deficiency was to cost them many lives when the fighting began.

With regard to the actual selection of the battalions, it should be noted that the two chosen were in Class C. Those listed in Class A were certainly not regarded as perfectly trained either, but only as "sufficiently advanced to enable them to be despatched abroad and continue their training independently". The Royal Rifles and Winnipeg Grenadiers were two classes behind this category.

The Winnipeg Grenadiers were the earlier mobilized of the two units. They had had a reasonable amount of training before going to Jamaica, especially in the Vickers machine-gun. This was ironic, as when they were redesignated a rifle battalion and ceased to be a machine-gun unit, all Vickers guns were handed in and never re-issued. Unfortunately, their stay at Jamaica was under such conditions as to seriously hamper training. A War Diary entry for October 1940 notes: "Due to duties and sickness only 100 men available to train—50 at Up Park Camp, 50 at Newcastle." Almost all of this was individual training on weapons with no firing involved. One company was detached to Newcastle Camp in the hills for one month at a time to train, but it does not appear that many section, platoon, or company exercises were carried out. When sickness became widespread, men had to be brought down from Newcastle to fill guard duty committments around the harbour and town of Kingston.

In March 1941 each company began, in turn, a two-week course in tactical training at a specially constructed camp at Montpelier. The first week of the training, however, still concentrated on individual subjects. Section and platoon training took place in the second week. Two company exercises were carried out.

In July 1941 two mock general alerts were staged. The first was not particularly successful, the second went a bit better. If enthusiasm was lacking, it was quite possibly because the troops were never turned out with ammunition.

The Battalion's only experience of air attack was just before it left Jamaica. Two old and slow RAF aircraft carried out a mock attack on the column as it marched to the ship. The men stayed in bunches, all on one side of the road—"Casualties estimated as high". The men also had trouble following the aircraft with their weapons.[1]

Lieutenant Colonel Sutcliffe submitted a detailed report on the state of training of his battalion when he returned to Winnipeg in September. Individual training in the main infantry weapons had reached the TOET level. Some tactical training, but no range work, was done with the Bren gun and the Boys anti-tank rifle. Bayonet work was taught but without an assault course. As far as the handling of Thompson guns, 2-inch mortars, and 3-inch mortars, as well as grenades, was concerned, almost nothing had been done due to the scarcity or total absence of these weapons. The Anti-Aircraft Platoon had been trained up to but not including firing, the Mortar Platoon had hardly been trained at all, and the Carrier Platoon had done neither tactical nor drill training. The Signal Platoon was reported as trained, but no personnel from the rifle companies had been taught. The Pioneer Platoon was trained and trade tested. Cooking, despatch riding, and Mechanical Transport training schools had all been held. Sutcliffe also noted that the 75 recruits sent to him in June appeared to be extremely raw. They were put in a special class and had reached the sixth week of their course by the time of embarkation.

In summary, Sutcliffe said that while garrison duties were onerous, "the many and varied duties did however furnish both the officers and OR's with a far more extensive general training than this report would indicate. . . . Morale, discipline, and *esprit de corps* has been maintained at a very high level."[2] General Stuart, in his testimony before the Commission, also claimed that the Winnipeg Grenadiers, because of their service in Jamaica, had learned to be self-reliant. They were the only troops there, and had done their job very effectively for over a year. They had, in addition, become acclimatized to the sub-tropics.[3]

Interpreting the Winnipeg Grenadiers' training report, Lieutenant Colonel Graham, the Officer Commanding an Advanced Training Centre at Winnipeg, stated, at the Commission, that the Winnipeg Grenadiers' rifle training appeared to have reached but did not include actual field firing with machine-gun support. He also said that judging from the report the men sent to the Winnipeg Grenadiers in October 1941, and the Grenadiers themselves would not have been capable of using mortars in combat.[4]

A corporal, W.J. Middleton, who had been with the Winnipeg Grenadiers since demobilization also testified. He had left the troop train without permission at Sicamous, British Columbia, on the way to Vancouver where the unit was to embark for Hong Kong. He had already been told by a medical board and the Battalion Medical Officer that he should be in the hospital for stomach ulcers. In spite of this the Regimental Sergeant Major had put him on the train, and Middleton had therefore taken matters into his own hands. He suffered no punishment for his action except that his pay was withheld for the time he was absent without leave. He was discharged from the army in February 1942 on medical grounds.

In his testimony, Middleton conveyed a rather poor impression of the training the Winnipeg Grenadiers had received in Jamaica. The two weeks at Montpelier was their only period of real training as the camp at Newcastle was really too small to be of any use. At Montpelier the company incorporated Lewis guns into the tactical schemes but not Bren guns, and never so much as saw a 2-inch mortar. Middleton saw a 3-inch mortar once, but was not allowed to examine the sight as he was told that it was too delicate. This prohibition applied to the men of the Mortar Platoon as well. There was no grenade training whatsoever, to say nothing of the fact that there was no fieldwork, little camouflage training, and no carriers. The Government and Commission counsels tried to demolish his credibility because of of his "desertion", but to no avail. Middleton thought that the Medical Officer in Jamaica had rather unwisely ignored his pains, but he had nothing at all against the other officers. Middleton also recalled that at Banff Lieutenant Colonel Sutcliffe had read out a letter from Brigadier Lawson, saying that they were going "where there was a war, not yet our war, but it might be our war at any time."[5]

The Grenadiers, after being warned for overseas, had the St. Charles Ranges at Winnipeg set aside for their use for a week. During this period many of the men fired off an average of 35 rounds apiece in practice. About 10 men of the Carrier Platoon were also given a week's course at an Advanced Training Centre. No further training was done before embarkation.

Additional officers joined the battalion prior to sailing. These were described as excellent and fully-trained. The first statement may well be true—the reinforcement officers did very well in the actual battle. But the officers themselves, the weekend before leaving, confided to T.C. Douglas (later to be the Premier of Saskatchewan and leader of the federal NDP), who had earlier participated in a training course with them, that they felt "that they were not in a position, nor had they had sufficient experience of operational manoeuvres, to take men into a fighting zone."[6] They were very happy to go nevertheless. If these officers, who proved to be quite useful, regarded themselves as under-trained, we may wonder what the position of the original Winnipeg Grenadiers' officers was, particularly with regard to that one aspect—operational manoeuvres or tactics—in which the Canadians were most at a disadvantage at Hong Kong.

When we turn to the Royal Rifles, we find a battalion that had mobilized 10 months later than the Winnipeg Grenadiers but seems to have had more opportunity to train. The Rifles had also had their share of garrison duty, though not the Grenadiers' 16 months, and their duties in Newfoundland were not as demanding as those undertaken by the Grenadiers. They had also been much more in touch with National Defence Headquarters than the Grenadiers, and were part of the large organization of a Canadian Command. They therefore had more feedback, assistance, criticism, and inspections, all of which undoubtedly helped them. This is not to say, however, that they were fully trained by any means.

The unit was officially mobilized 28 June 1940 at Quebec and for the first two months recruits were drilled as they came in. There were no weapons. When the battalion moved to Valcartier Camp in September 1940 training began in earnest. Unlike the Winnipeg Grenadiers, the battalion was built up almost from scratch as far as other ranks were concerned. It was often necessary to select a "likely-looking lad" who was a raw recruit and make him an NCO. Before he could teach the other recruits, the officers had to take the newly-promoted NCO, "who was to take a squad in some subject the following day", and "give instruction to him the night before". Nevertheless, some progress was made before the unit moved to Sussex Camp in October 1940. The camp at Sussex was considered inconvenient because, among other reasons, the parade ground was much too small for a battalion. The ranges themselves were on a riverbank, and on wet days in autumn the firing points were underwater. Tactical schemes were held for the first time at Sussex, and many route marches also. The unit picked up fieldcraft quite easily—the diary noted that "most men have hunted before and do this well." Night schemes were also carried out.

In November 1940 the Royal Rifles went to Newfoundland and were split up. Half the battalion and the Headquarters were at Gander, and the other half under the Second-in-Command at the seaplane base in Botwood. At the latter, before the harbour froze over, guard duties continually required the service of 50% of the men. After the harbour froze and air activity consequently ceased the Botwood detachment had a good deal of time to train. They fired Lewis guns at stationary and moving balloon targets, trained in taking up defensive positions, and continued rifle practice on the 30-yard range.

Junior officers and NCO's were given considerable latitude in forming their own area defence shemes.

At Gander Airport the defensive duties were rather more onerous, but, as they mainly consisted of providing guards and sentries, could hardly be considered training in any sense. On relief days, however, the different platoons trained intensively. In February 1941, the companies at Botwood and Gander changed places. Bren and Lewis gun firing continued to be carried out, including night firing, and when TOET's were taken in rifle and Bren, most men passed.

Winter camping was undertaken as well as training on skis, and some companies were able to find an opportunity for tactical training. In May 1941 the battalion moved to St. John's and was reunited.

During the Royal Rifles' stay in St. John's, blackout practice and alarms were a feature. The latter consisted of a full defence scheme requiring the whole battalion to turn out and take up positions in the area. Range firing was recommenced and more men were put through their TOET's. Reconnaissance work and map reading started to appear in the training syllabus. The seven carriers which arrived were incorporated into the defence scheme. Nevertheless, the unit's War Diary records that "in Canada almost anywhere training is less handicapped than here."

During this period more Brens arrived, allowing platoons to get their own complement. Thompson submachine-guns were issued, though only a very few, and one 2-inch mortar was loaned to the battalion for a week. A four-day course in the latter was held for Warrant Officers and NCO's.

In August 1941 the Royal Rifles were moved back to Valcartier and then almost immediately to Saint John, New Brunswick.[7]

One thing that emerges with abundant clarity is that blame for any deficiencies in the training of the Royal Rifles of Canada and the Winnipeg Grenadiers cannot be laid at the door of the officers, NCO's, or men of these units. They trained hard and enthusiastically to the limits of the time, opportunity, and facilities available and paid it far more than mere lip service. Whether the training that they were actually able to undertake had brought them to a level of being even remotely ready for battle is an entirely different question.

At the Commission hearing, many officers gave testimony as to their impression of the battalion's training, particularly that of the Royal Rifles. Brigadier Philip Earnshaw, the Officer in Command in Newfoundland, called the Rifles a "good average unit". He recalled that Lieutenant Colonel Home had spent most of his service in the Army connected with training in one way or another. The Second-in-Command, Major Price, was a natural leader as well, he claimed. Earnshaw said that junior officers and NCO's were given actual operational responsibility during the duty at Newfoundland. The battalion had a reasonable amount of training up to the company level, but little or none as a battalion. Grenade training was carried out, but only with dummies. Earnshaw admitted that live grenades were a far better way to build confidence.[8]

A report submitted in September 1941 summarized the Royal Rifles' training to August 1941. It was filed as Exhibit 122 and bears the following information:

TOET's	Rifle	79% of strength
	LMG	63% of strength
	Gas	49% of strength
	Judging distance	57% of strength
	Grenade (dummy)	41% of strength

This perhaps gives a better idea of the actual state of training. The Royal Rifles seem to have been the opposite of the Grenadiers, having received more tactical training than weapon training. One must also remember what the Tests of Elementary Training meant: they did not mean that the soldier had necessarily even fired a weapon, indeed he had to pass the test before he could be allowed to fire it, but only that he knew how to load, aim, and clean it to a minimum degree. What these percentages indicate if looked at negatively is that, of the two main weapons, the rifle and Bren, 21% and 37% of the men had not yet demonstrated that they were sufficiently trained to fire their first shot! As the battalion was almost constantly on the move from September until it arrived in Hong Kong in late November, little more training could be done. Again, as with all the battalions in Canada, there was virtually no chance to train at all with mortars, grenades, anti-aircraft weapons (twin Brens), submachine-guns, and signal sets, because these weapons only became available in Canada to any extent at the end of 1941.

Confirming Sutcliffe's observation in regard to the Grenadiers, Lieutenant Colonel Harry Lamb, who was with the Royal Rifles until October 1941, testified that the battalion's stay in Newfoundland was useful training in a general way. Newfoundland was a potential theatre of war—it was not just a place to do sentry duty. The many alarms and scares which occurred during their stay kept the men of the Battalion on their toes and gave them experience in a defensive role. Lamb also claimed that the men were very fit, a statement which does not agree with the battalion's experience during the actual fighting in Hong Kong. This discrepancy can be blamed on the fact that there was, unfortunately, little opportunity to maintain fitness in the months immediately before the battle.[9]

Major Duncan Laurie gave testimony concerning reinforcements and the recruits who joined the battalion before October (when it was further reinforced). Laurie was in command of the Rifles' Regimental wing in Quebec in late 1941, and despatched 62 men to the battalion from there. No weapons at all were available and the recruits were only trained in squad, platoon, and company drill.[10] In any calculation of the percentage of men with less than 16 weeks training, these men should therefore be included, even if their date of enlistment goes back further. As was brought out many times at the inquiry, training is a matter of fact, not time, and these would have received their first rifle training in June 1941 at the earliest.

From evidence of fact the Commission often descended to evidence of a most subjective nature. The Government called many witnesses from among the senior ranks of the Army, who all testified in glowing terms to the quality of both the Rifles and the Grenadiers. One piece of evidence to this effect pre-dated the despatch of C Force and therefore seemed to have greater validity. Colonel Gerald Berteau, who was acting District Officer Commanding of Military District No. 5 (Quebec) in September 1941, sent in a report to NDHQ 15 September 1941, stating that the Royal Rifles was "one of the most efficient ever mobilized in this District". He also recommended that it be included in an overseas formation, where it "would prove of great value". It transpired, however, that Berteau wrote the letter because Lieutenant Colonel Home was anxious that he should. Home's men were getting very restless, and he was afraid he would lose some of his best officers and NCO's through transfers if he failed to get his unit into a divisional formation in the near future. It has already been noted that the Second-in-Command was also engaged in an exchange of correspondence to this end with C.G. Power at this time. Berteau's letter was probably written in all sincerity—he seems to have had a good deal of respect for Home—but he hardly had a chance to know anything about the Royal Rifles' training, beyond seeing them on parade for the Governor General in September 1941, and observing their mobilization in the summer of 1940.[11]

General Stuart appears to have uttered more nonsense during the Commission than any other witness. In his second appearance he proceeded from the particular to the general, and went off on an abstract discourse regarding military training. Like a French *Marechal* before the First World War, he told the Commission that morale, character, and *esprit de corps* were the things that mattered most. The General was hurt because he felt that "the evidence I have heard so far has been trying to bring out just the condition of the battalions . . . in respect to their individual and sub-unit training . . . that is only part of the training of a unit . . . that is superficial." Stuart explained carefully to Duff that the moral and mental training of a unit was what really mattered. If this was at a high peak, "these alleged short-comings that we have heard about, which are all very simple and do not take very long to adjust, can be adjusted." The two battalions could easily have made up these deficiencies by 8 December;

> . . . it is not as though these units had no training whatever. . . . they had a considerable amount of weapon training. It is true in the case of the Winnipeg Grenadiers they lacked the actual firing of these various weapons, but they had done a certain amount of preliminary training with respect to weapons. Some of them missed, it is true . . .

And so on.[12] Duff accepted this line and even quoted some of it in his official report, despite the fact that any officer who genuinely believed that sort of stuff in 1941 should have been drummed out of the Army. It is difficult to credit that Stuart did believe it, but he certainly managed to convince the Commissioner. The examination of the whole question in 1948 (see Appendix C) gives a clear analysis of this matter based on wartime experience. Training is almost every-thing in the production of an efficient unit. *Esprit de corps* grows out of efficiency, not vice versa. As the Minister, J.L. Ralston, who had commanded a battalion in action during the First World War and knew whereof he spoke, said in a speech on 7 November 1941, "The man who has to stop to think how to adjust his respirator or remedy a stoppage in an automatic weapon will probably have no need of either before he has arrived at the answer." Also, "not until every section of a platoon is efficient as a section can a platoon carry out useful training as such . . ." No section could be considered efficient without extensive practice with the 2-inch mortar, no battalion without well-trained mortar, carrier, anti-aircraft, signal, and pioneer platoons, et cetera.[13] It is depressing, in summary, to read such things being said by the Chief of the General Staff.

And what of Major General H.D.G. Crerar who had been Chief of the General Staff and who recommended that the Royal Rifles of Canada and the Winnipeg Grenadiers be the units to go to Hong Kong? To do him justice he did not beat around the bush in his written testimony. He said that the two battalions "in my opinion were generally adequately trained to undertake defensive responsibilities such as those in prospect in Hong Kong." He then became even more specific and positive. "I would say that Force C was certainly fit to meet an attacking force, even in superior numbers, and to give a fine account of itself by December 8, 1941."[14]

Despite the suggestion that the two battalions had been "half-way to the war already" (Crerar) and were therefore well trained, Brigadier Macklin admitted that the units of the 4th Division were "more ready for immediate battle than those two battalions". In mitigation, the General Staff were convinced that time for the necessary refresher training would be available at Hong Kong. Possibly it was not coincidental that the Commander of the force was the Director of Military Training, either. For his part, Lawson was very pleased with the appointment and showed no anxiety about the quality of the troops. He was, by all accounts, not a "yes" man, and would have said something if he thought it necessary. The most probable judgement on Lawson's attitude is that he knew the state of the battalions, honestly felt that there would be time to train before war broke out, and welcomed the opportunity to whip a brigade into shape and bring it up to his standards.

In the final analysis, however, the whole controversy must be viewed and judged in the light of the two Battalions' experience in battle. As one British officer, who escaped from Hong Kong on the night of 25 December 1941 said, "Both Canadian battalions sent to Hong Kong consisted of magnificent material, both officers and men. On arrival we were appalled at their lack of training . . ." There is little doubt that in many cases the Canadians' lack of training cost them unnecessary lives, and this was a subject the Duff Commission was charged specifically to investigate. In view of this it is unfortunate that the Commissioner tended to accept, as expert testimony, the evidence of men whose professional reputations would have been injured if their choice of these battalions had not been upheld.

Young Men Full of Enthusiasm...
—the force is organized and strengthened

The Canadian government had agreed in principle to the despatch of two battalions on 23 September, and, after Ralston was consulted, the substance of this decision was communicated to the United Kingdom government. No time had then been set for the actual sailing of the force, but its selection had, to all intents and purposes, already been made. The final draft proposing the Royal Rifles and Winnipeg Grenadiers was submitted by Crerar to the Minister the next day.

On 9 October 1941 the Dominions Office despatched a telegram to the Canadian government which informed them that the British government "now feel that in all circumstances it would be most desirable if the two Canadian battalions could be despatched at a very early date . . ." The Dominions Office suggested that future discussion of the matter be on the military level.[1]

This was obviously the cue for the British War Office to move. That same day Canadian Military Headquarters (CMHQ) in London sent a telegram to National Defence Headquarters relaying an inquiry from the War Office, who wished to know whether the force would be able to embark on the transport *Awatea* (capacity 2000 troops) in late October. As the next opportunity for direct sailing would not be for another two months, the War Office was very keen that the units go on the *Awatea.* The Department of National Defence was also informed of what the requirements were for the units to be sent to Hong Kong. The battalions were to be up to full war establishment, though possibly a reduced scale of MT [Mechanical Transport] would be acceptable. Some non-standard items such as tropical clothing and mosquito nets would also be necessary, and the War Office wanted to know which of these Canada would not be able to supply.[2]

On receipt of these telegrams, Colonel Gibson (the Director of Military Operations and Intelligence) arranged a meeting of National Defence Branch Directors to discuss what measures would be taken regarding the despatching of the battalions, which was held at 3 pm on 9 October 1941. The final approval of the selection of the two battalions had not been given (this arrived at the end of the meeting), but arrangements were to proceed as far as possible. Lieutenant Colonel Spearing, Movement Control (Quartermaster General Branch), stated that as rolling stock was needed at that time for other important moves, the westward movements for the Royal Rifles should start about 23 October and for the Winnipeg Grenadiers about 25 October. In view of the fact that it would be very difficult to reinforce the units in the event of war, it was decided that extra men should go as first reinforcements. For the medical inspections necessary before the departure of these units it was thought that the standard required should be the same as that for garrison units. As for MT, further information was needed from CMHQ in London, but meanwhile preparations were to be made for the transportation of full scale and ship-boxed MT. Most of the weapons needed could be supplied by Canada. For administrative purposes at least a Staff Captain and possibly a Force Commander should accompany "C Force", as the units were now designated.[3]

After this meeting similar warning orders were sent out to the two battalions—"Serial 1042 Royal Rifles will be ready to move from 0900 hrs 23 October to carry out duties in semi-tropical climate. Further instructions will be issued by QMG. Acknowledge."[4]

The following two days saw a flurry of messages containing requests, queries, information, and advice pass between National Defence Headquarters and CMHQ, the latter acting as the liaison for the War Office. The British advised that men down to medical category C2 could be taken[5] (Gibson testified that in fact no man below the much higher B1 category actually went). National Defence Headquarters informed the United Kingdom that a senior Canadian administrative officer would probably be appointed.[6] Enough Thompson guns to bring the unit up to established strength were obtained from the United States by a special release, and commercial Marconi sets replaced the standard No. 18 set.

On 11 October CMHQ relayed to National Defence Headquarters a request originating from the General Office Commanding Hong Kong for a Brigade Headquarters, to consist of a Brigadier, a Brigade Major, a Staff Captain, and 94 miscellaneous all ranks including 2 medical officers, 2 nursing sisters, a Signals Officer, a Workshop Officer, and a Pay Officer. It was stated that if Canada could not find these quickly "despatch two battalions should not repeat not be delayed on that account."[7] General Crerar and the Minister of National Defence were leaving for England that day and were no longer in Ottawa when the telegram arrived, but Brigadier Kenneth Stuart, the Acting Chief of the General Staff, immediately telephoned the airport at Montreal and reached them before they left. He suggested Colonel J.K. Lawson, the Director of Military Training, as Brigade Commander and Colonel Pat Hennessy as the Senior Administrative Officer. Crerar and Ralston concurred both in the request for the Brigade Headquarters and the suggested appointments. Stuart then obtained official approval of this decision from C.G. Power. Power later informed the Cabinet War Committee of the action, but there does not appear to have been any discussion on the subject.[8]

Thus, the request was approved the same day it was received. Macklin replied to CMHQ informing them of the decision to accept the British request and adding that a Senior Adminstrative Officer (Hennessy) would be going with the Force. The Brigade Headquarters would go with the battalions and the "whole sailing will not be delayed on this account".[9]

Three days later a second meeting of Directors was held at the instigation of the Director of Military Operations and Intelligence. Everything seemed to be under control at this meeting. It had been decided earlier to take full scale MT with 12 months' reserve. The representative of the Director of Mechanization (Captain James) stated that arrangements were being made to send 212 vehicles. Although this is not recorded in the minutes, Lieutenant Colonel Spearing, Brigadier Lawson, and Gibson discussed the practicality of getting all the vehicles on one boat. Spearing agreed to check the freight capacity of the *Awatea* after the meeting.[10]

On the 16th October the War Office sent back a telegram saying that they had "learned with gratification the quantities of equipment which will be taken with Canadian units to Hong Kong. Any of the few deficiencies mentioned can and will be made up at Hong Kong."[11]

Before C Force was sent overseas the Brigade Headquarters, consisting of 83 all ranks, was organized. Most of the other ranks were tradesmen of one sort or another and most had over 16 weeks in the Army; only 4 had less. The C Force administrative personnel were drawn from all across Central and Western Canada, and rather hastily assembled. Lieutenant Colonel Home got the impression that they were a rather inexperienced lot, particularly the Staff Captain, H.S.A. Bush.[12] This is borne out to some extent by an entry in Brigadier Lawson's diary for 19 November; "Tell 2 Ech [Colonel Hennessy] to keep away from Bde in order to give S.C. [Staff Captain] a chance."[13]

Two nursing sisters accompanied the force, despite the fact that the GOC at Hong Kong had stated that medical orderlies were what were really needed. Likewise, two extra RCAMC doctors were attached, although at a full British Command base in a colony of 1½ million, which had a University with a medical school, doctors were not exactly at a premium. The other attached officers appear to have been well trained for their jobs, particularly Captain G.M. Billings, the Brigade Signals Officer, who was made responsible for training Punjabis, Rajputs, and Royal Scots at Hong Kong.

More messages passed across both the Atlantic and Pacific before the troops sailed. On 31 October 1941 the War Office informed National Defence Headquarters, " We are very grateful to you for despatching your contingent to Hong Kong at such short notice. We fully realize the difficulties of mobilization and of distance which have had to be overcome. The moral effect of their arrival in November will be much greater than it would have been two months later."[14] During October, however, there had been a few problems associated with the despatch of C Force that had not been entirely overcome. These related specifically to the matter of reinforcements and mechanical transport.

Because the force was being sent to form part of a distant garrison, the units carried with them full establishment for all their stores and weapons, plus reserves. The same principle applied to the men. In addition to the normal full war establishment of an infantry battalion, 150 men and 6 officers were attached to each unit as what the military termed "first reinforcements". Under normal conditions these would remain at the Regimental Wing and be sent out as required, but Hong Kong was much too far away for that.

The normal establishment for a battalion plus attached personnel was 34 officers and 773 other ranks (807 total). With 156 reinforcements this came to 963 all ranks. When the two battalions arrived back from their garrison duties in Newfoundland and Jamaica, the Royal Rifles were slightly over strength while the Winnipeg Grenadiers were under strength by just over 100 men. The Grenadiers, in addition, had men who were in the process of transferring to the RCAF. Before sending the units to Hong Kong, all ranks in both battalions had to pass a medical inspection which also resulted in a certain reduction in strength, especially among the Grenadiers, who had just spent 16 months in the tropics. In the end 436 new men were required—136 to bring the units up to strength and another 300 for the reinforcements.

Responsibility for this task fell to Colonel Pat Hennessy, the Director of Organization (Adjutant General's Branch) who was later chosen as C Force's Senior Administrative Officer. In obtaining the new men Hennessy worked with Brigadier Riley, the District Officer Commanding, Military District No. 10, and in the case of the Royal Rifles with Lieutenant Colonel Home. Hennessy was sure that he could get the men. The criteria used were, first, to obtain the best men possible under the circumstances (the need of speed and secrecy), and secondly, transfers to the C Force regiments had to be voluntary. It was decided that reinforcements for the Grenadiers should come from Military District No. 10 (the Winnipeg area) while reinforcements for the Royal Rifles should come from Military District No. 2 (Toronto, Camp Borden, and adjacent areas).

Obviously, Hennessy was hoping to fill the ranks with "trained men", that is, men who had completed the 8-week Basic and 8-week Advanced Training courses. In fact, there had been a routine order in effect since 18 August 1941 that men were not to be sent overseas unless they had the full 16 weeks of training, without prior authority from National Defence Headquarters. At that time, of course, the order applied only to the Canadian Corps in England, but it should be safe to assume that it was meant to be a general rule (which, in fact, all routine orders are). Ironically, the order was written and distributed by the Director of Military Training, then Colonel J.K. Lawson, who as Commander of C Force was to take with him to Hong Kong more than 100 men who had not received the required training. The Adjutant General, Major General B.W. Browne, claimed at the hearings that these men were replacements, not reinforcements, and the order did not therefore apply. In addition, he claimed, prior authority had been obtained from National Defence Headquarters in the person of Colonel Hennessy. As Hennessy had given his instructions to the Military Districts over the telephone because of the pressure of time, no documentation of this existed.[15]

In Winnipeg, meanwhile, Lieutenant Colonel Sutcliffe could not be certain as to the precise number of men he would need. The men currently on his battalion strength still had to pass medical inspection, and some were waiting for transfers. The situation was further confused because the last group from Jamaica had only returned on 10 October and, having been granted 14 days leave, had promptly scattered. These men all had to be contacted and told to report back immediately. Sutcliffe at first thought that 150 men would do, then he asked for (and got) 220. After the medical inspection of the battalion, however, it was found that 50 or 60 more were still required.

The first contingent for the Winnipeg Grenadiers was taken from Advanced Training Centre No. 15 at Winnipeg. The Commanding Officer there, Lieutenant Colonel R.G. Graham, asked Lieutenant Colonel Sutcliffe to visit the Centre, which he did on the 10th or 11th of October. Sutcliffe said he was badly in need of signallers and other specialists. Graham gave him 30 trained signallers, two or three 3-inch mortar personnel, 12 driver mechanics, three or four carrier drivers, plus some NCO's who were willing to revert to privates in order to go overseas immediately. In response to a request for volunteers, 150 at the Advanced Training Centre came forward. Later Graham was asked for some more men. Sutcliffe gave a talk on the regiment to the men at the Centre, after which 35 more volunteered. Four more men from the Centre were to join later. Of the 189 men who joined the Grenadiers from this Advanced Training Centre, 30 had only three months in the army; the rest had the requisite 16 weeks.

Graham also supplied 12 officers to the Winnipeg Grenadiers. He had a high opinion of all of them and said they were fully trained. These included the ones who had talked to Tommy Douglas the weekend before they left. All in all reinforcements from this Centre were good; Brigadier Riley later claimed they were the cream of the reinforcements earmarked for the Princess Patricia's Canadian Light Infantry, Queen's Own Cameron Highlanders, and South Saskatchewan Regiment. Some of the NCO's were former instructors and these subsequently proved very valuable. Riley also stated, in regard to the Grenadiers, "it was quite clear that the specialists were not adequately trained. . . . The signalling section could not be classed as trained. . . . No training done as a battalion . . ."[16]

The Winnipeg Grenadiers found that they still needed men, so an Advanced Machine-Gun Training Centre at Dundurn, Saskatchewan (in Military District No. 12) was asked for volunteers. Thirty men, all with over 16 weeks' training, came forward and were taken off to join their new battalion in Winnipeg by a Grenadier lieutenant.

As it appeared that both the Winnipeg and Dundurn training centres were exhausted as sources of reinforcements, recruits were sought from a Basic Training Centre (No. 100) at Portage-la-Prairie, where 17 men volunteered. About half these men had less than eight weeks' training.

Finally, about 22 October, it became apparent that the battalion was still not up to strength. Men were obtained from the Military District No. 10 District Depot in Winnipeg, which was a holding unit for men waiting assignment. About half these men had completed basic training, while the other half had gone through advanced training. Of the 38 men taken from the Depot, 23 were originally with the 18th Reconnaissance Battalion and had been left behind when this unit moved east. They had not been taken because the Second-in-Command of the 18th Reconnaissance Battalion, who was Acting Commanding Officer at the time, did not think they were suitable for his unit due to low mental capacity or inability to learn. Brigadier Riley protested against the strength of this assertion when it was later brought forward by George Drew and said that they were not struck off as inefficient—they were just thought unsuitable for a reconnaissance battalion. The Second-in-Command at the Depot considered them much better material than the 18th Reconnaissance Battalion's Second-in-Command gave them credit for and thought that they had been unfairly treated. [17]

All together, 63 of the men who joined the Winnipeg Grenadiers in October 1941 had less than 16 weeks' training. The senior officers who testified at the Commission claimed that this was not particularly important because the officers of the battalion had been personally involved in the recruiting of these men. These senior officers also stated that the need for secrecy prevented National Defence Headquarters from combing all the Districts in Canada. It was pointed out, however, that the trained men were there—1513 men had completed the 16-week course and were in the training centres in October 1941. Of these, 388 were at Camp Borden and at Winnipeg. The reason for emphasizing this last point in testimony at the Commission was purely politics. George Drew, the chief critic of the government concerning the Hong Kong affair, was rabid for compulsory service, and was always on the lookout for anything that would prove that Canada's volunteer system was a miserable failure. This was a point that R.B. Hanson, Tory Leader, wanted written into the Commissioner's terms of reference. Hence the attempts by the officers to show that "other considerations"—secrecy, speed, and the value of having the Commanding Officer inspect the men, and not the lack of trained soldiers—were responsible for the scraping of the bottoms of certain barrels to find reinforcements.

The impression was also given at the hearings that Colonel Hennessy was constantly informed of the reinforcement situation and that he assented to all the transfers, although Riley and Sutcliffe did most of the work. In fact, Hennessy remarked on board the *Awatea* that Military District No. 10 had been instructed to call on other Districts as far as the coast if enough men could not be found.[18] When this was done, as at Dundurn in Military District No. 12, the results were good. As for the Military District No. 10 men, "only a very small percentage were sufficiently trained for overseas service," however the officers supplied by this District were "splendid material and well trained".

The Royal Rifles did not need as many reinforcements as the Winnipeg Grenadiers, because they had been slightly over strength before medical re-examinations. It was decided to get the necessary men from Military District No. 2. No explanation for this was asked for or given, but it is curious when it is recalled that Military District No. 5 was home ground for the Royal Rifles. The probable explanation lies in the fact that the Rifles were an English unit from Eastern Quebec. Problems in recruiting in their home district may have been foreseen, as by 1941 their main sources of recruits, English Gaspesians, Lac St. Jean, and Quebec City men, must have been almost exhausted. This factor was undoubtedly known and taken into consideration at National Defence Headquarters, where it was feared that as a result of a heavy battle, the unit might lose its regional character.[19] It seems most likely, therefore, that the reinforcements for the Royal Rifles were taken from Ontario because in the time allotted the necessary Quebec men could not have been found.

There was one attempt made to get Quebec men for the Royal Rifles. The Regiment's Second (Reserve) Battalion was paraded and Home asked for volunteers. Out of these 250 men, most of whom were conscripts for Home Service only in the "Non-Active" battalions, only one stepped forward—a Rifleman Fleming. This man subsequently deserted at Kamloops, British Columbia, before the troops embarked for Hong Kong.

The first call for volunteers was made at Camp Borden where there were two Advanced Training Centres, A-10 and A-11. At A-11 the Commanding Officer, Lieutenant Colonel Richard Denison, was asked via the Camp Commandant, Brigadier McCuaig, for men to transfer to a unit for overseas duty. He was also told that Hennessy would accept men with one month or more in an Advanced Centre, in other words, men with 12 weeks' training or better. There were 89 volunteers from this camp, who were taken to the District Depot in Toronto to be looked over by two Royal Rifles officers. Two were rejected. Of those accepted, 38 had 16 weeks or more training, 3 had 15 weeks, 1 had 12 weeks, 43 had 11 weeks, and 2 had ten weeks. The Commanding Officer of Camp Borden looked them over, and thought they were good potential for any battalion. Major C. Goodday, the Commanding Officer of the A-10 Advanced Training Centre, was also asked to recruit volunteers. He assembled his men together and told them that a Quebec regiment wanted men. No men came forward. When he reported this to Brigadier McCuaig, the Brigadier asked if he had told the men it was an English, not a French, unit. No, Goodday hadn't; he re-assembled the men and made a further pitch. Five men came forward that day; 11 came forward the next morning. Of these 16, 11 had over 16 weeks, while 5 were in their 12th week of training. When he was calling for recruits, Goodday was not aware that they were destined for overseas.[20]

In January 1942, when this whole question was being looked into by National Defence Headquarters on its own initiative, the Adjutant of A-10 informed the Camp Commandant that "there was merely a call for reinforcements" to the Royal Rifles, "no information as to whether they should have completed their advanced training."[21] Goodday defended those recruited from his Centre in a letter, saying, "they were young men full of enthusiasm to get into a fighting unit, and had received training in rifle, LMG, and gas."[22]

Although there appear to have been 388 men in Camp Borden who had completed Advanced Training, only 49 had actually volunteered. The reason for this is quite simple. Men, on enlisting, signed up with a particular regiment and after training were posted to it, where they usually had friends, relatives, or people from their own area. Most of the men in the Advanced Training Centre at Borden were earmarked for regiments already overseas. The 11th draft to England had been warned already, and the men who were not on it were quite confident that they would be on the next draft to their own units. They were therefore not too interested in service with the Royal Rifles.

The Royal Rifles still needed a number of men to complete their war establishment with first reinforcements. In hopes of obtaining those men the District Officer Commanding contacted Brigadier Stevenson, Officer Commanding the 10th Infantry Brigade, who asked Lieutenant Colonel Joseph C. Gamey, Officer Commanding the Midland Regiment, to have 52 men ready to go to the District Depot the next day. As the Midland Regiment was strung out on guard duty over four counties in the Niagara region at the time, Gamey had to let his company commanders select the men. When the offer was made nearly everyone in the battalion volunteered, as the unit had been on either Coast Defence or guard duties for many months.

All the men chosen by the Company Commanders had been in the army for a considerable time—two had joined in 1941 (March), the rest in 1940. They had all done TOET's in rifle, Bren gun, grenade (dummy), PAG (protection against gas), and judging distances, yet had rarely fired a rifle. When, on one of their brief and infrequent trips to the range, they fired a classification, 11 of the 52 had failed, 5 had qualified as 3rd class shots, and 9 had either not finished or never actually fired a rifle. This accounts for almost half the men sent. No 2-inch mortar training, anti-tank rifle, or Thompson submachine-gun training had been given them. Gamey said in his testimony that the men were as good as any in Canada. He later qualified this and said they were as good as any who had had the same opportunities for training. Gamey explained that Coast Defence and guard duties left him very little time to train. At Saint John, New Brunswick, he could train two companies at a time (including the Headquarters Company) but at Niagara there was no opportunity to train at all; guard duties had kept them completely busy the whole time.[23]

A further comment on the men from the Midland Regiment, which was no more than rumour, was that all the men selected were the trouble-makers of the unit. This was repeated in a letter to Drew from George White, a Tory MP, dated 26 February 1942.[24] White's source of information is unknown, and it is difficult to place much credence in such a sweeping assertion without more evidence. The possibility of its being at least partially true cannot, however, be ignored. A more reliable source in this regard was the father of a Winnipeg Grenadier who wrote to Drew 19 January 1942 (before the Commission was appointed): ". . . after nearly two years of soldiering, he was not a soldier yet. Their stretch in Jamaica was a joke as far as training was concerned." This is probably a legitimate comment on the battalion's state of training. The father also spoke of the reinforcements to the Grenadiers, "three of whom I know personally. Some soldiers!!"[25]

Altogether the two battalions received 115 men as reinforcements who had had less than 16 weeks' training. If we add to that the 75 "raw" men who joined the Winnipeg Grenadiers in Jamaica in June 1941 (who, on the move from September onward, could not have received much training between June and October) and the 62 men sent to the Royal Rifles from the Regimental Wing (where there was not even a rifle), we arrive at a larger figure—something around 250 men. These latter 137 men were never considered by the Commission at all; as they were Royal Rifles or Winnipeg Grenadiers in October, they simply did not count as reinforcements.

In arriving at a finding on the reinforcements, the Commissioner accepted the testimony of the senior officers who claimed that such a small number of partially trained reinforcements, estimated at 6%, would not seriously affect the quality of the troops. The figures in the foregoing paragraph, however, give a percentage of 12½%. In other words, one man out of eight was only partially trained. Apparently the Commissioner was particularly impressed by the testimony of Lieutenant General A.G.L. McNaughton, who dropped in to give his "unbiased" expert opinion. The General was not being investigated, so his testimony was seen as valid in the extreme, however it is obvious to anyone who has read Crerar's correspondence with McNaughton that they were old friends. When the training of the reinforcements being sent to the Corps in England was receiving criticism, Crerar asked McNaughton to lend him support. McNaughton released a bulletin praising extravagantly the quality of men coming out of the Canadian training camps and wrote back to Crerar, "I hope this suits the purpose" or words to that effect.[26]

McNaughton went into the familiar "character and morale" routine. The Commanding Officer of the units had been given the chance to inspect the men, and as the men were keen on seeing action, and full of character, the matter of training was secondary. For a battalion to absorb 10% to 15% recruits was no problem, and implied no unfairness either to the recruits or to the original members of the unit.[27]

Taking into account McNaughton's testimony, the need for secrecy, the need for speed, and the desirability of choosing men from only a few Districts, Duff concluded that the business of reinforcement was done competently and that no unfairness resulted to the men from this aspect of the expedition. Besides, said Duff, with Lawson around, the 3 weeks on the ship and the 3 weeks at Hong Kong would have sufficed to train the newcomers adequately. Duff also made it a point to emphasize that the requisite trained men were in fact already in Canada; that is, the volunteer system was working well.

What Duff unfortunately did not stress in his 1942 report was that many of the volunteers should never have been accepted as adequately trained for overseas service. Between the acceptance of the British request and the sailing of the *Awatea* only one month was available for finding reinforcements for the two battalions, and perhaps this was considered justification for the lack of complete training. In any event, between 9 October and the end of the month, two insufficiently-trained battalions were reinforced, united, and put under the command of a newly-organized, unfamiliar, and partly inexperienced Brigade Headquarters, and sent to Hong Kong to fight for their lives.

They've Despatched J.K. Lawson Without Even a Wheelbarrow...

—the force is equipped

The second most common epithet after "poorly trained" that has been applied to the hapless men of C Force is that they were "poorly equipped", particularly with regard to transport. As with most such sweeping generalities this is far from totally accurate, but the lack of transport was tragically all too real. In dealing with the question of equipping the force it is necessary to divide the matter into three component sections—Technical Ordnance Stores (dealing with such items as weapons, ammunition, and wireless), General Ordnance Stores (such items as blankets, boots, and uniforms), and Mechanization Services of National Defence all come into play. In providing the first two types of equipment the job was done quickly and efficiently, despite many problems due to shortages. In the case of the third type, the vehicles never reached the ship. The circumstances leading up to this situation were exhaustively investigated by the Commission, and its censure of the handling of this matter was the only wrist-slapping it indulged in. Even then, the Commissioner doubted that any harm had been done to the troops as the 20 priority vehicles despatched in advance would probably not all have gone on the ship and, even if there had been sufficient space, he could not positively find that they would have been much help. On both these points the findings of the Commission were directly contrary to the testimony and evidence given. Perhaps more than any other point raised at the Inquiry, the decision on this issue gives the impression that the whole thing was a whitewash. When considering questions such as the probability of a Japanese attack, the exact state of training of a battalion, or the effect of reinforcements on a unit, there are bound to be some grey areas. But when three immensely experienced men who were present at loading testified that the vehicles could have been loaded, and the Commissioner preferred to believe a man who was not there and who stood to gain by saying the opposite, it is difficult for anyone who has read all the testimony to believe in Duff's impartiality. The Commission also saw as exhibits reports from Hong Kong stressing the critical nature of the transport situation during the battle. Ignoring these, the Commissioner wrote in his report, "There is no evidence, however, that the troops suffered from the lack of them . . ."[1] In this matter, as in others, the Commissioner showed himself remarkably selective when it came to weighing the evidence.

General and Technical Ordnance Stores can both be dealt with briefly. The evidence submitted at the hearing established that everything went smoothly and there were no complaints about the supply of these stores.

Out of a voluminous list of General Ordnance Stores needed for C Force, only four things could not be supplied, because they were not available: strings for bugles, disinfectant for dishes, an oil cabinet, and heel plates for shoes (nails were supplied instead). All clothing supplied to C Force was brand new and of the latest pattern. Major Robert McColm, who had been in charge of General Ordnance Stores at the time, felt that this force was the most well-equipped of any that left Canada. McColm had assembled the stores required from 12 different depots in Canada, mostly in small quantities. He stated that if any stores had not arrived either he or the Special Ordnance Officer in Vancouver, Colonel Henderson, would have completed stores from the Vancouver Depot or else would have raided battalions in the Vancouver vicinity. The only check used by McColm on the smooth functioning of the supply system he had arranged for C Force was the sending of a message to the local Ordnance Officer giving the scheduled date of arrival of any shipment. If it did not arrive in time, the Ordnance Officer was to telephone McColm immediately. This seems to have been effective.[2]

Technical Stores, that is, weapons and ammunition, were supplied equally efficiently. Colonel Gordon L. Ross, the Director of Supply, Technical Stores, testified that the most notable deficiencies were in Boys anti-tank rifles, and 2-inch and 3-inch mortar ammunition. Instead of having 22 anti-tank rifles each, the battalions only had one each, and there was no mortar ammunition at all. In no way could these deficiencies be laid at the door of military ineptitude unless one traces it back to the failure to convince pre-war Canadian governments of the desirability of a well-equipped army and an indigenous armament industry. As there were, at that time, only 300 rounds for the 3-inch mortar in all of Canada, it is not altogether surprising that none could be spared for C Force. Echoing McColm, Ross also said that, on the whole, C Force was the most well-equipped group that had left Canada.[3] There is no reason to doubt McColm's and Ross's estimate. A British officer noted when the force disembarked that they appeared "unusually well-equipped".[4]

The third type of equipment supplied to the force was mechanical transport (MT), and its provision did not go as smoothly. The evidence on this subject at the hearing was voluminous, and the Commissioner's criticism of Lieutenant Colonel Spearing for his lack of energy was the only censure of the report. This aspect of equipping C Force had already been the subject of an extensive departmental investigation, as a result of which the Quartermaster General (QMG), Major General Schmidlin, and Lieutenant Colonel Spearing had been retired.

The failure to fill the troopship *Awatea* with as much MT as she could carry was the result of a misunderstanding between the QMG's Branch and the Master General of the Ordnance (MGO) Branch, with the civilian Controller of Transport adding his bit to the confusion.

On 9 October the first Directors' meeting was held at National Defence Headquarters in order to begin preparations for the Hong Kong expedition. The British War Office had advised that a reduced scale of MT might be acceptable, but at the meeting it was decided to make the full scale available. The name of the ship, the *Awatea,* was made known that day, but Lieutenant Colonel Spearing, in charge of Movement Control in the QMG's Branch, did not take note of this. Captain F.D. James, Acting Director of Mechanization, MGO's Branch, undertook to make the necessary MT available.[5]

The following day Captain James, after ascertaining the established complement of vehicles for an infantry battalion, made arrangements with the major automobile manufacturers (Ford at Windsor and General Motors at Oshawa) to have the necessary vehicles boxed for shipment and ready to load on flatcars.[6]

James's subordinate, Lieutenant Findlay, wrote a memo the next day to Movement Control, stating that the Royal Rifles and the

Winnipeg Grenadiers would take no MT with them from their districts.[7] This memo was a routine one, complying with a February 1941 QMG directive requiring that Movement Control be kept informed of what MT a unit kept when it moved, but Lieutenant Colonel Spearing wrongly inferred that neither unit would take MT to Hong Kong.[8]

On 13 October James gave Major Gwynne of Movement Control a list of the MT which was to go. The next day, having learned from the manufacturers that rail permits were still lacking for the vehicles, James phoned D.C. Connor, the Assistant Controller of Transport in Montreal, to find out what was causing the delay. When Connor told him that this was the first he had heard of the matter, James arranged for Spearing to phone Connor immediately. James had already given Connor the information on MT, and Spearing gave Connor information on the general and technical stores.[9] Connor then worked out the space required for MT (100-125,000 cubic feet) and the other stores (70,000 cubic feet).

On 15 October Connor gave rail permits to the motor companies. It may be noted in passing that the Office of Controller of Transport was created late 1939 to have control over the passage of goods by rail. The Controller could stop or embargo a shipment if in his opinion the rolling stock was needed more urgently elsewhere or if there was not enough shipping available to take a cargo. The prevention of rail congestion in dock areas was one of his prime responsibilities. That same day Connor's superior, the Controller of Transport T.C. Lockwood, learned from the Naval authorities that the *Awatea* had only a 45,000 cubic foot freight capacity. Realizing that the force's MT required approximately three times this capacity he therefore placed an embargo on the shipment late that day, thus preventing it from leaving the factory. He informed the motor companies the next day of his action, but his office did not pass the information on to National Defence Headquarters.

James found out about the embargo on 16 October direct from the motor companies. He phoned Movement Control every day thereafter to ask about moving the MT and Lieutenant Colonel Spearing kept talking about getting another ship. James claimed at the Commission that, by this time, he was getting "pretty disgusted" with the whole thing.[10]

Following a second Director's meeting on 14 October, Spearing, Lawson, and Macklin held a brief conference. Having learned that not all the MT could go on the *Awatea,* they decided to list the priority vehicles and load as many on as possible. The priority vehicles were 6 Universal Carriers, 12 fifteen-hundredweight trucks, and 2 fifteen-hundredweight water tanks which occupied a total space of 11,571 cubic feet. On 18 November Macklin gave James the list of priority vehicles, which totalled four carloads, and the latter then phoned the motor companies. James left a memo for Lieutenant Findlay to inquire about the permit situation and then left Ottawa that weekend, telephoning back the next week to check on progress. The second time he called, on 21 October, he was told that the priority shipment had been allowed to proceed, and the rest of the MT would go the next day.

The shipment of priority vehicles had been released the day before when Lieutenant Colonel Spearing ascertained, by totalling up the volume of general and technical stores, that 12,000 cubic feet would still be available. Mr. Connor was still sceptical, and wired to P.B. Cooke, General Manager of the Canadian Australian Line, owners of the *Awatea,* to confirm this. Cooke's return telegram was rather unclear, but the shipment of MT was released nonetheless. It went out the morning of 21 October, and in normal circumstances would have reached Vancouver late 27 October. Due to congestion of rail traffic on the prairies, however, the MT did not roll into Vancouver until the afternoon of 28 October, by which time the *Awatea* had sailed.

Brigadier Lawson was far from happy about this. He had talked to Macklin a few times about the MT situation and it had been agreed that the ship would take all she could. In a report dated 15 November 1941, written on board the *Awatea,* Lawson complained: "Despite my repeated representations at NDHQ regarding the necessity for at least a proportion of our transport to accompany us, none of the MT had apparently arrived at Vancouver by 27 October, and it was therefore necessary to sail without it, though there were two holds practically empty."[11]

There is no question that Lieutenant Colonel Spearing, on 9 October, should have ascertained the exact capacity of the *Awatea* and acted accordingly. As it was, he did not begin to look for another ship until 16 October. That was two days after he had talked to Macklin and Lawson, and agreed that all the MT for C Force could not possibly go on the *Awatea.* He seemed confused over his responsibilities, and claimed his organization had not been responsible for movement of vehicles crated for overseas since March 1940. The Controller of Transport told the Commission, however, that "Movement Control advises that Controller of Transport of any equipment which is going forward on troopships."[12] Whoever was responsible for the actual movement of the vehicles, Spearing was the only man in a position to know how much space, if any, could be used for MT, and he was exceptionally slow in acquiring this absolutely essential data.

For their parts, neither Lockwood nor Connor made any real effort to inform National Defence Headquarters that an embargo had been placed on the shipment. Captain James found out, almost by accident, from the motor companies. He talked to Spearing about the matter several times between 15 and 17 October, but there is no evidence that Spearing was particularly concerned as a result. Having agreed, on 14 October, that as much MT as possible should be shipped, he made no move until 20 October to inform the Controller of Transport of this decision. One telephone call would have been sufficient to get four carloads, out of a total of approximately 50, moving to the coast. Until 20 October the Controller of Transport was not aware that there was a distinction being made in the MT, and that some were set aside which it may have been possible to load. During those five days, the MT sat on the motor company sidings gathering demurrage charges.[13]

One excuse for the "lack of energy" on Spearing's part was that he was involved with 10 other troop movements concurrently with C Force, one totalling 30,000 men. During this period he was talking to Halifax and to the Controller of Transport's Office two or three times a day, and it was therefore difficult to remember everything that passed between them. Be that as it may, the Movement Control Chief appears to have been quite confused during this entire period, and extremely slow in passing on information. This could probably not have occurred in the case of anything but crated vehicles as there was a definite routine laid down (Routine Order 318) for the shipment of goods overseas. The Order was unworkable in the case of MT because of its bulk, and when a special case such as the despatch of C Force cropped up no one seemed to know what to do or what their responsibilities were, and demonstrated no great urgency in finding out. On 18 October, for instance, Spearing knew that 12,000 cubic feet would be empty on the *Awatea*, he also knew that this space could be filled with priority vehicles, and he knew that the MT was crated and ready to be shipped to Vancouver whenever permission was received from the Controller of Transport. He did nothing, however, until two days later, as he thought that it was James's job to inform the Office of the Controller of Transport, despite the fact that the QMG's Branch was quite clearly responsible for any long-distance movement of Army material.

At the Vancouver end, neither the Ordnance officers nor the Movement Control Officer (Major Gwynne, who had been sent out temporarily) were troubled by the non-appearance of the MT. They knew by 25 October that another ship had been found (the American freighter *Don José*) and therefore believed that everything was going well.[14] According to Major Gwynne, Brigadier Lawson was not too worried either, as he probably knew by 25 October that the MT would not be loaded, but made no complaint.[15] This impression is certainly not corroborated by Lawson's report of 15 November quoted earlier.

The Commission also looked into the question of whether the priority MT could have been loaded even if it had arrived on time. Conflicting evidence was heard, many witnesses asserting that room could have been found for 10 or so vehicles at most.

The Controller of Transport, T.C. Lockwood, testified that the problems of stowing the vehicles in the *Awatea* would have been very great, due to the size of the hatchway on her No. 1 hold and the fact that MT uses a great deal of space over and above its nominal requirements.[16] Chief Justice Duff was quite impressed with Lockwood's testimony, and he referred to Lockwood as a "man of immense experience in the shipping business before the war as well as in his present office."[17] Duff quoted his testimony at length in his report.

The Commissioner also heard evidence from Mr. P.B. Cooke, who stated that the MT could all have been loaded quite easily, even after the other gear was stowed, and proceeded to explain in detail just how it could have been done.[18] Sir Lyman simply noted in his report: "I do not accept Mr. Cooke's evidence that it was a simple matter to load these vehicles . . ."[19] Yet Cooke was the General Manager of the Line that owned the *Awatea.* He had loaded military vehicles and civilian cars on that very ship before. He was present the whole time the ship was loading. Most important, however, is the fact that he had no vested interest, as did Lockwood, in the outcome of the Inquiry. Lockwood's Office was the possible subject of a censure by the Commission, and it was obviously in his interest to show that the

MT could probably not have been loaded. In addition, Lockwood had never seen the *Awatea* and had never supervised the loading of MT before. On the other hand, Cooke's testimony was corroborated by two independant witnesses, both of whom had much more knowledge in this regard than Lockwood. In signed affadavits, Henry Scarisbrooke, the Wharf Superintendant, and Adam Watson, the Marine Surveyor, gave evidence in detail to show that the MT could have easily been loaded.[20] The former had held his position for 20 years and was directly responsible for leasing the *Awatea.* He knew the ship well. The latter, a former captain and holder of the highest certificate in the British Empire, was responsible for issuing a certificate of seaworthiness to all foreign-bound ships in Vancouver after loading. That the Commissioner chose to ignore the evidence of these experts in favour of Lockwood's seems on the face of it a very curious thing.

The Commissioner then went on to speculate about any possible deleterious effect the lack of MT had on C Force. To anyone studying the battle it soon becomes clear that MT would have been very useful at Hong Kong even though it would not have altered the final outcome, and that the trucks and especially the water-carriers would have alleviated a great deal of hardship among the troops. This evidence, however, was not brought before the Commission. What was included was a cable of Lawson's to National Defence Headquarters of 24 November 1941 which said that "Transport hired as required".[21] Duff quoted this in the report (p. 60) to show that no injury was caused by the lack of MT, although a careful reading of the entire telegram makes it appear likely that this transport was mentioned only in the context of "breaking down, checking, and distribution of ordnance stores" from the ship to the barracks. The vehicles hired for this job certainly did not go into battle.

Situation reports demonstrate clearly that the extra MT would have been valuable in the battle. A report from the General Officer Commanding dated 22 December states: "Water and transport situation critical".[22] One of 23 December says: "Troops now very tired, Water and transport situation still very grave."[23] In the light of these reports, it is difficult to understand Duff when he reported, "In the absence of evidence, I can make no finding as to whether or not the force suffered from lack of these two [water-carrying] vehicles." It would probably be hard to overestimate the value of even two of these vehicles in the last few days of fighting, when the pipelines from the reservoirs had been destroyed by Japanese shellfire. As to the carriers, the Commissioner reported that both the Bren gun and the 3-inch mortar, the normal load of these vehicles, were designed to be carried by the troops. Evidence pointed out, however, that in the case of the mortars (and the six priority carriers were those for the Mortar Platoons) this was impractical except over very short distances, as the loads were quite heavy. Lack of the carriers or shortage of trucks would seriously hamper the use of the 3-inch mortars, and this was admitted by officers at the hearings.[24] To the Commissioner, however, whether detriment to the force resulted could only be a matter of "speculation". This might have been so as none of the members of C Force were in a position to appear before the Commission and testify, dearly as they might have liked to. There is a world of difference, however, between Sir Lyman's matter of "speculation" and the definition any reasonably objective person would apply—a "virtual certainty".

All 212 vehicles were eventually loaded on the second ship, *Don José*, which left Vancouver 4 November. It was originally scheduled to sail Shanghai—Hong Kong—Manila, which would have brought it to Hong Kong on 6 December. However the vessel's master was given instructions by the US Navy (as it was an American ship it was subject to US Navy orders) to proceed via Honolulu and Manila first. It is interesting to note that the US Navy was, even at this early date, taking extensive precautions. On the route from Honolulu to Manila, the ship was instructed not to proceed directly, but via Torres Strait and the Molucca Passage. These are well to the south of the direct route—Torres Strait is between New Guinea and Australia. The master of the *Don José* was told to "darken ship after passing the Hawaiian Islands" and "maintain radio silence west of 160° West". The ship, which normally sailed at 8½ knots, passed south of Port Moresby on 2 December and arrived in Manila on 12 December, several days after the outbreak of war. Since it was impossible to deliver the MT to Hong Kong it was decided to turn the vehicles over to the United States military authorities in the Philippine Islands, with the understanding that if a chance presented itself, they would be delivered to Hong Kong. The United States authorities agreed to pay for them, but it is doubtful that the money was forthcoming quickly, as the Philippines were soon under full siege themselves. At the time of the Commission's hearings the Americans were still resisting but were obviously very near the end, and the Canadian vehicles presumably ended up in the hands of the Imperial Japanese Army.*

One case of spare parts failed to make the connection with the *Don José* due to the inability of the automobile company to collect the necessary parts on time. It was loaded onto the SS *Fernplant* on 22 November 1941, and by 10 December had reached Los Angeles. This shipment appears to have been eventually returned to Canada. The Canadian authorities were exonerated from any blame for the failure of the cargo of the *Don José* and the *Fernplant* to reach Hong Kong. It may be argued that a second ship should have been obtained earlier, but evidence submitted by two west coast representatives of the United Kingdom Ministry of War Transport stated that, even if they had started looking on 9 October for a second ship, the *Don José* was the first available. This may be so, but it appears that Movement Control was blameless in spite of itself; Spearing ought to have known that a troopship could not take most of the MT, and he knew by 9 October that the *Awatea* was proposed.

When the Minister of National Defence was advised in December that no MT had gone with the force, he instituted an inquiry into the matter. In early January he took personal charge of this investigation. During its course, the officers of the QMG and MGO Branches kept dumping the problem into each other's laps. The Quartermaster General, Major General Schmidlin, protested that "the 10,000 feet [of available space] was nominal. It wouldn't have taken more than eight or ten vehicles." Ralston said with considerable clairvoyance, "Somebody will say these vehicles might have been useful". Later on he became extremely angry: "I can't find any branch taking responsibility. The Master General of Ordnance has the stuff on the rails. The Transport Controller says the stuff is moving. Whose responsibility is it to tie it up?"[25] Macklin, the Director of Staff Duties, put in a gloomy word:

> I said I had a feeling that people did not appreciate the necessity of making that ship as self-contained as she could be. I still have that impression—that Mr. Lockwood and everybody was (as Mr. Lockwood says) jubilant when they got the second ship. Everybody but me. I wasn't jubilant. And when I knew that ship had sailed without the transport I remarked that they had despatched J.K. Lawson without even a wheelbarrow and nobody could tell where he might end up.[26]

---

*The total value of the MT was set at $845,562. The United States planned to buy it outright, but the American Quartermaster General officer who had the papers was soon afterward a POW himself. There is no record of the money being paid.

Ralston came to the conclusion that Spearing was primarily at fault and the Quartermaster General's Branch was therefore partly responsible. Lieutenant General Stuart, the Chief of General Staff, "felt that this situation alone was not sufficient to take drastic action regarding the Quartermaster General but agreed that there was a cumulation of incidents respecting the Quartermaster General's attitude in matters of responsibility and decided [that it was] desirable to have the Quartermaster General take a District."[27] Schmidlin was offered Military District No. 12, but preferred to retire instead (announcing that it was for ill health). Lieutenant Colonel Spearing was also retired and his superior, Colonel H.O. Lawson, the Director of Supplies and Transport, followed soon after (although he had little to do with it, he got caught up in the general shake-up in the Quartermaster General's Branch). No other action regarding personnel was taken. In all, three officers were retired for a muddle that caused untold hardship and an indeterminate number of casualties to the two battalions.

Equipment and Training

—a summary

The answers to the dual question respecting the quality of the equipment and the training of C Force are, respectively, simple and complicated to reach.

In the case of equipment, the force was admirably looked after in both general and technical ordnance stores. The only deficiencies, anti-tank rifles and mortar ammunition, were due solely to there being none available in Canada. The fact that the battalions were fully equipped with such rare items in Canada as grenades, Thompson guns, mortars, and wireless sets is a tribute to the Ordnance personnel concerned and an indication of the effort that was made to properly equip C Force. In all respects except Mechanical Transport (MT) it was almost certainly the most well-equipped force to sail from Canada.

If the force had received its full complement of vehicles it would have been better equipped than any other portion of the Hong Kong garrison in that regard. The lack of energy shown by Movement Control at National Defence Headquarters and the lamentable communication gap between National Defence and the Office of the Controller of Transport might not have been solely responsible for the late shipment of the bulk of the MT—there would probably not have been another ship available before the *Don José*. It is puzzling that Sir Lyman Duff in his Royal Commission Report criticized the military but not the civilian participants. One can hardly help suspecting, as well, that it was not wholly coincidence that the only people the Commissioner chose to censure in the entire report had

Major General A.E. Grasett (*right*) and General H.D.G. Crerar. These two men between them share much of the responsibility for the despatch of Canadian troops to Hong Kong.

(Public Archives of Canada [PAC] PA116456, PA804282)

Prime Minister Winston Churchill. He was initially opposed to reinforcing Hong Kong, but changed his mind. (PAC PA22140)

Hon. J.L. Ralston (*below left*) and Hon. C.G. Power, Minister and Associate Minister of National Defence. Neither man questioned the desirability of concurring with the British request. Power may have been instrumental in having the Royal Rifles of Canada go to Hong Kong. (PAC PA501268 & PA124812)

The Rt. Hon. W.L. Mackenzie King, Prime Minister of Canada. He had no objection to Canadian troops going to Hong Kong as long as it did not furnish an argument for conscription. (PAC C42725)

Colonel (later Brigadier) J.K. Lawson (*below left*) and Colonel Pat Hennessy. These two experienced staff officers suddenly found themselves the senior officers of the Canadian Hong Kong force. Their deaths in the first days of the battle for the Island left the Canadian troops without representatives in the higher echelons of the garrison. (PAC PA501269 & PA114521)

A group of Royal Rifles at embarkation with the battalion mascot, acquired during their stay in Newfoundland. (PAC PA116791)

The Winnipeg Grenadiers entraining at Winnipeg. (PAC PA116790)

The departure scene at Winnipeg. (PAC PA116793)

C Force's staff officers on board the *Awatea; (l to r)* Major C.A. Lyndon, Brigadier J.K. Lawson, Colonel P. Hennessy, and Captain H.S.A. Bush. Only the latter would survive the battle. (PAC PA116457)

The ship on which most of C Force sailed, the *Awatea*, calls at Manila en route to Hong Kong.   (PAC PA116288)

C Company of the Royal Rifles on board HMCS *Prince Robert* and disembarking. They were the first Canadian troops to go into action on Hong Kong Island.   (RCN photos)

Winnipeg Grenadiers on board *Awatea*.   (Imperial War Museum [IWM] K1370)

Canadian troops disembarking from *Awatea*.   (IWM K1381)

C Force marching through Kowloon to Shamshuipo barracks.   (IWM K1378)

Major General C.M. Maltby takes the salute as C Force marches past.
                                    (IWM K1366)

already been dealt with by the military. In any event, while there was undoubtedly bad management, it was primarily due to ill fortune that the MT did not reach Hong Kong before the Japanese attack.

The fact that the twenty or so priority vehicles did not sail on the *Awatea* was the result of inefficiency and nothing else. What is far more inexplicable is the uncertainty of the Commissioner as to whether the absence of these priority vehicles had any effect. In this area, in particular, Sir Lyman appears to have had a remarkably shaky grasp on the facts of military life—one cannot avoid the impression that he felt that vehicles were not really necessary, but were simply provided for the enjoyment of the soft and pampered soldiery. It is blatantly obvious that the learned Chief Justice had never carried any portion of a 3-inch mortar over rough country. If he had, he would assuredly have descended from the bench and, with his own hands, hurled from the room any person who had the impudence to suggest that one could only "speculate" on the effect on troops of the absence of the tracked vehicles designed to carry the mortar.

As to the question of training, the enormous amount of verbiage devoted to the subject at the Commission gives a very detailed account of the state of training of both battalions. Whether the correct conclusions were drawn is another matter.

There can be no doubt that in both the Royal Rifles and the Winnipeg Grenadiers, the quality of officers, NCO's, and men was quite high. If events had dictated that one or both battalions had been incorporated into one of the divisions that fought in Europe, they would have undoubtedly had a record to equal that of any similar unit. The late mobilization of the Rifles (due probably to a rather narrow recruiting base) and the reduced requirement for machine-gun battalions such as the Grenadiers led to their assignment to garrison duties early in the war. Almost all the men in both battalions who had joined soon after the outbreak of war were not products of the Army's training establishments, but had of necessity been trained within the units themselves. Despite the best endeavours of all concerned, both individual and unit training was very difficult under garrison conditions. As a result, both battalions on their return to Canada were in a condition described by the Director of Military Training as "not recommended for operational consideration".

It seems possible that a suggestion made by the Associate Minister of National Defence, C.G. Power, led to one and consequently both of these units being selected to go to Hong Kong. In that event, all the testimony concerning training at the Commission was simply a verbal smokescreen designed to blind a militarily ignorant Commissioner to the exact status of these victims of a *fait accompli*. Following are some of the·brutal facts. None of the Winnipeg Grenadiers had fired a shot for nearly eighteen months, between April 1940 and October 1941. During the latter month most men had a chance to fire 35 shots. As far as the Grenadiers' tactical training was concerned, two Companies spent two weeks each in Montpelier Camp in Jamaica where, during the second week, they conducted section and platoon tactical training and one company exercise. The Royal Rifles had had somewhat more opportunity for tactical training, but in August 1941 (after which they did little training until they embarked for Hong Kong) about one-fifth had not yet passed their Tests of Elementary Training on such a simple and basic weapon as the rifle, and over one-third were in the same unhappy situation with the other standard weapon, the Bren light machine-gun. The implications of these figures should be apparent even to a reader without personal military experience. For additional confirmation let such a reader ask any friend or relative with Army experience for an opinion of the battle-worthiness of a unit of whose men 20% and 40% respectively had not passed the TOET's on the rifle and light machine-gun and then wait for the guffaw. When these melancholy facts are combined with the negligible experience the men had had with grenades (the Rifles had done a little with dummies, the Grenadiers nothing at all), mortars (the Grenadiers had never seen a shell, the Rifles had watched some go off once), and anti-tank weapons due to their non-availability, the actual state of the units' training is obvious. To say that these units were even close to being ready for action is arrant nonsense, although several senior officers who unquestionably knew better said exactly that before the Commission. Unfortunately, the Commissioner lacked the personal knowledge to treat their statements with the contempt they deserved, and instead, accepted them as expert testimony.

In 1948 General Foulkes stated during his highly lucid review of the situation (see Appendix C) that the concept of training for battle underwent considerable evolution during the Second World War. This is quite true, but the only question that may be asked in making a judgement is: were these battalions adequately trained *by the standards of the time*? They were not, and to say they were made a mockery of the words spoken and written earlier by these same officers in scores of circulars, manuals, and military pronouncements emphasizing the importance of training.

The Commission's detailed examination of the state of training of the October 1941 reinforcements was largely the pursuit of a red herring. In some cases their training had reached a higher level than that of many of the men already in the battalions, particularly the recruits received over the summer whom the Commissioner never took into his calculations. In any event, it was the training standard of each battalion as a whole that was the point at issue.

The heavy emphasis certain officers placed on the importance of morale over training was an obvious ploy to distract attention from the units' training weakness. If this testimony is taken at face value and then brought to its logical conclusion, why bother to train at all?

There *were* battalions in Canada whose men were better trained not only in personal military skills but in functioning and operating in battalion sub-units in the field as well. It was the weakness of the two Canadian battalions at Hong Kong in this latter area that was to cost them particularly dearly.

Any admission made at the hearings that the Royal Rifles and Winnipeg Grenadiers were less than adequately trained was usually tempered by the allegation that it was honestly thought that there would be sufficient time during their garrison duties at Hong Kong to rectify any deficiencies in training. This thesis seems also to have been accepted by historian C.P. Stacey.[1] Probably the most gaping loophole in this reasoning is that, if during ten months and sixteen months respectively on garrison duties in Newfoundland and Jamaica the battalions had not become ready for operational employment, what reason was there for assuming that similar duty in Hong Kong would do the job? Did they suspect the existence of some exotic oriental training potion?

So what remains? Simply this; those officers who spouted their pious platitudes at the Royal Commission about the importance of morale and *esprit de corps* were right in one way. The men of the Royal Rifles of Canada and the Winnipeg Grenadiers were all volunteers and so were the reinforcements who joined them. Their *esprit de corps* was undoubtedly high, and ill-trained as they were, at Hong Kong it was almost the only thing they had. Morale is no substitute for training, but they made it do. Fighting as strangers in a strange land, split up, and thrown into attack after attack against overwhelming odds over appallingly rough terrain, they never broke, they inflicted savage losses upon their enemies, and they put up a fight which, despite Canadian ignorance and British mud-slinging, deserves to live forever. But did the odds *have* to be so heavily stacked against them?

A Canadian Force Has Arrived
at Hong Kong
—C Force sets sail

When the Royal Rifles of Canada returned from Newfoundland after ten months and learned that they were to continue coast defence and guard duties for an indefinite period, they were extremely disappointed. Major Price set to work on C.G. Power, and it would appear that he got rapid results, though almost certainly not the results he had expected. When the warning order of 9 October reached the unit the next day, all ranks were, quite naturally, highly excited. Rumours about their prospective destination proliferated, and when Captain W.A.B. Royal and an advance party were sent off to Vancouver, most of the men in the battalion guessed that they would shortly be heading for Singapore. Lieutenant Colonel Home was soon privately informed that his battalion was going to reinforce the Hong Kong garrison.[1]

Shortly after the warning order arrived, a group of Ordnance officers from National Defence Headquarters descended on Valcartier (where the Royal Rifles had moved on receipt of the order) and went through the unit's stores in what appeared to the regimental officers to be a very rushed and haphazard fashion. All men in the battalion were given 48 hours leave in rotation. This was barely enough time for the men from Gaspé, who, in some cases, had to spend half of it travelling.

The officers in particular had a great deal to do over this period, preparing for the move. Two, Captain Dennison and Lieutenant Blaver, were sent down to Toronto to meet the reinforcements and go over their records. As mentioned, an attempt to get "R" recruits from the 2nd Battalion of the Royal Rifles of Canada to go "active" with the 1st Battalion was a dismal failure, with the single man who volunteered later deserting.

As for the Winnipeg Grenadiers, there is very little in the records which tells of their last few days in Canada. The St. Charles Range near Winnipeg was set aside for them for a week to fire musketry classifications. Officers were summoned back from leave, and the men returning from Jamaica were given short leave. Like the Royal Rifles, the Grenadiers were reboarded medically and issued with new drill uniforms. Lieutenant Colonel Sutcliffe began to suspect during the last few days that many men were going to miss the sailing.[2] When the battalion entrained on 25 October 1941 for Vancouver the Grenadiers did, in fact, have 40 men absent without leave. The number of these absentees has occasionally been cited as an example to give an exaggeratedly dismal impression of the battalion's morale. These men were almost all from the rear party that had been the last to leave Jamaica. They had arrived back in Winnipeg on 10 October 1941 after 18 months without leave. Their leave had been cut short when the warning order came in, and, in consequence, many of them stayed away over the weekend (25 October was a Saturday). None, apparently, were trying to avoid overseas service—they simply wanted more time with friends and relatives, and, because they had not been informed of the sailing date, they felt sure that they would be able to catch up with their unit on the coast. Of the 40, the vast majority returned to the Depot of their own volition. In the event, they were not severely punished.

The Royal Rifles entrained 23 October 1941 and headed west. The personnel of C Force Headquarters were picked up in Ottawa and elsewhere along the way. The two senior officers, Brigadier Lawson and Lieutenant Colonel Hennessy were among those who boarded the train at Ottawa. Four days later the train arrived in Vancouver. Lieutenant Colonel Home had been made responsible for the military administration of the *Awatea*. Captain Bush, the Staff Captain, had already flown out to Vancouver a few days earlier to commence this administrative work. The elements of C Force Headquarters who were not on the train were, in many cases, from the Vancouver area, and all joined the ship directly.

The Winnipeg Grenadiers rolled in on 27 October as well, minus four men who had deserted the train at Kamloops. The absence of the four men was not immediately noticed—a reflection of the fact that the Grenadiers had a large number of new men and officers on strength who were unfamiliar both with each other and with the original members of the battalion.

At the wharf the scene was one of intense activity as stores were loaded and the men embarked. Brigadier Lawson (according to Captain Bush and in contradiction to Major Gwynne's testimony at the Commission) "was extremely disappointed that no unit transport was aboard ship. He was advised that it was aboard a freighter lying along side of us . . ."[3] Either Bush is mistaken or someone had not told Lawson the truth because neither the MT nor the second ship was in Vancouver on 27 October.

Further trouble soon broke out with the troops. According to Lieutenant Colonel Home, Major Gwynne, the Embarkation Staff Officer, was only interested in getting the men on the ship as soon as possible.[4] It was very crowded in the men's quarters, and their resentment was in no way diminished by the fact that the officers' quarters were comparatively spacious. In the words of one soldier, Rifleman Skelton:

> October 27—After breakfast we finished packing our kits ready to detrain at Vancouver. We passed through Vancouver to the docks, detrained, formed up and marched off to the ship which was waiting for us. It was a great sight, but of course there were no bands, few people, but a bunch of officers and NCO's, snapping orders all around . . . Expecting a good meal it turned out to be salted ham, bread without butter, and nothing to drink but water . . . We walked around deck and nearly everywhere was *Out of Bounds, No Smoking Below Decks,* [underlined in original] and only smoking in rooms, —officers had the smoking rooms, indeed the officers had everything . . . Things begin to look bad. Supper came and the lads waited hours for it and it turned out to be tripe and onions, and it really was tripe. One thing led to another and all the troops were going to march off the boat. The lads of the Winnipeg Grenadiers were just barely back from Jamaica and had served sixteen months guard duty. They had been treated rotten all the time and they swore they would not take any more. Fifty men got off and the first time arguing was all the result they got. The third time the plank was raised and there was nearly a riot. The officers had everything and the rest nothing, so you can hardly blame them. Finally everyone calmed down and all the excitement was over. Late the same night we crowded the rails as we pulled out of Vancouver harbour . . . We were the first Canadian troops to leave Vancouver.[5]

Skelton's impressions are largely confirmed by the reports of senior officers. Lawson stated:

While the officers, W.O.s and N.C.O.s and the men generally realized that conditions would improve, some 30 or 40 men determined to break ship. They were, however, restrained, force being necessary at one period to do this. The men implicated were, I understand without exception, those who had not been with the unit long enough to get to know, or be known by their officers.[6]

Major Gwynne reported that approximately fifty men forced their way off the gangway into the shed, but were "persuaded by their officers and NCO's to return in a matter of about 20 minutes."[7]

C Force sailed that same evening of 27 October. Its personnel strength was 1,975—96 officers, 1,877 other ranks and two civilian Auxiliary Services supervisors. Included were two nursing sisters, two medical officers in addition to the regimental medical officers, two officers of the Canadian Dental Corps with their assistants, three chaplains, and a detachment of the Canadian Postal Corps. The force was short 51 men who were absent without leave, all but one from the Winnipeg Grenadiers. In addition to those who had not embarked in Winnipeg or had jumped the train *en route* were a few who, employed in such duties as loading stores on the ship, simply did not board and their absence went unnoticed until after the ship had sailed.

After this inauspicious embarkation things improved, including the food. An entry in Brigadier Lawson's diary—"Issue Trg Order"—shows that training was started the next day, but not without some difficulty: "29 October—A little trg commenced, but have to put on pressure. 30 October—Trg Winnipeg Grenadiers going well, but Royal Rifles of Canada still sticky."[8] Rifleman Skelton records the same picture: "1 November—I was just up on deck and we had drill on 2-inch mortars. 8 November—We have been drilling every day, Bren guns, 2-inch mortars, and anti-tank rifles. They keep us busy with that plus boat drill, fatigue duty, etc."[9] A certain amount of actual firing of the Brens was done and lectures were given on Hong Kong, the Japanese Army, and other subjects.

Captain Billings of the Royal Canadian Corps of Signals gave very intensive training to his personnel on ship as "Brigadier Lawson had warned all ranks that we might be at war when we landed at our destination."[10] This belief is reflected in Lawson's diary: "10 November— News says war in fortnight. Hope our transport arrives. 12 November—Winston Churchill says the United Kingdom will declare war if Japanese do so against US. Wish he would let us get to Hong Kong first."[11] Lieutenant Colonel Home said later that, on the whole, the training carried out on shipboard was very beneficial, but the crowded conditions of the ship handicapped the process to some extent.[12]

Of the men in the force, not all were on the *Awatea*. 105 men of C Company of the Royal Rifles of Canada were on HMCS *Prince Robert,* the armed merchant cruiser which acted as *Awatea's* escort. On this ship training was even more greatly hampered, but they did get the benefit of the Royal Canadian Navy's opinion, which was that "the balloon will go up before we reach the Far East".[13]

On 1 November the ship reached Honolulu and tied up near a Japanese ship. No one was allowed ashore, but the dock authorities had arranged a show of hula girls on the wharf for the men. One of the nursing sisters recalled that "The troops went wild—threw money and cigarettes to the girls."[14]

The night after leaving Hawaii, Brigadier Lawson disclosed to the officers that Hong Kong was their destination. This puzzled some of the Royal Rifles officers who had attended a course at Kingston in August 1941. Colonel Dewing, General Staff Officer at Singapore, had lectured to them on the Far East. He had stated quite explicitly that Hong Kong would not be defended in case of war. "Was policy . . . changed . . . or was there no policy at all?" they quite naturally asked themselves.[15]

One Rifleman, D.M. Schrage, died at sea. It was reported as a case of heart failure, but in fact the man was a diabetic and did not tell the medical officers in time. He died from lack of insulin. Schrage was a Toronto volunteer and had apparently had the impression that he would not be allowed to go if he was a known diabetic.

There was also one stowaway, a Royal Canadian Army Medical Corps private who had helped store medical supplies at Vancouver and decided to stay on. Every report on this man, Private Harvey J. Perry, from Captain Bush, the nursing sisters, and the medical officers, was very good, and medical orderlies were needed in Hong Kong. The Brigadier applied to National Defence Headquarters for him to stay with C Force, but he was ordered back on the *Prince Robert.*

On Friday 14 November the *Awatea* and *Prince Robert* pulled into Manila harbour. There they picked up an additional escort, HMS *Danae,* a British cruiser. *Danae* had been provided as the result of a message from the Admiralty to the Commander-in-Chief of the Royal Navy's China Station which stated, "In view of altered circumstances request you will provide cruiser escort for *Awatea* from Manila to Hong Kong."[16] George Drew, at the inquiry, claimed that the message proved that the United Kingdom authorities were aware of the imminence of war in late 1941.[17] Whatever the "altered" circumstances, the most likely being the new Tojo government in Japan while another was a German merchant raider in the area, the troopship steamed into Hong Kong on 16 November with two warships beside her and the antiquated aircraft that represented Hong Kong's air strength—all five of them—roaring overhead. The ship tied up at Holt's Wharf in Kowloon as the men gazed around at the oriental city.

Back in Canada, National Defence Headquarters was clearing up a few administrative details. The Vice Chief of the General Staff, Brigadier Kenneth Stuart, wrote a memo to the Minister advising that the maintenance of C Force, with the exception of men, should be undertaken by the British. Sailings from Canada to Hong Kong were too irregular, he argued, to permit the efficient replacement of material from home. The British could work out the cost and send the bill from London.[18] A preliminary report was ordered on the reasons for the MT missing the boat for Hong Kong. A memo from Major General Crerar suggested that the War Office should be asked to supply such papers as a map of Hong Kong (!), Defence Scheme papers, and information on artillery forces there. Crerar thought that, "We should keep 'up-to-date' on Far East, especially Hong Kong, in view of our particular military committment there."[19] It is astounding to contemplate that only after the two battalions had been sent to Hong Kong did it seem desirable to learn something about the place. Even more incredible is that most of what Crerar had requested was already available at National Defence Headquarters!

On the political level the Canadian government prepared to reap the Public Relations harvest associated with the landing of the troops. It was arranged that the General Officer Commanding, Hong Kong would send a one-word signal—"Zebulon"—when the men had landed safely. The discussion went on from there to the wording of the public communiqué, which the British had agreed to let Canada release first. The Canadian government wanted a big splash with a long message issued, including the sentence "Hong Kong constituted an outpost which the Commonwealth intended to hold." The draft was sent to the United Kingdom for approval, and the Canadians were probably somewhat crestfallen when the reply requested that the communiqué should not "be on such a scale as to over-emphasize the strength of our defences in Hong Kong."[20] This should have given the Canadian government cause to think, but there is no indication that it did so. The final statement agreed upon was rather bald:

> A Canadian force, under the Command of Brigadier J.K. Lawson, has arrived at Hong Kong after a safe and uneventful voyage, the Canadian government announced at Ottawa today. The Canadian troops will serve with other units of His Majesty's Forces making up the Hong Kong garrison. The strength of the force was not disclosed.

London was supposed to release the news three and a half hours after Canada, but there was a leak somewhere. On 11 November the *Daily Telegraph* successfully pinpointed Hong Kong as a future Canadian theatre of involvement but no one appears to have noticed. 15 November this paper again hinted at "expected developments in Canadian participation in Far Eastern defence." In Ottawa, officials were a little disconcerted and annoyed, feeling that it would "destroy the value of the news announcement of the Hong Kong arrival of Canadians. . . . You will appreciate the trouble we have had in this regard in the past, and we had hoped that on this occasion, it could have been avoided."[21]

The announcement nevertheless went off quite well. Mackenzie King made a little speech saying that defence against aggression anywhere meant protection for Canada.[22] Some Tory papers actually lauded the Liberals for the action—King and his cronies, although not bringing in overseas conscription, were finally commencing to take the war seriously. The Kingston *Whig-Standard* described Hong Kong as "essentially a strong point inside Japanese lines".[23] King was delighted to observe all this favourable publicity. Canada now had her forces on three continents, and was doing her full share in Commonwealth defence.

We Were Going to Fight a War
—October/November 1941

October 1941 saw a great increase in tension between Japan and the United Kingdom/United States front. As George Drew pointed out in his argument before the Royal Commission, at the time the Canadian battalions were requested the situation had supposedly improved. Earlier it had not been felt right to send more troops to Hong Kong. In October 1941, with the situation once again deteriorating, why did the Canadian government not reconsider?[1]

There are two answers to this question. Diplomatically, it would have been almost impossible for Canada to refuse to send the two units after Tojo took power, as it would then appear that Canadians were only willing to go where there were no risks involved. Also, the information on the situation in the Far East being received by the Canadian government was of a very conflicting nature—some of it pointed to an early war, while other evidence tended to indicate that the situation was not as serious as it might be. The government also continued to think of the little Canadian force as a "deterrent", even after Tojo's accession to power. This illusion operated at high military levels as well.

Early October was rather calm in Japan. The British Ambassador, Sir Robert Craigie, who had earlier been rebuffed by Eden for suggesting that Japan was weakening (see page 38), reiterated that a swing away from the Axis was occurring. Prince Konoye, the Japanese Prime Minister, was sincere in his efforts to avoid war, but Sir Robert warned that if there were no real signs of progress in the United States-Japanese talks the extremist elements would become more vocal.[2] Perhaps Konoye (who used to dress as Hitler at fancy dress balls) really was a "moderate", whatever that might mean in Japan, but like one of his predecessors, the "moderate" Prime Minister Yonai, he fell from power for being too soft. His War Minister, General Tojo, took over as Prime Minister on 16 October 1941.

Craigie, the eternal optimist, was still able to take a cheerful view of this event, which had given most other knowledgeable westerners a nasty shock.* He reported to London that the new cabinet was not as extreme as it appeared at first sight. Although Japanese demands would become more strident, war in the near future was still unlikely.[3] (Sir Robert was again indulging himself in what appears to have been his favourite pastime—picking out the least objectionable ministers, labelling them "moderates", and assiduously looking for the smallest hint that they were "gaining control".) The new cabinet, in fact, contained extremists in every vital portfolio. The holdovers from the Konoye cabinet (hardly a conciliatory group itself) were mainly in unimportant posts. Tojo, reported to Mackenzie King as "much more likely than Prince Konoye to seek a solution by positive action," was an undoubted extremist, "quite capable of making a prompt decision to break off the talks and launch upon further aggression without warning."[4]

The change of government in Japan does not seem to have been discussed at the next meeting of the War Committee of the Canadian Cabinet, which was held on 22 October 1941. There was, however, a lengthy discussion of measures to be taken in the event of war with Japan.[5] Whatever the official position of the respective governments, a growing number of people felt that time was running out. Lieutenant A.R.S. Woodside, the Intelligence Officer of the Royal Rifles, recalled, "During that time I had a number of talks with A.D.P. Heeney [who was then Clerk of the Privy Council and Secretary to the War Committee] about the changing situation. And it is clear to me that he knew, I knew, and the Canadian government knew before we left that we were going to fight a war."[6]

Soon afterward the British decided to throw another "deterrent" into the ring. This was HMS *Prince of Wales,* accompanied by HMS *Repulse.* The former was the pride of the Royal Navy, while the latter was also a formidable fighting ship. Churchill wrote Mackenzie

---

*The fall of the Konoye cabinet on 16 October 1941 resulted in an alert being sent to the United States Pacific Commanders that war was imminent and measures should be taken accordingly. The Canadian government was never told of this warning.

King on 5 November 1941 telling him of these new actors in the drama, saying, "I am sure she [*Prince of Wales*] will be the best possible deterrent to Japan."[7] The tragic sequel to this need not be enlarged upon.

The diplomats seemed unsure all through this period of Japan's eventual course of action. A cable from Canadian Military Headquarters to National Defence Headquarters of 26 October 1941 contained the latest information from Japan, and said, "Concensus [of] opinion [is] that war in Far East unlikely at present. . . . when time arrives . . . initial movement of Japanese forces will probably be northerly against Russia and not to south against our forces."[8] The direction and time were wrong, but the prospect of hostilities was definitely considered probable. In his Royal Commission report Sir Lyman Duff quoted only the first sentence of this message, presumably to establish that war was not really expected.

On a less exalted level, there were many who were more knowledgable than their superiors. The former Military Attaché for the United Kingdom in Tokyo, Colonel Mullahy, continued to pump out reports on the Far East which observed correctly that the Japanese army was getting out of hand, that Japanese public opinion was being railroaded into approval of the war, and that "things have been allowed to drift to the point where it is difficult for Japan to soften up without losing considerable 'face'."[9] Another man, who did not want to be identified, but who was apparently a businessman, gave an interview to Canadian Military Intelligence officers in Victoria, British Columbia in mid-November 1941. He had recently returned from Japan. Among his observations he noted that German influence in Japan was getting stronger. Reports belittling Japanese naval gunnery were false—it was deadly accurate. Japanese naval warfare, the man said, would not be conventional, but would "exhibit a pronounced element of surprise". The officers also noted: "Informant definitely says that no troops should have been landed [at Hong Kong]. Rather he says we should evacuate. He says it is not possible for us to conduct a defence for any length of time. He has learned from Japanese sources that no attempt will be made to capture Hong Kong by naval action alone."[10] The forced migration of Chinese into Hong Kong "would simplify a land attack". Such reports as these were usually buried somewhere in National Defence Headquarters. Lieutenant Colonel Murray, GSO 1 (Intelligence) at National Defence Headquarters, was in charge of their collection and distribution, but it does not appear that even he made any attempt to read them with any consistency. The higher-ups as a rule were only interested in reading the observations of such optimists as Sir Robert Craigie. (As an aside, it is interesting to note that George Drew received a letter from a Major A.M.K. Hobbs in 1948 which claimed that Murray had recognized Japanese intentions. Hobbs, who worked in the National Defence Headquarters Intelligence section from 1942 to 1945, contended that it was common knowledge in late 1941 in the Intelligence section that war was imminent. He said that Murray had been intercepting messages from Japan and "was convinced that Japan would attack the United States in December 1941." Murray supposedly informed Norman Robertson and Hugh Keenleyside of External Affairs, but they apparently thought that he was crazy. He then relayed his information to the G.2 of the United States Army. Only Murray's lifelong attachment to the Liberal party had prevented him spilling the beans to the public after the war.[11] Hobbs' story seems to have little basis in fact. Murray did intercept two uncoded messages from Japan but could make nothing out of them at all.)

Also in November 1941, the Dominions Office sent the Department of External Affairs a copy of the instructions given to the new Commander-in-Chief Eastern Fleet, Admiral Sir Tom Phillips. These instructions contained phrases such as, "While Japan remains neutral", "An outbreak of war with Japan", and "It is possible that a part of the Eastern Fleet may be assembled in Eastern Theatre before outbreak of war with Japan."[12] Scarcely any doubt was displayed in this telegram that war was on the way, and sooner rather than later.

The minutes of the Canadian Cabinet War Committee throughout November and early December reflect a growing concern over the situation in the Far East. The brief period of hope in early October soon died away, and the Allies prepared for war. It was reported at the meeting of 27 November 1941 that the United States Secretary of State, Cordell Hull, had told the United Kingdom that "the chance of Japanese acceptance of American proposals for a *modus vivendi* was slight. War and Navy Departments [are] impressing on United States Administration the military values of delay."[13] The news from then on worsened. In all the messages, telegrams, and reports of these last few weeks before war, there is not the slightest suggestion that the Canadian reinforcement of Hong Kong had had any diplomatic effect whatsoever. The strengthening of the colony had not "tipped the balance" as some had hoped it would. By the time the

Canadians arrived the situation had deteriorated irretrievably and the Japanese probably took no notice of the arrival of the Canadian troops whatsoever, except on the most local of levels.

In Hong Kong the news that Canada would furnish two battalions and a brigade headquarters was undeniably a tonic. It also caused the War Office to become slightly more generous to the fortress. Major General Kennedy at the War Office sent a memo to the Director of Anti-Aircraft and Coast Defence saying that, in view of the decision to send the Canadian battalions, "I consider that the existing ruling that Commander-in-Chief Far East may not allocate anti-aircraft equipments to Hong Kong should be cancelled immediately."[14] As there were no more than 30 anti-aircraft guns in the colony at that time, most of which were obsolete 3-inch weapons, this step promised a very great improvement in its defences. Unfortunately, no new anti-aircraft guns reached Hong Kong before the Japanese attack.

The British Chiefs of Staff, however, were not getting sentimental. On 5 November 1941 they dealt with a memo which seemed to indicate that the Commander-in-Chief, Far East thought that the policy on Hong Kong had changed. On 6 November they told him, "Our policy regarding defence of Hong Kong remains unaltered. It must be regarded as an outpost and held as long as possible."[15]

In Hong Kong, however, the immediate defence policy *was* being altered. When the General Officer Commanding, Hong Kong, Major General C.M. Maltby, heard that the Canadians were coming, the Gin Drinkers Line was brought back into the defence scheme. Nevertheless, work on it did not start until 14 November, two days before the Canadians arrived. It was not in good condition and a great deal of construction and repair was needed.

Japanese activity in the Hong Kong area increased during October and November. About 20,000 extra troops were landed in South China in October 1941, bring the total to four divisions and one independent mixed brigade. A Japanese transport was stopped in Hong Kong waters and was found to have a Japanese general and his staff on board, presumably making a reconnaissance. They were allowed to proceed after a warning. The Japanese Navy was said to be fully mobilized and ready for war, although Japan's armies were reported to be still in a position where sudden moves were unlikely. These events were seen by British Intelligence as "a tightening up to concert pitch rather than the final touches before plunging off the deep end."[16] (The mixed metaphor seems to be a standard form in military writing.) Japan was still thought to be fence-sitting.

The next month British Intelligence in Hong Kong reported that a move against Russia was unlikely. Troops were massing in Indo-China, possibly for an attack on Thailand. Closer to home, Japanese troops were reported as having established a lookout station on a small island near Hong Kong. The same report also noted an air attack on an airfield near the Chinese city of Namyung. The Japanese dropped 43 bombs from 14,000 feet and every one landed on the target. Despite this evidence, General Maltby maintained, right up to the time of the battle, a belief that the Japanese air force was poor, with inaccurate bombing and no aptitude for night flying. This opinion was shared by many British officers.[17]

The senior naval officers in the Pacific were also putting their heads together. On 12 November 1941 the Commander-in-Chief, China Station and Admiral T.S. Hart of the United States Asiatic Fleet based at Manila issued plans for a defensive strategy in the Southwest Pacific. They decided to "defend" Hong Kong, most of the Philippines, and most of the Netherlands' East Indies and to "hold" Luzon (Philippines), Malaya, Singapore, and Java. "Defend" meant to continue resistance as long as possible, "hold" indicated the intention to repulse all attacks. Thus it was not considered feasible to retain Hong Kong indefinitely "if . . . attacked on a major scale".[18] These naval plans were made with the knowledge that the colony would soon be reinforced, but it is evident that a successful defence of the Island was still not viewed as likely, while the Chiefs of Staff telegram of 6 November 1941 attests that the arrival of the two extra battalions had not altered military policy.

Meanwhile, as the diplomatic and military prospects continued to darken, the Canadian troops sailed on into a death trap.

Hardly a Combination Likely to Make an Efficient Fighting Force
—the Hong Kong garrison

The man under whose command the Canadian Force was to serve was Major General C.M. Maltby, who had taken over from Major General Grasett as General Officer Commanding, Hong Kong in July 1941. Maltby was an Indian Army Officer who had at one time commanded the Indian Army Staff College at Quetta. He had the reputation of being an efficient soldier, which is not surprising considering his background, but many found him difficult to get along with. He is reported to have been rather unimpressed by one of his original battalions at Hong Kong, the 2nd Royal Scots,[1] and his initial low opinion of the Canadians was to mean that he took a very jaundiced view of their actions during the battle.

Maltby seems to have fallen heir not only to his predecessor's command, but also to his optimism. He, too, had a low opinion of Japanese military capability, and tended to believe only the most understated reports of Japanese strength in South China. To do Maltby justice, however, he was meticulously thorough in his defence preparations and surveyed all the ground personally. Over-confident he may have been, but negligent he most definitely was not.

The piece of real estate that Maltby was charged with defending presented many difficulties both to the defenders, and, apparently, to any potential attackers. By far the greatest land area was the mainland portion of the colony, the leased "New Territories". The bulk of this land mass of approximately 360 square miles consisted of a peninsula, stretching 15 miles from the city of Kowloon at its tip to the Chinese border at its base. Most of this area was mountainous and sparsely populated. The Island of Hong Kong had an area of 32 square miles averaging approximately eight miles from east to west and four miles north to south. The south coast was broken by several prominent peninsulas and deeply indented bays. The capital, Victoria, occupied most of the north coast directly opposite Kowloon, and the famous Hong Kong harbour was formed by the passage between the north coast of the Island and the Kowloon peninsula. Most of the Island terrain was mountainous with steep-walled valleys, gaps, and passes between the mountain ridges.

The official total strength of the Hong Kong garrison in early December 1941 was 13,981 all ranks and in all corps, however this figure included such groups as nursing sisters, the St. John Ambulance Brigade, and the Hong Kong Mule Corps. The actual number of regular infantrymen was 5,422. Approximately 6,000 others, such as the Royal Artillery, Royal Engineers, Hong Kong Volunteer Defence Corps, and Royal Navy, could be considered part of the fighting forces.

The Royal Navy component of the defence was only a pale shadow of the powerful China Squadron of the peacetime years. Until the day before the Japanese attack the principle units were three First World War "S and T" class destroyers, the Royal Navy's smallest and oldest destroyers. However, during a discussion in early December between senior British and American naval officers, the United States agreed to send four destroyers to Singapore if Britain would reinforce Singapore with its three Hong Kong destroyers. The Royal Navy was probably only too happy to salvage something from what promised to be a futile defence, and HMS *Thanet* and HMS *Scout* sailed for Singapore on the night of 7 December. The third ship, HMS *Thracian*, was undergoing repairs and could not leave the harbour. A flotilla of eight motor torpedo boats (MTB's) were also on hand for the defence of the island, but these were very early models with little more than machine-guns and depth charges to use against the enemy. The remaining naval defence consisted of four river gunboats and a number of minelayers and auxiliary patrol vessels. The total number of naval personnel was 1,300 British and 300 Indian and Chinese.

The air strength of the garrison has often been derided, but its weakness may be an indication that the Royal Air Force took a more realistic view of Hong Kong's prospects than the other two services. At the tiny Kai Tak airfield on the mainland were three Vickers *Vildebeestes*, former torpedo bombers now used as target tugs, and two Supermarine *Walrus* amphibians. These latter aircraft are usually credited to RAF strength, but it is more likely that they belonged to the Royal Navy. These five aircraft represented an RAF and RN Station Flight maintained for the peacetime training of the garrison only and were not regarded as part of the defences.

The fixed defences of the colony were primarily designed to counter an attack from the sea, and in the event of such a purely ·naval attack could probably have withstood anything short of a major battle fleet.

The fixed coastal guns consisted of eight 9.2-inch, fifteen 6-inch, two 4.7-inch, and four 4-inch weapons. There were also six 18-pounder and four 2-pounder beach defence guns. Around the coast of the Island was a ring of 72 pill boxes, field works, and barbed wire entanglements. The strongest portion of these defences and all the coastal batteries were designed to counter a seaborne attack from the south. An enemy landing from this direction would have had to deal with the heavy guns of the fixed defences, go through minefields that were reputed to be sown more thickly than those protecting the Firth of Forth, break through the beach defence guns and pill boxes, and then contend with land mines, barbed wire, and the infantry. The defences on the north side of the Island facing the mainland across the harbour and the Lye Mun Passage (approximately 450 yards at its narrowest point) were not nearly as formidable. The big coastal guns would have little effect on a landward assault or a crossing in small boats, not because they were unable to fire to the north—they were able to do so—but because, as in the case of Singapore,* they lacked suitable ammunition. Most of their ammunition was designed to pierce thick armour plate to reach the magazine of an enemy warship. While a 380-pound, 9.2-inch armour-piercing shell would have a distinctly traumatic effect on a Japanese soldier if it hit him directly, with its thick casing and relatively small bursting charge it could do little damage if it exploded deep in the ground or water. The supply of ammunition suitable for use against troops was only sufficient to furnish 25 rounds per gun. This was unfortunate as the mobile artillery was far less formidable, consisting mainly of obsolete weapons—four 60-pounder guns and twelve 6-inch, eight 4.5-inch, and eight 3.7-inch howitzers. Anti-aircraft guns were in even shorter

---

*Contrary to popular myth, many of Singapore's guns (including the huge 15-inch weapons which were capable of 360° fire) did not "face the wrong way", they simply lacked the correct ammunition.

supply and able to provide very little defence. The troops manning these vehicles were the 8th and 12th Coast Regiments, 5th Anti-Aircraft Regiment, and 965th Defence Battery of the Royal Artillery, all containing many Indian personnel, and the 1st Hong Kong Regiment of the Hong Kong and Singapore Royal Artillery, consisting of Indian troops under British officers. Another important component of the garrison was formed by the 22nd and 40th Fortress Companies of the Royal Engineers, many of whose men were Chinese.

The backbone of the defence should the Japanese establish a foothold in the colony consisted of the six battalions of infantry—two British, two Indian, and two Canadian. The senior battalion, both in the Army List and in service in Hong Kong, was the 2nd Battalion, Royal Scots, which had arrived in Hong Kong from India in 1936. Most of the men of this battalion were Lowland Scots. They had the reputation of being excellent fighting men, but the general concensus of opinion seems to be that their long stay in Hong Kong had taken the edge off their efficiency, and there is no doubt that their sickness rate, particularly from malaria, was regrettably high. Furthermore, the Battalion was split between three locations, and while some field training had been carried out, "the periods in which the Battalion could train as a unit were too short for the liking of experienced senior officers."[2] This hardly seems to show Hong Kong as an ideal posting for the Canadians to complete their tactical training.

The other British battalion, the 1st Battalion, Middlesex Regiment, was recruited from the London area and had been overseas since 1931 and in Hong Kong since 1937. It, too, was growing stagnant from overlong garrison duty at Hong Kong—probably the "softest" posting in the Empire—and, like the Royal Scots, had lost experienced personnel in postings away from the unit and from Hong Kong due to the expansion of the wartime army. The 1st Middlesex had been converted to a machine-gun battalion and its primary duty was to man the static defences around the Island.

The two Indian battalions were the 5th Battalion, 7th Rajput Regiment and the 2nd Battalion, 14th Punjab Regiment. Both were regular battalions of the Indian Army with long and honorable histories. While they had not been exposed as long to the enervating Hong Kong garrison duty, the Indian battalions, even more than the two British, had lost many of their officers, NCO's, and trained men who had been transferred, and replaced by partially-trained recruits.

This had changed them from crack regular battalions equal to the best in any army to units of far more dubious reliability. The Rajputs were a particularly sad case. They had been in Hong Kong since October, 1940, but had not received vehicles and mortars until August 1941. 40% of the men were partially-trained recruits who had arrived in October 1941. It is easy to see why, in the eyes of some Canadian officers, the Winnipeg Grenadiers and Royal Rifles were not markedly inferior to other units in Hong Kong.[3]

A not inconsiderable part in the defence was played by the Hong Kong Volunteer Defence Corps. Conscription had been introduced for British residents of Hong Kong in early 1941, and most men of military age had ended up in the Volunteers. In addition, substantial numbers of European nationals, Chinese, and men of other Asian races had voluntarily enlisted. The Volunteers, who trained part time before the Japanese attack, provided no less than five batteries of artillery and seven infantry companies in addition to other arms. The ranks of the Volunteers embodied men from all walks of life, many of them men who were well aware that they would be fighting in the most direct way for their homes and families and so threw themselves into their duties with intense determination. Indeed, one group of men who were over 55 years of age, and so ineligible for service in the Volunteers, formed their own group. Unfortunately there were others who were conscripts in the most reluctant sense of the word. As a result, in the test of battle, many Volunteers fought with a courage and determination equal to the best of the regular garrison, while others were merely an encumbrance to the defence.

All told, including non-combatants, the garrison comprised 8,919 British, Canadian, and colonial personnel, 4,402 Indians, and 660 Chinese. As the C Force records state, it was "hardly a combination likely to make an efficient fighting force".[4]

Before Maltby had received word of the despatch of the Canadians, defence plans had envisaged the main effort being devoted to the Island, with little more than a delaying action being fought on the mainland in order to allow demolitions to be carried out. The action was to be fought by a single battalion, the 2/14 Punjabs. As the Gin Drinkers Line had been abandoned before completion and was, in any event, far too long for one battalion to hold, it played little part in the proposed delaying action. The Punjabs were only intended to fight rear guard actions astride the main defiles leading up to it. It was essential that they be able to disengage on the mainland with minimal losses as they would be required to help defend the Island. The defence of the Island itself was based on an all-round scheme. Even with the loss of the mainland, the possibility of a seaborne landing on the south coast was to haunt Maltby right to the bitter end.

The news that two Canadian battalions were being sent to Hong Kong was responsible for a marked change in these plans. One of the reasons for requesting reinforcements was that the single battalion on the mainland simply could not provide sufficient time for an effective program of demolition to be carried out. This argument obviously carried some weight as it was repeated by the War Office in the minute to the Prime Minister. In January 1941 Brooke-Popham had estimated that the Punjabs might have to be evacuated after 48 hours, but "if the one battalion could be multiplied by three the period of resistance would in all probability be multiplied by six."[5] If Maltby concurred with this assessment, as he must have, his decision to detach three of his six battalions to the mainland made sense—the increased time they might win for him would probably be worth the risk inherent in attempting to evacuate a force of that size back to the Island. What is questionable is the way he chose to use them on the mainland. Maltby intended to man and hold the Line with three battalions up, less one company to cover demolition teams between the Gin Drinkers Line and the frontier, and negligible reserves. General Bartholomew had estimated in 1937 that it would require four battalions to fight a delaying action and seven to have even a chance of holding the Line. Maltby's decision to attempt to hold nearly eleven miles of incomplete defensive positions with three battalions could only have been based on a faulty appreciation of Japanese military ability. Yet if the Japanese succeeded in breaching the Line, the weak defence, lack of reserves, and proximity to the harbour would crush any hope of continuing resistance on the mainland, and the only recourse would be a hasty evacuation in front of the advancing Japanese. In short, from a delaying action on the mainland, Maltby had gone to an "all or nothing" defence of the area.

Maltby's new plan entailed the division of his infantry force into two brigades, an Island Brigade and a Mainland Brigade. Brigadier Lawson was to command the Island Brigade, which consisted of the garrison's machine-gun battalion, the 1st Middlesex, which would be deployed all around the island manning the 72 pillboxes and other static defences, and the two Canadian battalions, which would take up positions to defend against a landing on the south coast. The

Mainland Brigade was to hold the Gin Drinkers Line with, from west to east, the 2nd Royal Scots, the 2/14 Punjabs, and the 5/7 Rajputs holding approximately equal portions of the Line. These were to be supported by about half the available mobile artillery. The Mainland Brigade was commanded by Brigadier Cedric Wallis who had previously commanded the 5/7 Rajputs. Wallis was a dedicated and energetic officer whose personal courage was beyond question, but some of the Canadians, particularly the Royal Rifles, were subsequently to question his military judgement.

The plan for the defence of the mainland envisaged the three battalions manning the Gin Drinkers Line with the exception of one company of the Rajputs as brigade reserve, one company of the Royal Scots as local reserve, and one company of the Punjabs to initially operate forward of the Line in the New Territories. This last unit was to fight a short delaying action and assist in demolitions before retiring to the Line, which was to be held as long as possible. Maltby estimated this at a minimum of seven days. Should the Line be penetrated the brigade would be evacuated to the Island with the exception of the Rajputs, who were to hold Devil's Peak commanding the Lye Mun Passage as long as possible.

The Gin Drinkers Line was a system of entrenchments protected by barbed wire and reinforced at critical points by concrete pillboxes. Construction had been abandoned in 1937 and, except for parts of the centre, the defence work was largely incomplete. In addition, there had been considerable deterioration over the intervening years. As soon as the new plan was formulated, working parties from the three battalions of the Mainland Brigade commenced repair and construction activities. Once the Canadians had arrived, the battalions of the Mainland Brigade took up their positions in the Line in order to facilitate this work.

Thus the Canadians arrived in Hong Kong to find themselves part of an exceptionally heterogeneous force which, due to an entirely new defence plan, was in an uneasy state of flux.

Sano Force

—Japanese invasion plans

General Maltby was not the only man to have the defences of Hong Kong on his mind. They also figured prominently in the thoughts of Lieutenant General Sakai, who commanded the Japanese 23rd Army, and Lieutenant General Sano Tadayoshi, commanding the 38th Division in that army.

Japanese preparations for the capture of Hong Kong had been in hand for some time. The freezing of Japanese funds in the United Kingdom, United States, and Netherlands East Indies in July 1941 soon began to hurt Japan, and by the fall Imperial General Headquarters had commenced preparations for war. The Tojo government confirmed this policy and on 5 November 1941 decided to definitely go to war if negotiations with the United States had not succeeded by 25 November. Orders were sent to Imperial General Headquarters to have operational planning completed by the end of November.

The Japanese had always maintained a close watch on the state of the Hong Kong defences. In September 1941 the Japanese General Staff estimated that the Hong Kong garrison consisted of 13,500 regular troops plus 5,500 volunteers. This estimate, made before the arrival of the Canadians, was over 50% too high. The General Staff estimate of the air and naval strength was more realistic—they credited the air force with ten training aircraft and the navy with three destroyers and 33 other vessels.

On 6 November 1941 the Japanese Imperial General Headquarters ordered its Commander-in-Chief, China to prepare plans for the capture of Hong Kong. He was instructed that the 38th Division of the 23rd Army was to form the core of the force and that all preparations were to be completed by the end of November. He was also informed that the attack on Hong Kong was not to imperil the areas of China already occupied and that therefore the remainder of the 23rd Army would deploy to protect the rear of the assault force in the unlikely event of Chinese intervention. Operations against Hong Kong were to commence as soon as word was received of the Japanese landing in Malaya.

The plan of attack prepared by Lieutenant Generals Sakai and Sano was an uncomplicated one, with a straightforward basic design which demonstrated a typical Japanese flexibility and willingness to exploit the favourable aspects of a situation as they developed. Before the ground attack commenced, the enemy air and naval forces were to be neutralized by bombing. The Japanese were well aware of the reactivation of the Gin Drinkers Line and expected that the main military resistance would be encountered there. Their intention was simply to cross the border, advance to the Line, and launch a full-scale attack. If necessary the navy could be called in to transport troops in a flanking movement. After the Gin Drinkers Line had been passed the mainland would be completely occupied and installations on outlying islands eliminated. The Island of Hong Kong itself was then to be invaded and captured. The Japanese troops were to land and form a beach-head on the north shore and simply enlarge their gains from there.

If the Japanese really believed their September estimate of the strength of the Hong Kong garrison, they showed considerable confidence as they only allotted a single division, albeit a heavily reinforced and supported one, to the capture of the colony.

In overall command of the operation was Lieutenant General Sakai, who was to control all elements of the operation, including those detailed for the rearguard. The 23rd Army (which in Western parlance would have been designated a Corps) had been operating in the Canton area of South China for some time. In December 1941 it consisted of four divisions plus a mixed brigade and two infantry regiments.

The actual attacking force was known in the Japanese fashion as the Sano Force after Lieutenant General Sano Tadayoshi, who commanded the 38th Division. The infantry component of this division (38th Infantry Group) was commanded by Major General Ito Takeo and consisted of three regiments of three battalions each.

They were the 228th under Colonel Doi, the 229th under Colonel Tanaka, and the 230th under Colonel Shoji. The remainder of the division was under the direct control of Lieutenant General Sano and included a Light Armoured Car Unit with ten cars, the 38th Mountain Artillery Regiment of three battalions, the 38th Engineering Regiment, the 38th Transport Regiment, and Signal, Ordnance, Veterinary, and Medical Units plus two Field Hospitals.

Attached to this already formidable basic division were two Independant Mountain Artillery Regiments, the 10th and 20th, two Independant Anti-Tank Gun Battalions, the 2nd and 5th, the 21st Mortar Battalion, the 20th Independant Engineering Regiment, three Transport Regiments plus 3 companies of another, and two River Crossing Companies. These units greatly augmented the fire support, transport, and engineering capabilities of the 38th Division and made it even more suited for its assault role. Supporting the 38th Division's own and attached artillery was the entire Army artillery of the 23rd Army which included a Siege Unit with a regiment of 150-mm howitzers plus two independant battalions equipped with 9.4-inch howitzers.

Strong air support was available. Acting directly in conjunction with the 23rd Army was a light bomber regiment with about 40 Kawasaki *Ki.32* single engined bombers. After December 16 a heavy bomber regiment of 18 aircraft was also available to support the attacking forces. "Popular" historians automatically assume that the formidable *Zero* naval fighters were operating over Hong Kong. This was not the case as it was purely an army operation and no fighters of any type were employed—they were unnecessary.

The supply of the Sano Force and the protection of its rear was undertaken by various groups—the Kitazawa, Kobayashi, Sato, and Araki units, all named after their commanders. The Araki Unit, of approximately brigade strength, was the one specifically detailed to prevent any interference with Sano Force.

Sano Force was definitely a formation to be reckoned with. That such an aggregate of military strength could be spared from the Japanese forces in China without any apparent difficulty implies a very serious underestimation on the part of the British Intelligence whose reports implied that the Japanese were too occupied in China to be able to attack Hong Kong, to say nothing of being able to make troops available for invading Malaya and the Phillipines. Sano Force was distinctly superior to Maltby's Hong Kong garrison, particularly in mobile artillery. The numerical superiority of the cutting edge of the division, the infantry, was not as marked—nine Japanese battalions against six British, Canadian, and Indian battalions, plus at least a battalion and a half of Volunteers. However, the Japanese would be able to concentrate their strength, and if they could succeed in breaking through the outer defences would be able to force battle on their own terms. In addition, the Japanese soldiers of Sano Force would obviously be formidable antagonists. While it is uncertain whether the 38th Division had participated in any pitched battles against the Chinese, its men had worked together in an operational environment for some time and were seasoned in anti-guerilla operations and security duties. Training of the Japanese soldier emphasized mobility in combat, co-ordination with other arms, the importance of close combat, individual initiative, particularly on the part of NCO's, and the importance of night combat.* In the case of the Sano Force men, this rigorous and thorough initial training had been augmented by the most valuable training aid of all—experience.

It was this well-equipped, fit, and experienced force that in early December was moving unobserved along routes to the Hong Kong border, which they would cross on 8 December to do battle with Maltby's ill-trained, polyglot garrison.

---

*When it is considered that Japanese training manuals and other information on training were available to the British and Americans, their persistance in cultivating the myth that the Japanese lacked initiative and were poor at night work is hard to understand.

Soon We Shall Be Fighting
For Our Own Lives
—the last three weeks of peace

When the *Awatea* tied up at Holt's Wharf in Kowloon the Governor of the Colony, Sir Mark Young, the General Officer Commanding, Major General Maltby, and the Naval Officer Commanding, Commodore Collinson, came on board to greet the Canadians. Some of the Canadian officers were not impressed; the British were "more English in their talk than was natural, and, brilliant in their trappings, seemed rather to be at some peace-time festival than on the verge of an outbreak of war."[1] This may be too harsh a judgement on men whose only aim, at that time, was probably to greet the Canadians and made them feel appreciated.

The Canadian troops disembarked, formed up, and marched through the city to Shamshuipo Camp on the northwest side of Kowloon. The men were confined to the camp for the first two days while they settled into barracks, but the march through the city was of tremendous interest to them.

Brigadier Lawson had been given instructions in an Order-in-Council to place his forces "in combination with" the British forces in Hong Kong, in accordance with the Visiting Forces Act of 1931.[2] This essentially meant that, for the purposes of military operations, he was to come under the direct orders of the General Officer Commanding. The integration of the Canadians into the defence scheme soon began. Although the British War Office had been well aware that any troops sent from Canada would probably only be partially trained, they had not seen fit to pass this information on to the senior officers in Hong Kong. These were shocked to find that their reinforcements had so little training. Indeed, it was found necessary to organize a training course for NCO's, so that they, in turn, could train the men. Captain M. Weedon of the 1st Battalion, Middlesex Regiment supervised the course.

Training started after only a few days, but first the battalions had to settle in. Transport was hired to carry the goods to the camp, but Lawson noted on 19 November: "Bns still far from unpacked. Stores chaotic."[3] The two Canadian battalions were in a camp that had been built on reclaimed land in 1927 at the time of some anti-foreign riots. The Royal Rifles were comfortably housed in Nanking Barracks, the Winnipeg Grenadiers in Han Kow Barracks, and the Jubilee Buildings at the top of the camp were set aside for officers and NCO's. The troops from 18 November to 6 December continued training, doing TOET's (in a potential theatre of war!), bayonet drill, and route marching. One platoon per company spent a few days in early December manning their positions in the defence scheme after a reconnaissance of these areas. Rifleman Skelton records: "We climbed mountains all day long and we are shown the many spots for which soon we shall be fighting for our own lives. Climbing is no joke, and these mountains are plenty hard on greenhorns like me." There was also something of a war scare:

> Nov 30: We were confined to barracks. Everything was to be packed and ready at a moment's notice. The Japs have declared war. We have been issued with ammunition and are waiting for the word to move. Dec 1: Japan declaring war another farce. Went over to the Island again tonight.[4]

Soon after their arrival the Canadian officers, and later the NCO's, were taken on a tour of the Island and shown the defensive positions. Lawson inspected what was to be his Brigade Headquarters, pillboxes, and other works. On 19 November General Maltby spoke to all the Canadian officers. They were struck by some of the salient points he brought out, such as the lack of an air force, the proximity of the Japanese, the pitifully small anti-aircraft defences, the lack of significant naval support, and the number of Chinese refugees in the colony.[5] Both the Governor and the General Officer Commanding were new arrivals in the Colony (September 41 and July 41 respectively), and some of the British troops had been there for over four years and had stagnated in consequence. As Lieutenant Colonel Home wrote:

How even the thought that the Island could be defended without any fighters of the Air Force is beyond one's conception. The one belief that was current after checking up on the detailed defences was simply that England did not expect war with Japan in the immediate future. Any other belief can only lead one to the impression that those in authority were sublimely unconscious of what it was all about. . . . All officers were soon wondering what conceivable difference to the defence of Hong Kong two battalions and a Brigade Headquarters could make.[6]

At the same lecture Major Bishop, who commanded C Company, Royal Rifles of Canada, had a run-in with the mainland Brigade Commander, Brigadier Cedric Wallis. Bishop had made a joke about the 6-inch guns at Lye Mun, which were, in fact, wooden dummies: "Well, they sure fooled me, but I bet they don't fool the Japs." Wallis was most definitely not amused.[7] After only two or three days in the colony the Canadians and British were already eyeing each other with mistrust, which was in no way to decrease before the capitulation. The Canadians began to believe that they had been thrown into the deep end as a political gesture: "Did England think she could bluff the Japanese from attacking Hong Kong by sending a token Canadian Force?"[8] The British, dismayed at the low level of training of the Canadian soldiers, were annoyed at their self-confidence and arrogance. There was friction amongst the lower ranks as the better-paid Canadians began to monopolize the sing-song girls in the Chinese areas and, as has been the wont of new regiments in a garrison since time immemorial, to generally throw their weight around.

The specialists in C Force Headquarters were immediately integrated, for the most part, into the British structure. Captain Billings became the Signals Officer for the Mainland Brigade. The Ordnance, Service Corps, and Provost details were tacked onto existing organizations. The medical personnel were similarly treated. At Hong Kong, instead of Regimental Medical Officers, there were Area Medical Officers. Captain S.M. Banfill, the Royal Rifles' Medical Officer, set up a medical post at Lye Mun in the east end of the Island on 10 December while Captain Reid was stationed in the Grenadier area in the west. Captain Gray stayed at Bowen Road, the main military hospital in Hong Kong, and the senior Canadian Medical Officer, Major J.N.B. Crawford, was made Second-in-Command of the Field Ambulance Unit on the mainland.

There had been no desperate requirement for additional doctors in the garrison. Their real need was for male medical orderlies. These had been specifically requested, but two nursing sisters had been sent instead. They could not be used in the Canadian camp and were therefore attached to Bowen Road. The only medical orderly who came with the Canadians was the stowaway, Perry, who had been shipped back to Canada despite pleas from all concerned that he be allowed to stay. The two nursing sisters proved themselves of "incalcuable worth"[9] when the fighting began, even though they found Bowen Road and its practices to be "inferior and definitely antiquated."[10] It was already overstaffed before the Canadians arrived. The two nurses settled in and were shown around the Island a week later by the senior British nurse and her boyfriend, Lieutenant Colonel Lamb (a Staff Officer). "We were told how strongly fortified the Island was; in fact, it was impregnable. Later we learned that the majority of people in Hong Kong felt the same way."[11] The only officer they talked to who thought there was going to be a war was a Canadian.

Despite some Anglo-Canadian friction, not all was gloom. The Canadian officers were apparently quite popular at the clubs and hotels, and gained reputations as good dancers. Many of the NCO's, such as Frank Ebdon, born in London, were soon drinking with the cockney sergeants of the 1st Middlesex. The men slowly began to fit into their unaccustomed surroundings. Chinese servants handled all the fatigue duties in Hong Kong, which pleased the troops. Few tactical schemes were undertaken before the attack, as both battalions were earmarked for a static defensive role—the exact opposite of the role they were eventually called upon to play. Summing up the last weeks before the war, "the general picture is one of co-ordinated and intense activity directed by a Commander [Lawson] who had no illusions of security."[12]

Meanwhile, amongst the senior officers at Hong Kong, a curious air of optimism had begun to prevail. The Commander-in-Chief, Far East in Singapore had already been infected, but his delusions were dispelled by the War Office message of 16 November. This also informed him definitely that no fighters were to be sent to Hong Kong; that policy, too, remained unchanged.[13]

At Hong Kong itself, the General Officer Commanding began to think even more positively, apparently helped along by Brigadier Lawson. On 19 November the Commander-in-Chief, Far East passed along a message to the War Office. This message stated that Lawson, then newly arrived in Hong Kong, had suggested that the United

Kingdom ask Canada for more troops, thus enabling him to form the Canadians into a Brigade Group. These reinforcements would include an infantry battalion, a field regiment of the Royal Canadian Artillery, a field company of the Royal Canadian Engineers, and more signals, medical, and ordnance personnel. Lawson is reported to have said, "They will be thrown at us."[14]

The original message from Maltby to Brooke-Popham explained why such a reinforcement would be desirable. The object was to be able to hold the Gin Drinkers Line permanently to ensure the safety of the Kai Tak airfield. In the future, a mobile brigade group could link up with Chinese forces. Maltby asked, "Is not the value of Hong Kong as a bridgehead increasing every day and Hong Kong becoming potential centre of ABCD [American, British, Chinese, Dutch] front?"[15] This message might cause one to suspect that Maltby was deranged. The Gin Drinkers Line had been designed for a full division to hold—Maltby would have seven battalions for the whole colony even if the extra men were sent. The Line was a weak one, where reserves could not be brought up quickly. Kai Tak, even if the Japanese could be held on the Line, would still be exposed to any weight of artillery barrage the Japanese cared to bring to bear on it (to say nothing of aerial bombing) because it was only a few miles from the Line, so the reason stated for holding the Line was patently absurd. As for Hong Kong becoming a centre for the ABCD front, Maltby must have let his imagination run away with him. It was not with hindsight, but before the war, that the Allies had realized that holding even Singapore and the Phillipines was going to be difficult!

After being studied at the War Office Maltby's message was passed on to the Chiefs of Staff. The first person to examine it noted that, while the additional artillery would be useful, it should be employed not for offense or defence on the mainland, but "to increase the powers of defence of the Island".[16] The Chiefs of Staff were either sceptical or bewildered and suggested that the General Officer Commanding, Hong Kong and Commander-in-Chief, Far East explore the reasons for this proposed additional reinforcement.[17]

On 24 November the Commander-in-Chief, Far East, Brooke-Popham, repeated the suggestion, followed by the recommendation that "If approval is given for this reinforcement scheme I think it should also be given in principle for the fighter squadron [that is, the squadron based at Hong Kong for which Brooke-Popham had been agitating]." The Air Chief Marshal ended with a not particularly subtle hint: "I leave to you the political aspect of having Dominion troops unsupported from the air."[18]

The War Office replied to Brooke-Popham on 27 November 1941. The Chiefs of Staff did not agree that the proposed reinforcements would enable the permanent retention of the Gin Drinkers Line or that Kai Tak would then be available for fighters. The provision of the full complement of a brigade group by Canada would, however, be welcomed, but it should be used to hold the Island, not the mainland. An approach would probably be made to the Canadian government, but only if the War Office could be assured that no one had given the impression to the Canadian government that air support for Hong Kong would be supplied, as otherwise they would make a decision on a false assumption.[19] The last sentence of Brooke-Popham's telegram had obviously not been lost on the War Office.

These assurances were forthcoming, and at a Chiefs of Staff meeting on 1 December 1941 it was decided that, as the Canadian government was not under any false apprehension, the way was now clear to invite Canada to complete C Force to a brigade group.[20] This was at least partially true, because the British, of course, never explicitly informed the Canadians that air support was definitely *not* available. For their part, the Canadian government would probably never have thought to ask! The chances are that Canada would have agreed to this proposal—Lawson seemed quite sure of it. In any event, the war mercifully put an end to these proposals and no request was ever sent.

It is difficult to know what to make of Brigadier Lawson's part in this suggestion. He was a distinguished veteran of the First World War, had been one of Canada's few professional soldiers between the wars, and was universally regarded as an efficient officer. His suggestion that more Canadian troops be sent to the isolated outpost of Hong Kong can only be explained by either personal ambition, which seems unlikely, or a grievous underestimation of the quality, determination, and number of the Japanese troops which might be sent against the colony.

In any event, Maltby had perforce to make do with what he had. The arrival of the two Canadian battalions had, he said, already "caused me to alter my plans to a certain degree",[21] that is, to decide to hold, at least temporarily, the Gin Drinkers Line. The Japanese, on their part, had already made their plans. In his post-war report on the fall of Hong Kong, Maltby stated that estimates at the time had suggested that two to four Japanese divisions were available for an attack on Hong Kong, but in his November lecture to the Canadians he claimed that the Japanese had only 5,000 troops, with very little artillery in the border area. Maltby seriously underestimated Japanese forces, abetted by his execrable intelligence organization, which submitted this gem on 7 December 1941: "The reports are certainly exaggerated and have the appearance of being deliberately fostered by the Japanese, who, judging by their defensive preparations around Canton, appear distinctly nervous of being attacked."[22] If Lawson accepted this appreciation, as Maltby seems to have, his suggestion makes more sense.

The detailed defence plan for Hong Kong was voluminious, and the Canadians scarcely had time to learn its basic points. They were also confused because,

> the defences of the Island were primarily constructed in anticipation of an attack taking place on Hong Kong from the direction of the sea, while paradoxically all tactical manoeuvres, etc, were always carried out in anticipation of a Japanese attack across the border of the New Territories and moving southwards to Kowloon and Hong Kong.[23]

The Canadians were not the only ones who were confused. In the previous plan, drawn up before the decision to send the Canadians to reinforce the garrison, the Gin Drinkers Line had been disregarded. One battalion, the 2/14 Punjabs, had been slated to fight a delaying action on the mainland, and the other three battalions were to stay on the Island. In the new plan, as Maltby admitted, only two out of the six battalions really knew their job: the 1st Middlesex on the Island, and the 2/14 Punjabs, who were still on the mainland. As the primary task of the Punjabs on the mainland had changed to one of static defence, only the role of the 1st Middlesex could be said to have remained unchanged.

Although the Canadians had ostensibly been rushed to the Far East because the threat of war was receding, by the time they set out for Vancouver the chances of hostilities had become much greater. No one, however, thought to reconsider the decision to send them. The original belief that plenty of time would be available for refresher training should have been dispelled by 27 October, yet still the troops were despatched. After 22 days in the colony, the first part of which was spent finding their way about, the Canadians were face to face with the battle-seasoned troops of Imperial Japanese Army; troops who had been in action in China for four years. Even counting the three weeks' boat trip and three weeks in Hong Kong, there were still men in C Force who had not been in the Army for 16 weeks.

The Battle for the Mainland
— 8–13 December

Though many criticisms can be levelled at General Maltby's defence plans and his appreciation of Japanese intentions and capabilities, he cannot be accused of having been caught napping. Although Japanese preparations and the advance of Sano Force to positions near the frontier had been made under maximum security conditions, reports had nevertheless filtered through to Headquarters, China Command of suspicious Japanese activity. Therefore, late on Saturday, 6 December Maltby issued a "warning of impending war", and next morning at 11am all units of the garrison were ordered to occupy their war stations. This decision is all the more to Maltby's credit when one remembers that he did not believe a Japanese attack was imminent or even possible. Because he accepted the optimistic reports of his intelligence organization (see page 125), he reported to the War Office on 7 December that he thought reports of Japanese troops massing near the border were exaggerated and were merely rumours being spread by the Japanese to conceal their numerical weakness in South China.[1]

When the manning order was issued to the Island Brigade on the morning of Sunday, 7 December,* the two Canadian battalions moved from their barracks in Kowloon and ferried across to the Island to occupy their defensive positions on the south coast, and the Middlesex fully manned the pillboxes around the Island. The Volunteers were deployed to their battle positions, mostly designed to

---

*Due to the International Date Line, the Japanese attack on Hong Kong was Monday, 8 December, while at Pearl Harbor it was Sunday, 7 December.

guard vital installations. Brigadier Lawson occupied his Island Brigade Headquarters in Wong Nei Chong Gap, a position which was at the centre of the Island's road network. General Maltby and his staff were already in Fortress Headquarters, a well-protected underground installation in Victoria. The three battalions of the Mainland Brigade were already in position in the Gin Drinkers Line, and Major G.E. Grey's C Company of the Punjabs, with its accompanying Engineer demolition teams (nearly all from the Volunteers), were on the alert just behind the frontier. All units of the Hong Kong garrison were at their war stations, ready and waiting, fifteen hours before the Japanese made their first move, thanks to Maltby's determination not to take the slightest chance.

At 4:45am on 8 December Fortress Headquarters picked up a Japanese message warning that war was imminent (in actual fact Pearl Harbor and Malaya had already been attacked. Immediately the troops on the frontier were ordered to commence the first series of demolitions. Two hours later the garrison was informed that they were at war.

The first hostile Japanese action was an air raid carried out by all available aircraft on Kai Tak airfield. The installation was severely damaged and all but one of the *Walrus* and *Vildebeeste* aircraft were destroyed. Although the garrison's tiny air force could not have markedly affected the outcome of the siege, the aircraft might have survived to fly a sortie or two if they had been dispersed·or protected by shelters or blast walls. Presumably, participation in the defence of Hong Kong had been so entirely discounted that no protective measures had been taken. While Kai Tak was still under attack, bombing and strafing runs were made on Shamshuipo Barracks. Here Japanese intelligence was at fault—almost all of the Canadians had moved to the Island. Although considerable damage was done and Mainland Brigade Headquarters was forced to move to its incomplete battle headquarters north of Kowloon city, the only casualties were two men of the Royal Canadian Signals, who were wounded.

The Japanese ground attack developed early that morning, with elements of all three infantry regiments of Sano Force crossing the frontier. By early the next morning all British forward troops had been forced back to the Gin Drinkers Line. By that evening they had taken up their positions in the Line.

There can be no question that Major Grey's Punjab company and the Engineers did as well as they could possibly have been expected to do. Their task was to carry out a series of demolitions on the roads, railway lines, and bridges between the Line and the frontier and to inflict what casualties they could, in order to impose the maximum delay on the enemy. Grey's main problem was to avoid becoming cut off. For their part, the Japanese expected and were prepared for such a move and were, indeed, surprised at how little resistance they encountered before they reached the Line. Their tactics were simply to move their infantrymen around any resistance, and their strengthened engineer units, who knew almost exactly what demolitions would be carried out, were fully prepared to replace or repair destroyed or damaged installations. Grey's little command was greatly outnumbered by Japanese troops flooding past on either flank, not hesitating to cut across country. In one case a party of 150 Japanese landed behind them in sampans. Under these circumstances, it is not surprising that some of the withdrawals were rather precipitate, and that it was often impossible to wait to confirm the result of the demolitions. It is very much to their credit that this little force was able to carry out sixteen major demolitions, inflict casualties on the Japanese,—for example, one Punjab patrol staged a highly successful ambush on the night of 8 December—and retreat to the Line with minimal casualties. On the other hand, there can be no denying that some of these demolitions, as Maltby was to write in his report, "failed to provide the measure of delaying action anticipated."[2] This can be attributed both to the need for haste and to Japanese preparedness. As an example of the latter, when the two bridges at the frontier were being readied for demolition the Japanese refrained from interfering, instead concentrating on the preparation of temporary replacements which they rushed into position almost before the dust had settled.

The Japanese forward elements had reached the Gin Drinkers Line by the early afternoon of 9 December. They had expected a greater delay in the advance to the Line than they actually experienced, and, as they anticipated considerable difficulty getting through or around the Line, they did not contemplate making an immediate assault. They were particularly handicapped because, due to the recent reactivation of the Line, they did not know in what force any portion of it was held or what improvements had been made to the works. The Japanese intended to halt in front of the Line to prepare for the next stage of their attack, which they anticipated would be ready "within a week".[3] Maltby had estimated that by holding the Gin

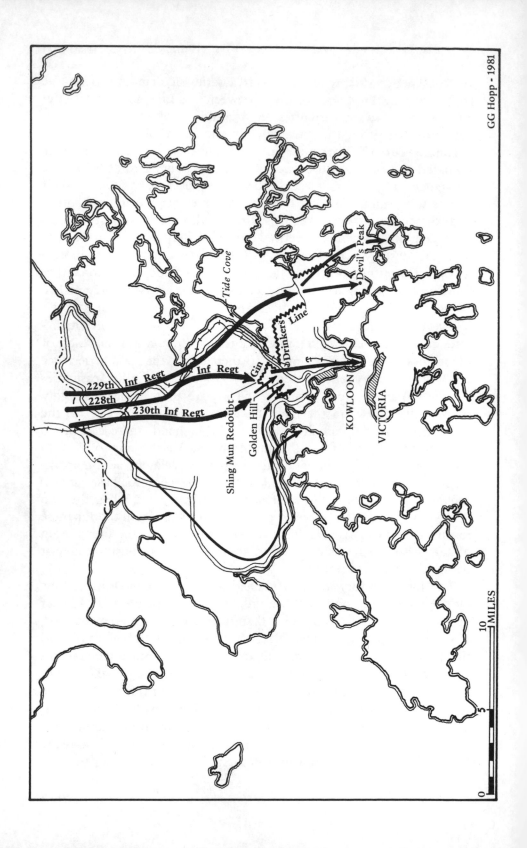

GG Hopp - 1981

Tide Cove

Devil's Peak

Drinkers Line

229th Inf Regt

Inf Regt

228th

Gin

230th Inf Regt

KOWLOON

Shing Mun Redoubt

Golden Hill

VICTORIA

MILES

10

5

0

Drinkers Line Japanese occupation of the mainland could be delayed for a week. He might well have been right if both his and Japanese plans had not been dislocated by the initiative of a Japanese regimental commander.

Beyond the fact that it had little depth and could be outflanked from the sea, the Gin Drinkers Line had other weaknesses. It was sited on very irregular, broken terrain which gave an attacking force considerable cover both from view and from fire and made it difficult for the defensive positions to provide mutually supporting fire. Probably the greatest weakness of the Line on 9 December 1941 was the fact that it was so thinly held. Instead of the optimum thousand yards defensive front per battalion, each of the Mainland Brigade battalions were responsible for over three miles, or almost five times that distance. Maltby, recognizing this, had ordered the Line to be defended by a system of "platoon localities" relying on "fire by day and patrolling by night" to cover the gaps.[4] In view of the extent and nature of the terrain, this was far more easily said than done.

The key position of the Gin Drinkers Line was the Shing Mun Redoubt, held by the Royal Scots. Situated in the western sector of the Line, it was a complex of pillboxes linked by fire trenches and underground tunnels. From the high ground on the north end of Smugglers Ridge it overlooked the Jubilee Reservoir and dominated the land approaches to Kowloon. Despite its importance, all that could be spared to hold it was a single platoon of Royal Scots plus a Company headquarters and an artillery observation post.

The Japanese infantry advancing on the Line consisted, from west to east, of elements of the 230th, 228th, and 229th Regiments. Colonel Doi of the 228th commenced a reconnaissance of the Redoubt position at 3pm on 9 December. With no interference from the defenders he was able to continue his survey for two hours until the weather deteriorated. Doi formed the impression that the Redoubt was lightly held and the garrison did not expect an attack. Therefore, having earlier obtained his divisional commander's permission to exploit any opportunities that might present themselves, and undeterred by the fact that he was poaching in the sector allotted to the 230th, he determined to organize an immediate attack.[5]

As soon as his troops had come up, Doi ordered his 2nd Battalion to reconnoitre on the left and the 3rd Battalion to undertake the actual assault with two companies leading. The men moved up through the darkness in single file without being detected by the defenders, while an obstacle-clearing team cut the wire in front of the Redoubt. The attack went in at 11:00pm preceded by a volley of hand grenades, and despite a fierce fight put up by many of the little band of defenders, by 1am on 10 December the Shing Mun Redoubt, the key to the Gin Drinkers Line, was in Japanese hands.

This was definitely a disaster, and Maltby, in his postwar report, laid the blame for the consequent early withdrawal from the mainland squarely at the door of the Royal Scots, although, he said, later fighting on the Island "did much to retrieve their prestige".[6] An officer at Fortress Headquarters stated that the loss of the Redoubt "caused real chaos at Fortress HQ. I have never seen General Maltby more shocked or angry." Maltby may have had some justification—probably either Doi's reconnaissance party, the wire-cutting team, or the approach of the 228th's 3rd Battalion could have been picked up by more aggressive patrolling, and Doi later stated that the defenders were overconfident and unready.[7] Nevertheless, it was very difficult country for a single platoon to cover, with or without patrols, and too many of the garrison, at all levels, believed the myth that the Japanese were poor at night work. In fairness to the Royal Scots, however, it must be said that given Japanese efficiency, the nature of the Line, and the numerical strength of the defenders, the Japanese could almost certainly have punched through the Line at any point and at any time they chose to make a serious attack. It was the garrison's hard luck that Doi's initiative had brought it about sooner rather than later, and at such an important point.

In the meantime, Maltby had to make up his mind what to do. As soon as it was known that the Redoubt was under attack, he had moved D Company of the Winnipeg Grenadiers over to Kowloon, but neither they, the Royal Scots reserve company, nor the Rajput company that formed the Brigade reserve were ordered to counter-attack because "the nearest troops were a mile away, the ground precipitous and broken, and the exact situation around the Redoubt very obscure."[8]

That same morning Colonel Doi must have been asking himself why he even bothered. He received orders to withdraw from the Redoubt and was told that he was in trouble for operating in the 230th's sector, despite the earlier permission he had obtained. He refused to move, and by noon, when his superiors realized what an opportunity Doi had handed them, he was told to remain.

The British made the next move—the Royal Scots withdrew

from their portion of the Gin Drinkers Line to try to establish a new defensive line running from Golden Hill to the coast. This was done with considerable difficulty between dusk and midnight on 10 December, but no interference was experienced from the enemy. Early the next morning the new positions were attacked by Colonel Shoji's 230th Regiment, which had moved forward into its allotted sector. The Royal Scots were routed in a battle on Golden and Black Hills. The Japanese simply threw in three well-supported battalions against a single, understrength one and took the ground. The entire left flank of the mainland defences had crumbled in two short encounters. The Japanese advance was temporarily halted by a counter-attack by D Company of the Royal Scots, but the lost positions could not be recaptured.

The Punjabs, who held the centre of the Line, were now in a hazardous position, particularly as the road to Kowloon ran almost parallel to the Line for a considerable distance. With the left flank gone the Japanese would be able to cut the escape route of the Punjabs and Rajputs, both of whom were being engaged in a desultory fashion by Colonel Tanaka's 229th Regiment, which had crossed Tide Cove in order to come up against the right flank of the Line. Faced with this situation, Maltby decided to bow to the inevitable and evacuate most of the Mainland Brigade to the Island. The order was issued at mid-day on 11 December. Earlier that morning D Company of the Winnipeg Grenadiers had been rushed up to fill the gap between the unbreached portion of the Line and the Royal Scots, who had formed a new line extending obliquely back into Kowloon. That afternoon the Grenadiers came under artillery and sporadic small-arms fire—the first Canadian Army unit to do so in the war—but suffered no casualties.

The evacuation took place that night. The Royal Scots moved back to Kowloon and crossed to the Island, as did many of the military vehicles. D Company of the Grenadiers covered the Royal Scots' withdrawal and followed them three hours later. Unfortunately, when the Canadians pulled back from their line they found that their vehicles had already departed, as an unidentified officer had told the transport NCO that D Company had been cut off. The company's support weapons and ammunition had to be manhandled as far as Kowloon, where two trucks were commandeered. There was no enemy pressure, though the Grenadiers reported some trouble with fifth columnists as they moved through the panic-stricken crowds in

Kowloon. The Punjabs and Rajputs also disengaged and headed southeast to the Devil's Peak Peninsula. There the Punjabs were to be evacuated while the Rajputs were to hold a previously prepared defensive line. The Punjabs' evacuation proceeded slowly and some were still on the mainland when the Japanese attacked the next day, 12 December. This assault took place in broad daylight unsupported by mortars or artillery, and was repelled by the Rajputs with the help of supporting fire from mobile artillery and from guns on the Island. The Japanese suffered losses and withdrew, after which the remainder of the Punjabs were successfully evacuated.

Stonecutters Island off Shamshuipo was also evacuated and the guns of the coastal battery there were destroyed. This did not prevent Japanese aircraft from attacking Stonecutters Island over the following three days and "silencing" the guns.[9] Apparently the Japanese Army Air Force was as accomplished as its Western counterparts at attacking non-existent targets with wildly successful results.

Despite the Rajputs' success on 12 December, Maltby decided early the next morning that the mainland should be completely abandoned. This was not according to plan, although Maltby did not admit as much in his postwar report. The Canadians had been told in their November briefing that the Gin Drinkers Line would hold for some time, and if it became necessary to fall back to Devil's Peak that position was to be held for as long as possible. It was a key position, as it dominated the Lye Mun Passage, and would afford an excellent artillery and observation post to the enemy. Maltby's original intention to hold Devil's Peak is indicated in the letter of one of his staff officers, who explained that the defence plan was "to withdraw this brigade [Mainland Brigade] less a detachment, which was to hold a mainland position to the last."[10] When the latest defence scheme was prepared Maltby had assured the Naval Officer Commanding, Commodore Collinson, that even if the Gin Drinkers Line fell Devil's Peak would be held for seven days. He apparently changed his mind because he feared the Rajputs might be completely stranded due to lack of sea transport. Collinson was less than happy about this alteration, but reacted admirably, and the mainland was completely abandoned by 9:20am on 13 December, with little interference by the Japanese.

The Japanese, in fact, were very much surprised to see the entire mainland evacuated so quickly, and this threw them into confusion for some time. They were far ahead of schedule, as they expected the main defence to be on the Gin Drinkers Line, and when the Line collapsed so quickly they were taken aback. Japanese casualties during the capture of the mainland were approximately 400 killed and wounded, which probably appeared to be a good bargain.

The Japanese were not the only ones who were surprised. Immediately before the evacuation Lieutenant Colonel Home and other officers were called to a conference with Brigadier Lawson. They were informed that things were not going well on the mainland and that the troops were to be evacuated and the garrison re-organized into two new brigades. A short while later Brigadier Wallis and his staff arrived and the re-organization took place. "The officers of the new Brigade Staff were in a highly nervous state and apparently very tired." "Troops withdrawing from the Mainland, tired, hungry, and disorganized. . . . tea was served to them as they passed through Tai Tam Gap."[11] The Canadians could get little information from Wallis and his staff, and were under the general impression that a large battle had been fought. But when Captain Banfill, the Royal Rifles' Medical Officer, set up an Advanced Dressing Station for two companies of Rajputs coming in, there was not a single casualty among them. (In the fight on the mainland and the shelling and bombing of the Island to 17 December, the garrison's casualties were 46 killed, 65 missing, and 93 wounded, totalling 204. Most of these were Royal Scots—the two Indian battalions had not been heavily engaged.) The Canadians, having been told that Devil's Peak, at least, could and would be held, were astonished to see the mainland handed over to the enemy in only five days, and judging by casualties, without much of an attempt to stop them. The British, they thought, were a little bit rattled.

The British officers reassured the Canadians that the demolitions on the mainland had been so extensive that it would be many weeks before the Japanese could bring up their artillery.[12] The next day the first heavy shells began exploding on Hong Kong Island.

The Island

— 8—17 December

When the Canadians moved into their battle positions during the afternoon of Sunday, 7 December, the threat of war did not seem unduly serious. The Royal Rifles' diary entry for the day records: "the general concensus of opinion here in Hong Kong by those who should know is that war will be averted." Captain Billings, the Canadian Signals Officer for the Mainland Brigade, was told the same day by the Brigade's Staff Captain that the manning exercise "had no special significance".[1]

Once war was officially upon the colony, the customary noble phrases were sounded. General Maltby's order of the day was:

> It is obvious to us all that the test for which we have been placed here will come in the near future. I expect each and every man of my force to stick it out unflinchingly, and that my force will become a great example of high-hearted courage to all the rest of the Empire who are fighting to preserve truth, justice and liberty for all the world.

J.L. Ralston sent this message to Brigadier Lawson: "Concurrently with Dominion's Declaration of War against Japan, I send you assurance of the complete confidence that Forces under your command will in the days that lie ahead worthily uphold the best traditions of Canadian Arms." Lawson answered: "All ranks much appreciate your message. We shall do everything in our power to maintain the best tradition of the Canadian Army."

The movement of the two Canadian battalions to their war stations was made more difficult by the lack of vehicles. Before the Japanese attack the Royal Rifles had "only five trucks available for all regimental duties,"[2] and the Grenadiers were little better off. Commandeered civilian vehicles became available after 8 December, but the Royal Rifles never had more than 12 trucks at one time, and although the Grenadiers had 30, they had to share these with Brigade Headquarters. What trucks were available were not the specialized army vehicles required and were inadequate in both number and quality. There were only twelve carriers in the colony, and one had been loaned to each Canadian battalion. These were retained right to the end. On 8 December men of the Royal Canadian Army Service Corps, working with their civilian counterparts, participated in collecting the commandeered vehicles—a total of 85 trucks and 25 cars.

With the exception of D Company of the Winnipeg Grenadiers, who were briefly moved to the mainland, the few days between the initial Japanese attack and the complete evacuation of the mainland were comparatively uneventful for the Canadians, who quietly manned their battle stations and waited. The Japanese air effort over the Island was begun on a small scale. After the bombing of Shamshuipo Barracks the rear echelon of the battalions, including the orderly room, battalion stores, and pay documents, was moved to the Island. Also on that first day of war, 3-inch mortar bombs were issued and at least one section of the Royal Rifles mortar platoon had their first chance to fire their weapons before the Japanese invaded the Island.

The civil population on the Island was beginning to create problems. The colonial government had become increasingly disorganized, and, even before the Japanese landing, fifth column activities commenced. There is little doubt that reports of sabotage by enemy sympathizers were considerably exaggerated, but some were true. Much of the sabotage was directed toward the transport, both by the drivers and others. Approximately 40 of the vehicles in the central military transport pool were reported as disabled on 9 December and the next day there were reports of "trucks wilfully damaged and several run into [the] large ditch surrounding the racetrack."[3]

With the beginning of the evacuation of the mainland there were changes in the military dispositions on the Island. Although Maltby stated afterward that he had not anticipated holding the mainland indefinitely, these changes nevertheless seem to have taken many of his subordinates by surprise, particularly the Canadians.

The operations on the mainland were, on the whole, a failure. No appreciable delay was imposed on the enemy. In addition, the British had a rude awakening with the realization that the Japanese soldiers were available in large numbers and possessed considerable initiative and expertise in night work, and that Japanese airmen were not, after all, near-sighted maladroits flying ancient aircraft. Probably the worst result was the effect on the morale of the defenders and the loss of "face" before the Chinese population, which could only encourage the opponents of the British regime. On the other hand, the demolitions of supplies and installations on the Kowloon waterfront before the evacuation had been very effective, and the Mainland Brigade and most of its equipment had been brought back to the Island with small losses.

Maltby was now faced with the problem of how best to defend the Island. Despite the fact that the enemy was in possession of the mainland he still considered an attack from the sea on the south coast of the Island a strong possibility. He therefore thought that he should dispose his forces so that they could counter an attack from almost any direction. The most obvious solution, the creation of a powerful counter-attack force at a central point that could be rushed to any threatened area, was impractical because of the poor roads, severe lack of vehicles, and Japanese command of the air. Maltby had two alternatives—either to concentrate a large proportion of his forces on the enemy's probable direction of approach or to provide approximately equal defensive strength at all points. He chose the latter.

Maltby decided to base his defence on the existing 72 pillboxes around the coastline, manned by the Middlesex and backed up by the two Indian battalions on the north coast and two Canadian battalions on the south coast, all four dispersed in company positions; The Royal Scots, whom Maltby considered in need of rest and recuperation, were kept in the Victoria area as Fortress Reserve. They had, however, manned the northeast coast for two days until the Rajputs were available to relieve them.

In addition to the redisposition of forces there was a command re-organization as well. Brigadier Lawson had commanded the Island Brigade during the fighting on the mainland, but he agreed that it was impractical for him to command all the forces available on the Island after the evacuation. On 12 December he made this entry in his diary: "Find I am in command of all troops on the Island. Quite impossible with Staff and facilities available. I got to Fortress HQ for discussion. Arrangements made for East and West commands."

The final organization distributed the garrison between two new brigades, East and West. East Brigade was commanded by the former commander of the Mainland Brigade, Brigadier Wallis, and included the Royal Rifles and Rajputs. West Brigade was commanded by Brigadier Lawson and included the Grenadiers, Punjabs, and Royal Scots. The Middlesex was under Fortress Headquarters but the pillbox detachments (each usually of nine men and two to four machine-guns) were under the operational command of the relevant brigade. In addition, most of the Middlesex men not assigned to pillboxes had been formed into a company and were entrenched on Leighton Hill just east of Victoria. The various Volunteer and artillery units, both mobile and fixed, were also under the control of the brigade in whose area they were located. The dividing line between the two brigade areas was a short distance to the east of the main north-south road, which ran from the north coast through Wong Nei Chong Gap to Repulse Bay. Brigadier Lawson continued to occupy his former tactical headquarters at Wong Nei Chong Gap. Brigadier Wallis established his at Tai Tam Gap where the Royal Rifles Headquarters was situated.

A major disadvantage of this new arrangement from the point of view of C Force was that its two battalions were separated and only one remained under Lawson's command. This seemed unfortunate at the time and was to prove increasingly so during and after the battle and in post-battle repercussions.

On 13 December a Japanese "peace mission" under a white flag crossed the harbour from Kowloon. It brought a demand from General Sakai for the surrender of the colony and the threat of heavy aerial and artillery bombardment if the demand was refused. The Japanese request was rejected almost immediately, and the enemy thereupon put their threat into effect. They possessed complete command of the air and so were able to bomb as and where they wished, and between over-hasty British road demolition and Japanese engineering efficiency, heavy artillery fire was coming down on the Island almost as soon as the Japanese surrender demand was rejected.

The artillery arm was one of the most efficient branches of the Imperial Japanese Army. In the bombardment of Hong Kong it was aided by the fact that the Japanese knew the exact position of most of the British fixed defences due to pre-war espionage. Counter-battery fire from the Island was largely ineffective. The Japanese

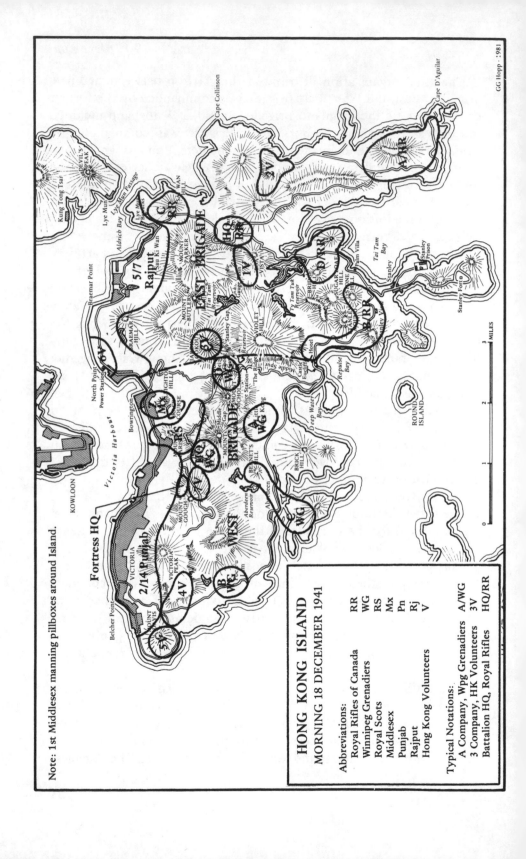

Note: 1st Middlesex manning pillboxes around Island.

Fortress HQ

HONG KONG ISLAND
MORNING 18 DECEMBER 1941

Abbreviations:
Royal Rifles of Canada   RR
Winnipeg Grenadiers   WG
Royal Scots   RS
Middlesex   Mx
Punjab   Pn
Rajput   Rj
Hong Kong Volunteers   V

Typical Notations:
A Company, Wpg Grenadiers   A/WG
3 Company, HK Volunteers   3V
Battalion HQ, Royal Rifles   HQ/RR

GG Hopp · 1981

were able to continually change their fire positions, thanks to the mobility of their guns, while the heaviest British guns, those of the coastal defences, were handicapped by their lack of suitable ammunition. It was at this point that the possibility that abandoning the Devil's Peak position had been a great mistake must have struck Maltby forcibly. Certainly, as long as it was held, the British would have possessed an excellent observation point on the mainland from which to direct their own fire, the enemy would have been denied this position, and they would also have seen an invasion of the north coast of the Island as a far more risky endeavour. With hindsight, it can be seen that the Rajputs would have contributed far more to the defence of the Island by holding on at Devil's Peak as long as possible than they could or did from their positions on the Island. To what degree this could have been deduced at the time is another question.

The rapid development and weight of the Japanese artillery bombardment was a shock to the many British, both military and civilian, who had held an exaggerated belief in the efficacy of the road demolitions and in Japanese military incompetence. Rumours were widespread, possibly the wildest of which was that the Japanese had before the war smuggled a 9-inch siege gun over the border in pieces (presumably in the suitcases of Japanese tourists) and assembled it surreptitiously in Kowloon! This rumour probably originated in the fact that the Japanese did site some of their light mobile guns in buildings during the bombardment, opening the doors for each shot.

The Japanese bombardment had an immediate effect on the civil populace and, in the city of Victoria especially, conditions deteriorated rapidly. Refugees from China had swollen the population of the colony in the years immediately preceeding the Japanese attack, and the government had neither done anything about the situation nor made allowances for it in planning for a siege. As soon as the bombardment commenced the roads became choked with Chinese streaming out of the city and across the Island to the comparative safety of the south. Rice distributions degenerated into riots. Chinese civilians who had been employed on defence work failed to report and most of those serving as military transport drivers deserted.

The military effect of the Japanese shelling and bombing was also considerable. On 13, 14, and 15 December several of the big coast defence guns (whose position was known to the inch by the Japanese) were hit. On the latter day a systematic shelling of the pillboxes along the north coast commenced and several were knocked out. In addition to these obvious preludes to invasion, the enemy was observed collecting small craft in Kowloon Bay, and this could have only one meaning. On the night of 14/15 December the sole destroyer, HMS *Thracian,* made a sortie and sank two vessels in this area, but the accumulation of boats continued.

Some of the Canadians were more exposed than others to Japanese action. At Bowen Road Military Hospital the shelling was very heavy. The hospital often shared the shells with the military targets surrounding it.

On 9 December some of the Royal Canadian Army Service Corps details had been moved to the Deep Water Bay area and were working around the clock from this depot, supplying the troops with what little transport they had. With this group were six members of the Hong Kong Volunteer Defence Corps, who apparently were far from being "volunteers": "Because of their attitude, [they] were more hindrance than assistance. They claimed that they had not volunteered for service, but had been 'conscripted', and they did not hesitate to tell us so. They would never go out on a night guard unless accompanied by a Canadian."[4]

The Winnipeg Grenadiers were in the southwest with the bulk of the Island between them and the enemy, and so were not directly affected by the Japanese artillery. This was not the case with the Royal Rifles, who were occupying an area extending from Repulse Bay in the south to Lye Mun in the north, almost all of which was exposed to Japanese shellfire. Commencing on 13 December, all company positions and Battalion Headquarters at Tai Tam Gap were the targets of a bombardment of increasing severity. Water, electrical power, and telephone connections were constantly disrupted. Indeed, the telephone system, which the Canadians had been informed was as good as that of the fortress of Gibraltar, was put out of action in the first stages of the bombardment.

Monday, 15 December saw a continuation of the bombardment. All Rifles' positions were shelled, and as always the northernmost position around Lye Mun, held by C Company under Major Bishop, was the most heavily hit. It was this company that was to participate in an event that is one of the minor mysteries of the siege.

At about 9:30 on the night of 15 December the Volunteer artillery battery at Pak Sah Wan on Hong Kong Island at the eastern entrance to the Lye Mun Passage opened up with artillery and machine-gun fire and illumination and were joined by other batteries firing into the Passage. After this heavy burst of fire, the Pak Sah Wan artillerymen precipitately abandoned their positions and headed south at top speed. Reaching Lye Mun Gap, they were halted by Major Bishop and informed him that the Japanese were "thick as leaves in the battery position". Realizing that this evacuation meant that his left flank was up in the air, Bishop immediately led a party to re-occupy the position and found it totally deserted, with no sign of friend or foe. Two hours later a platoon of Rajputs moved into the area, but C Company of the Royal Rifles still held their advanced positions until the next day when the artillery returned. The artillery officer in command admitted that his battery had sustained no casualties during the "Japanese attack".[5]

The story still persists that the Japanese had attempted a landing on the north shore that night. Carew and Ferguson in their luridly coloured narratives of the siege give detailed accounts of the attempt and its defeat by the garrison—including some Canadians.[6] Maltby also recorded the endeavour in his postwar report. No record of such an undertaking appears in any Japanese account—and the Japanese in their comments on the battle were markedly uninhibited in detailing both their successes and failures. No accounts, except of the false alarm described in the preceeding paragraph, appear in British or Canadian records—and surely they would not have been reticent in recording such an apparent victory!

What seems to be the most likely solution is that the "landing force" (if, indeed, there was *anything* moving in the Passage) were Chinese escaping from the mainland—a common event. Certainly the impressions of the officer commanding the battery, at any rate, warrant taking with a pinch of salt.

The previous day this same officer, a local magistrate, had been in to see Banfill at the Lye Mun Advanced Dressing Station. His battery had been shelled or bombed and several of his men were wounded. The officer himself had his head and arm dressed, but on examination he revealed no wounds at all. He asked Banfill, "Have I got to go back to that horrible place?", and when Banfill answered "yes" he jumped into his car and roared off, but returned to his post later. When the Japanese landed on 18 December his battery was quickly surrounded and captured, but he was to boast in the prisoner of war camp about what a great stand he had made.[7]

Banfill does not appear to have been a man to suffer fools gladly and a clash he had with the colonial administration on 17 December was another example of the increasing Canadian-British friction and mistrust, which seem to have been even more virulent at Lye Mun than elsewhere. On that day Banfill had phoned the Chief of Civilian Medical Services on the request of Mrs. Tinson, who ran the civilian first aid post next door to Banfill's Advanced Dressing Station at Lye Mun. Banfill told him that this post was not getting any cases to speak of, was in an exposed area, and should be moved, as the women and the Chinese helpers were getting nervous. The Chief of Civilian Medical Services accused Banfill of interfering and said that Lye Mun was no more dangerous than any other area. Banfill told him to come down and see for himself and hung up. The next day, 18 December, the Governor himself came down and gave Banfill a blast for sticking his nose in and for "addressing a representative of the Crown in a scornful manner."[8] Miss Lois Fearon, who was present, heard the Governor say that "the Japs wouldn't land".[9] The tragic sequel to that remark is recorded in the next chapter.

The two days following the invasion scare witnessed an increase in the enemy bombardment. The Japanese heavy bombers were now available and, with their help, by the end of 16 December more than half the pillboxes in the Rajputs sector of the north shore had been knocked out. The Royal Rifles recorded that their men were showing the strain of constant bombardment. C Company had been pulled back to Sai Wan and Lye Mun Gap, and now there were "no Canadians on North face of Island".[10] Nevertheless, 13 Platoon of C Company was dive-bombed at Sai Wan and suffered five casualties. The next day shellfire was landing as far south as Stanley, and this area was also bombed. In addition to artillery shells, mortar bombs were landing in the Royal Rifles area. When some of the mortar positions were located in the Devil's Peak area the battalion called for return fire, but none was provided. The Canadian Service Corps detachment at Deep Water Bay reported that by 17 December, in addition to vehicles immobilized through sabotage, no less than twenty had been put out of action by the Japanese artillery.

That same day another Japanese surrender demand was sent across the harbour from Kowloon. As it was essentially the same as the request received four days earlier it was rejected. As Brigadier Lawson wrote in his diary: "Jap envoy came over and said that all military installations have been destroyed, no use going on fighting. Governor told them to go back and destroy some more."

Despite these and other brave words from the defenders, there was little doubt in anybody's mind that the Japanese would shortly try their fortunes on the Island.

The Island

—18/19 December

Thursday, 18 December dawned fine and clear and the Japanese artillery and aerial bombardment increased in intensity. Although it still hit all parts of the Island, there was a very obvious concentration on the north shore. For what seems to have been the first time, the oil storage tanks at North Point were hit and set on fire, and other fires blazed on the north face of the Island. Fifth column activity also increased. Five West Brigade vehicles were destroyed by fire, and when the Canadian Service Corps men at Deep Water Bay commandeered twenty taxis that day, all but six were found to be inoperative due to sabotage. The Service Corps also reported that Japanese artillery fire made it very difficult to pass through the various gaps.[1]

Of all the infantry units the most exposed to the Japanese fire and the most affected by it were the Rajputs, holding the eastern sector of the north shore. The state of the platoon holding Pak Sah Wan was described by the battalion's commanding officer as "exhaustion from perpetual enemy fire".[2] When Brigadier Wallis visited the Rajputs' headquarters that afternoon, "it was jointly appreciated that the long and persistent fire of all natures, air attacks and the heavy pall of smoke drifting across the waterfront were almost certain to prelude an attempt to land after dark."[3]

There was little doubt that an attack was imminent and that it was coming from the north, yet Maltby and his brigade commanders made remarkably little attempt to alter their defensive postions to meet such an attack. The two Indian battalions on the north shore and the Middlesex in the pillboxes around the Island were presumably in the right position. Whether the position of the Royal Scots in

Victoria was the best one possible for the Fortress Reserve, however, is open to question.

What of the two Canadian units, posted to meet an assault from the south that appeared increasingly unlikely?

The Winnipeg Grenadiers were part of Brigadier Lawson's West Brigade. Lawson had established his headquarters in the vital Wong Nei Chong Gap in the centre of the Island. Three of the Grenadiers' companies were positioned to defend the west coast and western sector of the south coast—from east to west they were A,C, and B Companies at Little Hong Kong, Aberdeen, and Pok Fu Lam respectively. D Company, after its brief excursion to the mainland, was in position at Wong Nei Chong Gap to serve as a Brigade Reserve. Battalion Headquarters and Headquarters Company were at Wan Chai Gap just south of Victoria. Lawson had ordered three platoons formed from Headquarters Company to function as "flying columns", with two trucks per platoon. These stayed in the Gap during the nights and seem to have been the only mobile counter-attack force on the Island. As such, they might have been able to deal with an enemy reconnaissance party, but were woefully inadequate in the face of the invasion force the Japanese were about to fling at Hong Kong.

In East Brigade, the Royal Rifles were similarly strung out with a total battalion perimeter of 15 miles. Battalion Headquarters and Headquarters Company were beside Brigade Headquarters at Tai Tam Gap. Elements of Headquarters Company were, of course, with the other four companies as well. From north to south these companies were C at Lye Mun and Lye Mun Gap, A at Windy Gap and D'Aguilar Point, D at Obelisk and Red Hills, and B at Stanley View and Stone Hill. There appears to have been no provision for a Brigade Reserve.

At some time before the battle the Royal Rifles absorbed their first reinforcements directly into the battalion. A new platoon was now added to each company, identified by the suffix R, though whether these platoons consisted largely of reinforcements or whether the whole company was redistributed is unclear. In addition, Headquarters Company now disposed of several line platoons. The Winnipeg Grenadiers had absorbed their reinforcements as well, using some of them to fill vacancies created by the men who had not sailed on the *Awatea*. The remainder were absorbed directly into the companies, the majority going to Headquarters Company to enable it to form the "flying columns".

18 December seems to have held little out of what was now the ordinary for both battalions. In the Silesian Mission building at Sau Ki Wan in C Company area was Captain Banfill's Advanced Dressing Station. That day Major MacAuley, commanding Headquarters Company, visited Banfill and tried to persuade him to move as the location was so exposed. Banfill replied that as the Governor had refused to allow the women in the civilian first aid post to move, he did not feel that he could leave.[4] Other than this one attempt, there was little movement in East Brigade to counter the impending enemy incursion.

The Japanese had already completed their plans. Preparation for the invasion had commenced on 16 December with the organization of the landing forces and the issuing of plans to the various commanders. The three Japanese infantry regiments were to land on the Island in the same formation they had invaded the mainland, that is, from west to east, Shoji's 230th, Doi's 228th, and Tanaka's 229th. Each regiment would initially land two of its battalions, with the third being retained on the mainland as a reserve and for garrison duties. The 230th and 228th were to land between North and Braemar Points on the northernmost bulge of the Island, east of Victoria. After landing they were to swing right and advance westward over the northern half of the Island. The plan called for them to be south of the city of Victoria by daybreak of 19 December. The 229th would land further east on the north shore in the Aldrich Bay-Sau Ki Wan area and make a two-pronged thrust to the southern half of the Island, where it too would swing right and advance to the west. At some point, whether with the landing or after it, an engineering unit fighting as infantry, the Suzukawa Unit, was to take the right flank position and advance through Victoria. Although the Japanese had not attempted a landing in force on the Island before the night of 18 December, they had succeeded in landing at least one beach reconnaissance party of strong swimmers. The information gained by this group combined with pre-war espionage and plans captured on the mainland gave the Japanese a reasonably accurate idea of what to expect.

On the evening of 18 December, according to enemy accounts, the Japanese navy carried out a demonstration against the southwest coast in order to divert attention from the activities in the north. What form this diversion took is unknown, because nothing was noticed by the defenders.

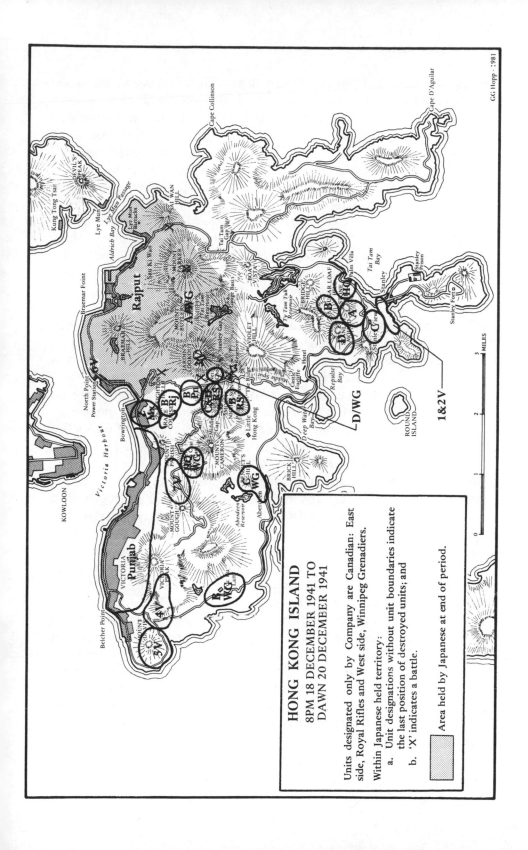

HONG KONG ISLAND

8PM 18 DECEMBER 1941 TO DAWN 20 DECEMBER 1941

Units designated only by Company are Canadian: East side, Royal Rifles and West side, Winnipeg Grenadiers.

Within Japanese held territory:

a. Unit designations without unit boundaries indicate the last position of destroyed units; and

b. 'X' indicates a battle.

▨ Area held by Japanese at end of period.

GG: Hopp- :981

By the time darkness fell, the weather, which had been clear earlier in the evening, had turned cloudy with occasional rain showers. Combined with the smoke from the burning oil tanks and other fires this weather made for an unusually dark night. The exact time of the Japanese embarkation and landing is uncertain—the British estimate is 8:30pm and the Japanese 9pm. The Japanese were transported in collapsible powered assault craft, assault boats propelled by oars, and commandeered civilian boats.

The full impact of the initial Japanese assault was to fall almost solely on the 5/7 Rajputs, who not only occupied positions along that section of coast, but also, for some reason, manned the pillboxes. In other words, approximately 700 infantry were supposed to defend almost three miles of coast, infantry that had been bombed and shelled almost incessantly for the last five days, and as the dark night and the smoke made it almost impossible to locate the crossing Japanese, even with the few searchlights remaining intact, it is no wonder that the Rajputs did little more than inconvenience the Japanese and inflict moderate casualties. British artillery did not intervene until after the first landings, and then with little effect as there were no Japanese in the target area at Quarry Point. All three Japanese regiments were somewhat disorganized after a water crossing under fire on a dark night, but each reached its designated landing area. As soon as the first waves of invaders reached the shore, they closed with the defenders. The 5/7 Rajput Regiment disintegrated. Some elements, particularly the officers and NCO's, put up a fierce resistance, and died to the last man. Almost half the battalion was composed of partially-trained recruits, and the strain of the previous days and the shock of the Japanese assault proved too much for many of them. Among the Canadians to report on this unfortunate unit was Captain Banfill, who stated that the Rajputs put up a good fight in isolated areas, but eventually broke and ran. The diary of C Company of the Royal Rifles recorded: "Between 2100 and 2200 hours there was a continual road race of Indian Troops running past without arms in the direction of Tai Tam. No information could be obtained from them, they would only say, 'Japs, thousands of Japs.'"[5] The early hour indicates that they had not put up a prolonged resistance. With the exception of a single company on the left flank that had not been engaged and a handful of stragglers, the 5/7 Rajputs took no further part in the defence of Hong Kong.

East Brigade—8pm, 18 December*

After the hapless Rajputs, the next infantry encountered by the oncoming Japanese was C Company, Royal Rifles of Canada. This was the most northerly of the battalion's companies. It was stationed in Lye Mun as a "Reserve and Security Force", but seemed destined to be in the forefront of the battle. Also, as in the case of the Pak Sah Wan "landing" of 15 December and the wooden gun episode, it tended to become involved in off-beat occurences and Major Bishop could not seem to get "on net" with Brigadier Wallis. The night of 18 December was to see this continued.

Despite the fact that he anticipated being relieved at 9pm by D Company, at 8pm Major Bishop, concerned at the weakness and exhaustion of the Rajput platoon at Pak Sah Wan and unaware that the Japanese were even then entering their boats, sent 15 Platoon under Lieutenant Scott forward to reinforce the position. Moving up, Scott and his men at 8:30 ran into a band of armed men in civilian clothes at the Lye Mun gate. There was a brief flurry of shots and bayonet thrusts. Scott held his ground and reported the incident to Bishop, who ordered the platoon to pull back to Lye Mun Barracks. Accompanied by Rifleman Gray, Bishop then left Company Headquarters at the Lye Mun Gap and made a personal reconnaissance. Moving up to Sai Wan Fort on Sai Wan Hill above the Gap, he encountered a party of artillerymen under a corporal who reported that the fort was now occupied by Japanese dressed as coolies, who had chased them out without even one shot being fired. The fort had indeed been occupied, although whether they were fifth columnists or Japanese in civilian clothes is uncertain. Being unable to contact the Rajput Commanding Officer (who probably had enough on his mind already) Bishop decided to deal with the matter himself and reported the capture of the fort to Battalion Headquarters who passed the information on to Brigadier Wallis. The Brigadier immediately telephoned C Company Headquarters and told Bishop, "there is no such thing as the enemy being at Fort Sai Wan. There are Canadians in the Fort." Bishop informed him that, as commander of the Canadians in the area, he could state that there had never been Canadians in the fort—indeed, he had not been allowed inside the place

---

*As the battle for the Island developed, it evolved into two separate conflicts, one fought by East Brigade and one by West Brigade. The narrative will alternate between these two sections of the battle.

himself. Wallis assured him, "I have definite information that there are friendly troops in the Fort." Bishop replied, "They don't act friendly. We are being raked by automatic fire from there this moment." He added that he was organizing an attack on the fort at once.[6]

Wallis undoubtedly thought that Bishop was unreliable, although he had done absolutely nothing wrong and was merely reporting the loss of a position by another unit and preparing to act. By this time it had become obvious that more was going on than a mere fifth column *coup*. Further to the north 15 Platoon had been attacked and pushed out of Lye Mun Barracks. Inspecting the bodies of a Japanese patrol they had cut down, 15 Platoon found three in uniform and four dressed as coolies. 14 Platoon at Sau Ki Wan had come under heavy attack from the left, been forced to extend its line to avoid being outflanked, and finally drew back to Company Headquarters. The Company had already been inundated with fleeing Rajputs. Bishop asked for reinforcements and artillery support to stage a counter-attack. This was referred to Brigade which refused permission to reinforce Bishop, but did provide an artillery barrage on call. Bishop, determined to at least get back the fort as it dominated most of his position, detailed 13 Platoon to go in from the northeast where the slope was gentlest, but at that moment a Captain Bumpas [or Bompas], Royal Artillery, arrived from Brigade Headquarters. Saying that he had "secret plans", he took charge of the attack and switched it to the east side, where the fort had a 20-foot perpendicular wall. The attack, now involving 15R Platoon as well, started and Bumpas stayed on the road, "Brandishing a revolver and shouting that he would shoot any men who attempted to retire." This was a rather inappropriate threat, as the only people who had retired from the area that night were the Royal Artillery. Major Bishop advised him to shut up and lead the attack if he was so bloodthirsty, but at this point Bumpas' enthusiasm wore off. He ordered Captain Gavey to stop after the enemy was driven into the fort, saying "we will take the Fort at dawn, according to plan".[7] The abortive attack had cost the company 9 men killed, and Captain Gavey was seriously wounded while attempting to disengage. During the attack, Bishop asked Brigade to have the Mount Collinson searchlight turned onto the fort, but was told the light came under another command. As the attacking force was retiring, however, the light did come on, giving the Japanese excellent targets. The entire fiasco was to set the scene for relations between East Brigade Headquarters and the Royal Rifles for the rest of the battle.

While C Company was being drawn into battle, there were various changes of position within the battalion. D Company was due to relieve C Company that evening, but the relief was cancelled and D Company stood fast except for 17 Platoon. This was ordered north to Battalion Headquarters at Tai Tam Gap and thence to a position at a ration store halfway between Lye Mun and Tai Tam to act as a second line of defence if C Company's front line fell back. A small party from A Company was ordered to Boa Vista at 9pm, B Company sent 12 Platoon up to Tai Tam Gap at 11:30pm, and Headquarters Company sent 5 Platoon and two sections from 3 Platoon, all under Lieutenant Williams, to Mount Parker. Mount Parker was the dominant feature immediately south of the Lye Mun area, and the force from the Royal Rifles was intended to reinforce a platoon of Volunteers that was holding the area. The Volunteers chose to believe they were not being reinforced, but relieved, and all disappeared except for an NCO and two men. The fact that they remained may indicate that the misinterpretation by the others was deliberate.

From midnight on, all of C Company was under heavy and continual attack by the advancing Japanese, who were from Tanaka's 229th Regiment. One of Tanaka's two battalions, the 3rd, had landed at Aldrich Bay and was heading for Mount Parker while the other, the 2nd, had landed further to the east and was moving south toward Sai Wan and the Tai Tam Gap. Major Bishop's men were the first serious resistance the 2nd Battalion had yet met, and it must have come as an unpleasant surprise. C Company possessed unusually heavy firepower—in addition to its own weapons it had acquired two Lewis guns, a Vickers machine-gun, and an extra Bren, presumably from decamped Volunteers or artillerymen. In addition, every officer had contrived to get his hands on a Thompson gun. As the Japanese advanced, the fiercely-burning fires in Sau Ki Wan threw them into relief, and they suffered severe losses. One Japanese officer told the Canadians after the capitulation that his company suffered 65% casualties in this action. C Company stopped Tanaka's 2nd Battalion dead in its tracks, forced the abandonment of its plan to head south for the Sheko Peninsula, and deflected its thrust to pass along the western slopes of Mount Parker toward Repulse and Deep Water Bays.

At 1:30am Captain Bumpas, apparently still on the scene, informed

Bishop that his company should retire as the enemy was circling to the rear and isolating them. Whether Bumpas was in touch with Brigade or not, his statement about the positions was undoubtedly true. The Japanese, unable to get past C Company, were moving around its left flank. By 2:45 each platoon had reported that it had successfully disengaged and was moving back to where Lieutenant Power was waiting with D Company's 17 Platoon. This withdrawal was difficult and slow as the wounded could not be left behind, and, at intervals, the platoons had to overlap and cover each other. The success of this is particularly notable when it is recalled that these men had not had a hot meal in five days, had manned their positions continuously under heavy shellfire for the same time, and had slept only in weapon pits. Men were falling down asleep wherever they stopped.

When the company reached its destination it was realized that two wounded men had been left at Lye Mun. Major Bishop, Lieutenant Scott, Sergeant Clayton, and a signaller went back through the advancing Japanese and after a sharp skirmish brought the men away. There is no question that, in the first hours of battle for the Island, C Company of the Royal Rifles put in a performance that few units anywhere could have equalled.

The withdrawal of C Company, though militarily the only course of action, left all remaining personnel from any unit at the mercy of Tanaka's men. Earlier that night when the Japanese had overrun the Volunteer anti-aircraft position on Sai Wan Hill, they took twenty prisoners and bayoneted them. Only two miraculously survived their wounds.

By dawn on 19 December Captain Banfill's Advanced Dressing Station was deserted, except for a few personnel from it and the civilian first aid post. They had just finished treating two badly wounded Rajput officers who had been shot on their retreat south,* when a party of Japanese occupied the building and led the men away, subsequently murdering all but four of them. The women were held for several hours and then released.

---

*These officers claimed to have been shot by Canadians and this story became widely circulated. Banfill did not believe this, with good reason, as the only Canadians had long since withdrawn. Presumably the Rajputs, moving through an area formerly held by the Canadians but now swarming with Japanese, were shot unexpectedly and leapt to the wrong conclusion.

Canadian troops after their arrival at Shamshuipo barracks.   (IWM K1375)

Major General Maltby and Brigadier Lawson confer after C Force's arrival.
                                                                  (IWM K1371)

Volunteers and Indian troops in camp.   (IWM KF176)

Volunteers prepare a machine-
gun position on the coast.
(IWM (K1325)

Chinese personnel of the Royal Engineers. These men were to fight with bravery and determination as infantry during the battle. (IWM KF138)

One of the coast defence guns. These weapons were handicapped by a lack of suitable ammunition. (IWM K1329)

A British advanced machine-gun position on the border looking into China.　(IWM K74)

British military convoy. This picture graphically illustrates how the high ground dominated the road system.　(IWM K1680)

Canadian troops establish a Bren gun position and put on a bayonet charge for the photographer. In a few weeks they would be doing this in deadly earnest over the same ground. (IWM KF193, KF189)

The Lye Mun battery showing Lye Mun Passage where the Japanese crossed. The high point in the centre background is Devil's Peak.   (PAC PA114877)

The Silesian Mission where Captain Banfill had his Advanced Dressing Station, with Mount Parker in the background.   (Canadian Forces [CF] PMR 79-167)

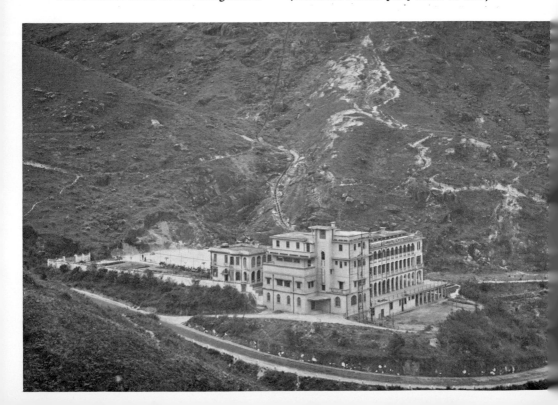

Lye Mun Barracks, the most northern point held by the Rifles' C Company.
(PAC PA116195)

Japanese machine-gun in action in Hong Kong.   (IWM SIT3306)

Mount Butler (*left*) and Mount Parker.   (CF PMR 79-169)

Japanese artillery in action on Jardine's Lookout firing over Wong Nei Chong Gap.   (IWM SIT3571)

While C Company was in its new position halfway between Lye Mun and Tai Tam Gap the Company Quartermaster Sergeant issued badly-needed ammunition and the Royal Rifles Adjutant, Captain Atkinson, came up with some hot food and was asked about the counter-attack Bumpas had talked about. "Captain Atkinson when questioned replied that there did not appear to be any plan as far as Brigade HQ was concerned re counter-attack, and doubted if ever there had been one."[8] Certainly there was no concerted plan for the Royal Rifles in the early morning of 19 December, as shown by the confused and futile battle for Mount Parker.

As Mount Parker was now held by only a single platoon plus two sections from another, the detached party from A Company (Lieutenant Blaver plus 20 men) which had originally been intended to hold 5 Platoon's vacated position was sent to Mount Parker as reinforcements. Then at 3am, Captain Clarke from Headquarters Company was ordered to take D Company's 16 Platoon (which a few hours earlier had been ordered up to Boa Vista), proceed to Mount Parker, take command, and co-ordinate the defence. In the meantime, the guide leading Blaver and his men had taken a wrong turn and they did not reach their objective until 7:30am. They found that the Japanese had possession of the crest and were assaulting the defence positions. From his position on the lower slope Blaver could see well over a hundred enemy but nevertheless he and his twenty men attempted an attack. They were hit by machine-gun fire from their right while the Japanese 100 feet above them on the crest of Mount Parker lobbed down grenades. After ten casualties they gave up the struggle and withdrew down the mountain. Firing continued on the crest until 8:30am at which time the last defence position must have been overrun. By this time Captain Clarke, making a personal reconnaissance from a ridge 500 feet below the crest, had seen Blaver and his men in their hopeless struggle. Clarke returned to Boa Vista, where he had left 16 Platoon, and telephoned Brigade. When Brigadier Wallis asked if Mount Parker could be retaken, Clarke replied that he didn't think so, but would try if reinforced.[9] Two additional platoons, one from B and one from D, were ordered up, but before the attack got underway it was cancelled. This is fortunate—all of Tanaka's 2nd Battalion was in the Mount Parker area and it is doubtful if a co-ordinated attack by the whole Hong Kong garrison could have ejected them. It would have been madness for three Canadian platoons to try.

Aside from the Mount Parker fighting, the only other early morning activity was a desperate attempt by Major MacAuley to reach Captain Banfill. The attempt failed but MacAuley did return with a truckful of wounded. Mortar fire was also brought down on the northeast slopes of Mount Parker.

It was decided some time in the early morning (whether by Battalion or Brigade is uncertain, but probably the latter) to bring A and B Companies forward to join Headquarters Company at Tai Tam Gap. B Company reached Tai Tam Gap at 8:30 and took up defensive positions there.

By 9:30am Brigadier Wallis had had time to take stock of the situation. As the Rajputs had been annihilated, his only effective infantry unit was the Royal Rifles. The Rifles had effectively blocked the Japanese thrust along the low ground from Lye Mun to Tai Tam, but the Japanese had siezed the high ground to the west. As there seemed no hope of organizing a co-ordinated counter-attack from the Rifles' present positions Wallis decided to concentrate his infantry and mobile artillery in the area around Stone Hill and Stanley Village, from where they could be used to best advantage.

Before issuing the order Wallis discussed the matter with Maltby, who had hoped instead that East Brigade be moved to the west to link up with West Brigade. Wallis did not think Maltby appreciated the nature of the terrain nor did Wallis consider the Royal Rifles capable of the move across the enemy-held high ground. He recalled later that it was at this time that "I realized that the Battalion was incapable of real fight".[10] As the only fighting Wallis had to base this opinion on was the successful fight of C Company against a whole battalion and the failure of a small party of men to drive another battalion off Mount Parker, it is obvious that he had failed to grasp the realities of the situation.

Orders for the move went out around 10am and, after various trials and tribulations, all Royal Rifles companies reached their new positions. Most of D Company was at Stanley Mound by dark; C Company was pulled back to Tai Tam Gap at 10:20am and had taken up defence positions at Stanley View by nightfall. B Company covered the withdrawal of the others and so had to take up its positions on Sugarloaf Hill in the dark—a difficult task as no path could be found. Headquarters Company personnel stayed to the last, evacuating company stores, covered by a single platoon of B Company under Lieutenant Ross. Tai Tam Gap was finally evacuated at 4:45pm.

During the last 45 minutes Ross and his men were continually under fire from almost 200 Japanese who were trying to surround the abandoned position. Eventually, Headquarters Company and Battalion Headquarters moved into Palm Villa, on the coast near Tai Tam Bay. It had been a particularly frustrating day for A Company. At 7:30 the company was ordered out of its positions at D'Aguilar and told to move up to Battalion Headquarters at Tai Tam Gap. They moved off with their only truck at 7:50am and were half a mile up the road when the order was cancelled. No sooner had they arrived back at D'Aguilar than they were ordered up again. On arriving at the Gap at 10:30 they were immediately instructed to move south to Stanley Mound, but halfway there Brigadier Wallis ordered Major Young to halt and march his company to Stone Hill, as all plans had changed and the force was going to "counter-attack the enemy and drive him back into the sea". There was no counter-attack, but the exhausted company was finally deployed around Stone Hill by 6pm.[11]

Whatever problems he might have had with the Royal Rifles, Brigadier Wallis had reason that day to think them paragons compared with his artillery. The coast defence guns at Cape D'Aguilar and Cape Collinson were supposed to continue fighting after the infantry had pulled back, but instead the guns were destroyed and abandoned. Even worse was the situation with the mobile artillery. When Wallis ordered one of the batteries to "get out of action" and leave, the gunners accidentally or deliberately took this as an order to put the guns out of action. Another battery stayed in action too long and lost the guns. As a result, the only mobile artillery left to East Brigade was one 18-pounder and two 3.7-inch howitzers.

The first day's fighting had been disastrous for East Brigade. The infantry force was halved, the artillery was nearly wiped out, and the whole force was concentrated in a small area of the south coast. The Canadians of the Royal Rifles were tired, but not disorganized, though they had suffered casualties. Nearly two platoons had been lost in the Mount Parker battle, and of the 177 men with C Company on 18 December, only 68 answered roll call at Stanley View the next evening.

West Brigade

The fight in the West Brigade area, even more than that to the east, was dictated by the ridge of mountains running east to west along the Island. In the eastern half of the Island the high points are, from east to west, Mount Parker, Mount Butler, and Jardine's Look-out, with the latter in the area assigned to West Brigade. On the west side of the Island, separated from Jardine's Lookout by Wong Nei Chong Gap, are, from east to west, Mount Nicholson, Mount Cameron, Mount Gough, and Victoria Peak. Therefore, when Brigadier Lawson located his Brigade Headquarters at Wong Nei Chong Gap, he had chosen not simply a strategic location from the point of view of control and communication, but what was probably the prime Japanese objective of the early stage of the invasion, Indeed, Lawson seems to have belatedly realized that the position, while admirable for control, was far from ideal defensively. On 18 December Major Lyndon, the Brigade Major, located a new site for Brigade Headquarters at Black Links, to the south of Mount Nicholson. The move was scheduled for the following day.

When Colonel Shoji's 230th and Colonel Doi's 228th Regiments landed near North Point and Braemar Point respectively, their initial experiences were much the same as Colonel Tanaka's. A certain amount of trouble was caused by the Rajput defences, but this was quickly dealt with, and both units headed inland. Unlike Tanaka's Regiment, both units advanced directly to the high ground and, skirting Braemar Hill, drove south toward Jardine's Lookout, over-looking Wong Nei Chong Gap, and to the Gap itself: Shoji's 2nd Battalion was to take Jardine's Lookout and his 3rd was to occupy the Gap. Doi had some communication problems, but his account indicates that his unit arrived at the foot of the Lookout at first light, took that position, and proceeded on to the Gap. The Lookout was held by two platoons of Volunteers. Some of their pillboxes were quickly overrun by Shoji's men, but others, on the southeast slope, held out until the afternoon.

The first action taken by Brigadier Lawson in response to the Japanese landings was to order the three Grenadier flying column platoons forward from the Gap to oppose any Japanese breakthrough. One platoon went to a road junction northwest of the Gap while another, under Lieutenant Birkett, was ordered to Jardine's Lookout and the third, under Lieutenant French, to Mount Butler. There *had* been a Japanese breakthrough, but in much greater strength than could be contained by such small bodies of troops. As in the battle on Mount Parker, Birkett's and French's platoons had as much success as one might expect of platoons sent to attack oncoming battalions. French's platoon found the Japanese already occupying

Mount Butler and, failing to dislodge them, pulled back. French was wounded, and then killed, covering this withdrawal. Birkett's platoon did not reach its objective until just before dawn. It, too, encountered an overwhelming number of enemy and was attacked. Birkett was killed while trying to cover his men with a Bren gun. Some of the survivors of his platoon reached the remaining Volunteer pillboxes and played a large part in enabling them to hold out until the afternoon.

Brigadier Lawson realized shortly after midnight that some of the enemy had penetrated as far as Mount Butler. D Company of the Grenadiers, which had been designated as Brigade Reserve, was holding positions in and north of the Gap. Not wishing to leave the Gap exposed by moving D Company, Lawson brought up A Company less one platoon from Little Hong Kong village. At 2:30am he ordered the Company Commander, Major Gresham, to take A Company plus one platoon of D Company (to replace the A Company platoon left behind), clear Jardine's Lookout, and, it would seem, occupy Mount Butler (although this last order is not recorded). The company did not reach its objective until dawn. A Company's last battle, though it resulted in the award of the only Victoria Cross of the Hong Kong fighting, is wrapped in obscurity, largely due to a lack of reliable witnesses and some ambiguity in Japanese records. The evidence indicates that the company did reach Mount Butler at dawn and cleared it of the enemy. A series of heavy Japanese counter-attacks forced the Canadians to withdraw in the late morning, and by mid-afternoon they were surrounded before they could complete their withdrawal. By the end of the fighting, almost the entire company had been killed, wounded, or taken prisoner. During their last stand, Company Sergeant Major J.R. Osborne, who had been a pillar of strength throughout the entire action, deliberately covered a grenade with his body, saving the lives of those of his men within its range at the cost of his own. After the war he was awarded a posthumous Victoria Cross.

It is difficult to fit this fierce little battle into the context of the Japanese accounts, which contain few details. Neither regimental commander mentioned fighting on Mount Butler, yet both claim to have taken Jardine's Lookout. However, control and communication that night and early morning was as difficult for the Japanese as for the defenders, and as the two features are very close together and part of the same hill system, a mistake could easily have been made, particularly in the fog and mist. Shoji mentions in his account that resistance from the Indian (that is, Volunteer) defenders was "slight", but at another point states that strong resistance was encountered on the Lookout. Shoji also recounts that as he was moving up "fierce rifle fire [was] heard from the direction of 2nd Battalion moving toward Jardine's Lookout,"[12] which sounds more like an attack on a company than on pillboxes or platoon positions (though it may have been Lieutenant Birkett and his men). Among the possibilities are that Colonel Doi's men attacked Mount Butler thinking it was Jardine's Lookout, that some of Shoji's 2nd Battalion did the same, or that some or all of A Company's gallant fight was actually on the Lookout.

At the same time as Colonel Shoji heard the firing from the direction of the Lookout he also heard the commencement of a similar heavy engagement in the direction of Wong Nei Chong Gap. Shoji's 3rd Battalion had made contact with 17 and 18 Platoons of the Grenadiers' D Company, which were in positions north of the Gap. After a fierce fight against vastly superior numbers both platoons were surrounded and overrun. A few men managed to escape over the rough country. The attacking force then headed for the Gap, and was soon joined by the bulk of the 2nd Battalion which Shoji diverted from Jardine's Lookout. Doi's 1st Battalion was also at the Gap and in action by daylight, and by the end of the day, no less than four Japanese battalions were attacking the Gap and the slopes above it.

By first light Brigadier Lawson must have been sickeningly aware of the precarious situation of both his Brigade Headquarters and the vital Wong Nei Chong Gap. A Company of the Grenadiers had vanished without trace into the hills, and one platoon of D Company with it. Once the two forward D Company platoons went under there was only D Company Headquarters, Brigade Headquarters, and the headquarters of West Group of the Fortress Artillery. On both sides of the Gap steel-doored anti-aircraft shelters had been dug into the cliff. D Company Headquarters occupied those on the west side while Brigade and Artillery Headquarters were on the east. One reinforcement, consisting of Lieutenant Blackwell and 20 Grenadiers, reported to D Company Headquarters at 7am. These men had originally been detached from Headquarters Company to guard the coast at Belcher's Bay. They were ordered to man a pillbox further up the Gap, but before they could set out the Gap came under heavy attack so they remained and fought from D Company Headquarters. This little group was to make a stand of epic quality. They were well-equipped with Bren and Thompson guns, had plenty of ammunition, and, as long as they held their positions, the vital Gap could not be passed. The Japanese account describes how their first troops "came upon a powerful group of sheltered positions . . . The enemy fire from these positions was so heavy that not only was the advance balked, but our troops were thrown into confusion."[13]

The morning was marked by a succession of attempts to relieve or reinforce the Gap. At 7am Brigadier Lawson requested a company of Royal Scots to attempt a breakthrough to the Gap. A heroic but futile effort was made by A Company, but the Scots came under Japanese fire which destroyed their trucks. Although they made a gallant effort to press on, less than a dozen reached the Gap, and the rest of A Company, now reduced to fifteen, was forced to fall back. Three naval platoons suffered the same fate. These men, from the disabled HMS *Thracian,* were on their way to Little Hong Kong to occupy the former Grenadier A Company positions but were instead ordered to clear the Gap from the south. They were ambushed before they could get out of their trucks, and lost most of their men without accomplishing anything. The remaining platoon from the Grenadiers' had earlier been despatched to establish a road block in the area of Tai Tam. Failing to reach their destination before the Japanese, they returned to Wong Nei Chong Gap to find it under attack. The platoon made several attempts to clear positions to the front and flank, but only succeeded in losing men. Around 1pm the survivors withdrew to Battalion Headquarters.

In the meantime the sands had run out for Brigadier Lawson. By 10am the Japanese had surrounded Brigade Headquarters and, unlike D Company Headquarters, the defenders did not have the firepower to keep the enemy at bay. After destroying essential records and the telephone switchboard, Lawson and his staff emerged from the shelter. Major Lyndon had earlier telephoned Fortress Headquarters that they were going to evacuate to the new Headquarters position at Black Links chosen the previous day, but Lawson had subsequently told Wallis that they were going outside to fight it out, presumably because Japanese proximity prevented a successful evacuation. Japanese fire commanded the Gap, and as Lawson's group entered the killing ground the Brigadier was hit and fatally wounded. The Japanese found his body several days later and buried it with honour.

D Company Headquarters continued to resist the enemy. Their

numbers were slowly augmented by stragglers and survivors, mostly from the Grenadiers but some from other units. These reinforcements balanced the losses in killed and wounded. No other reinforcements ever arrived. Captain Bowman of D Company led a counter-attack to clear the enemy from the front, where they were making gains. This attack achieved a temporary success, as Bowman's group got above the Japanese and forced them to retire. But it could not last, and Bowman was killed while withdrawing to the shelters, whereupon the Japanese re-occupied their positions.

Realizing that Lawson was, if not dead, at least not in a position to effectively command the Brigade, Maltby ordered a major counter-attack by West Brigade to halt the Japanese, clear the Gap, and link up the two brigades.

In the north the Punjabs, who had already made one unsuccessful counter-attack against the Suzukawa Engineering Unit at Caroline Hill just east of Leighton Hill and suffered 30 killed and wounded, were to attack east toward the North Point Power Station. This was still held by a party of Volunteers (including the group over military age) and other defenders with exceptional courage and determination against a number of Japanese attacks. The Punjabs do not seem to have received the order and the Power Station fell late that afternoon.

The Royal Scots were ordered to attack south to clear Jardine's Lookout and the Wong Nei Chong Gap. One company was to circle around Mount Nicholson and attack northward and the other two to head straight toward the Gap. These two companies came under fierce Japanese fire at the same point where A Company of the Royal Scots had been all but annihilated that morning. They suffered severe casualties and dispersed to wait for nightfall before continuing their advance.

The Winnipeg Grenadiers' contribution to this general advance was to be an attack by Headquarters Company, led by Major Hodkinson, who at 2pm was ordered to counter-attack at Wong Nei Chong Gap, clear the area, and proceed to Mount Parker! Between the support detachments which had been attached to other companies, Lieutenant Blackwell's 20 men now fighting with D Company, and the heavy losses in the flying column platoons, only 40 men could be found. A platoon of C Company was brought up from its position at Aberdeen and arrangements were made for A Company of the Royal Scots to participate. It is uncertain if either Hodkinson or Fortress Headquarters was aware of the hideous losses suffered by this unit that morning. As the Royal Scots failed to arrive on time, Hodkinson began the attack solely with his few Grenadiers. He detached a platoon under Lieutenant Corrigan to provide flank protection from Mount Nicholson. Corrigan's platoon fought its way to the top of Mount Nicholson, arriving with only five men unwounded, continued down the far slope above the Gap, and engaged the enemy until nearly midnight, by which time the ammunition was exhausted. Meanwhile, Hodkinson and the main force were continuing around Mount Nicholson on the Black Links Road when they came upon approximately 500 Japanese eating. The enemy's security must have been exceptionally poor as the Canadians achieved complete surprise and poured in accurate fire, dispersing the enemy with many casualties. This force was probably Shoji's 3rd Battalion. After this clash the Grenadiers pushed on until close to the junction of the main road where, at approximately 5pm, they were joined by the remnants of A Company of the Royal Scots, their fighting spirit still high despite the morning's ordeal. The party then split up, with Hodkinson and four men going across country to approach the Gap from the north and take over the old Brigade Headquarters, while Lieutenant Campbell cleared the Gap from southwest and west. On the way, Hodkinson's little group re-captured a Vickers machine-gun post. The assault was well co-ordinated, and the Gap was cleared by Campbell's men, aided by some good grenade throwing by Hodkinson. They made contact with the Grenadiers' D Company Headquarters, which at this time consisted of twenty wounded and seven unwounded men still holding out in the shelters. Hodkinson reported his successes to Battalion Headquarters which passed the information on to Fortress Headquarters. The latter then ordered Hodkinson's party to move south through the Gap, capture the police station which was built on a commanding knoll at the south entrance, and then proceed to Mount Parker "even without any artillery preparations".[14] It is difficult to judge which is the most incredible, the order given by a Headquarters that obviously did not have the slightest grip on reality, or the little group of men actually undertaking to carry it out. Hodkinson's force, now consisting of two officers and 24 other ranks, commenced an attack from the flank on the police station at 8pm. They charged up the hill to the station under heavy defensive fire and, when about ¾ of the way up the hill, about forty Japanese appeared on the skyline and lobbed a volley of grenades. Most of the attackers became casualties, including Hodkinson, who was seriously wounded. A small party under Sergeant Patterson was left to try to hold the position, but the attempt failed, and Patterson was killed. Thus ended possibly the most gallant and successful attack against the greatest odds of the entire battle.

The next force to approach the Gap was a small group of Indian artillerymen and two Volunteer armoured cars despatched from East Brigade. They approached the Gap from the south, reported the police station cleared (which seems strange, in view of the prior experiences of Hodkinson's men and the later experiences of the Royal Scots), and, coming under fire, dispersed.

Early the next morning, before dawn, the Royal Scots put in two attacks, each pushed home through fierce fire with great courage, great losses, and no success. The first assault was by the two companies to the north, straight through the Gap as far as the police station. The other was in conjunction with the company that had come around the south of Mount Nicholson. Two-thirds of the Royal Scots became casualties on 19 December and, at first light on the 20th, the remnants of two companies were in positions on the north-east slopes of Mount Nicholson and the other at the bottom of the southern slopes.

The day had not gone as badly for West Brigade as for East. West Brigade had not yielded as much ground, and two of its battalions, the Punjabs and Middlesex, had not faced the full force of the Japanese infantry. However, its Headquarters had been annihilated, the Royal Scots had been reduced to a fraction of its former self, and A, D, and Headquarters Companies of the Winnipeg Grenadiers had been almost wiped out.

The Island

—20 December

As this second day of the battle for the Island dawned, both sides had problems to solve. Colonels Shoji and Doi, with two battalions of each of their regiments milling around in the Mount Nicholson-Wong Nei Chong Gap area, had to get organized and secure these features before they could swing west, according to plan. Colonel Tanaka, now no longer directly confronted by the enemy, intended to drive his 229th Regiment through to the south coast at Repulse or Deep Water Bay, cutting the Island in two, before he moved west. Maltby, on his part, had to clear or dominate the Gap and, if possible, link up the two brigades.

A particularly tragic event for the Canadians on 20 December was the death of Colonel Pat Hennessy, the Senior Administrative Officer of C Force. The Japanese were still shelling the Island from the mainland and a heavy shell hit the house on Victoria Peak in which he was working, killing Captain Davies, the Field Cashier, and mortally wounding Hennessy. He was an able and popular officer and his death meant that the senior Canadians in Hong Kong were the two battalion commanders, each desperately busy and serving in separate brigades under British officers.

East Brigade

It was Brigadier Wallis' firm intention to push west at the earliest opportunity in order to link up with West Brigade. The most direct route, via Gauge Basin south of Mount Parker, was initially ruled out as the Volunteers in the area had been pushed back by Tanaka's

229th Regiment. Wallis therefore determined to move up the coast road to Repulse Bay and then advance north toward Wong Nei Chong Gap. He had urged Lieutenant Colonel Home to have the Rifles ready to move by 5am, but Home felt that it would be at least 8 before he could re-establish communications between his companies.* A Company, which had spent most of the previous day marching and counter-marching, was ordered to form the advance guard, and moved off. At almost exactly the same time as A Company of the Royal Rifles began to move, the first of Tanaka's men reached Repulse Bay. Having arrived at Wong Nei Chong Gap in the early morning and finding Doi's and Shoji's Regiments taking up position, Tanaka ordered his men to move south. By 8am the Island's defenders were effectively cut in two.

At the foot of the cliffs overlooking Repulse Bay stood the Repulse Bay Hotel, a palatial establishment with nearly two hundred civilian guests still in residence and a garrison of 50 Middlesex, Volunteers, and naval personnel. Some of Tanaka's men climbed down the cliffs and surrounded the hotel, occupying several outbuildings. The advancing A Company of the Royal Rifles was soon informed that the Japanese held the Hotel garage, and was ordered to brush this opposition aside and carry on. The company cleared the Japanese—who were in approximately platoon strength, but with machine-guns—from the garage by 11am. By this time there were two companies of the enemy on the hillside and more were on the way. A Company pushed on, under increasingly heavy fire, until it was forced to deploy into defensive positions in the area of Repulse Bay and Eucliffe Castle (a large mansion just before the junction of the coast road and the north/south road). Later that day a message reached the company that the Hotel was to be held at all costs for the sake of the women and children there.

Next to move forward was D Company. It was decided not to send this company by road—Wallis had recorded in the Brigade Diary that A Company's advance was "slow and over-cautious. Men were taking

---

*Little wireless was used during the battle by the defenders, who had to rely on either runners and despatch riders (who were handicapped by unfamiliarity with the ground and by its rugged nature), military field telephones, or the civilian telephone system. The Japanese did not make any attempt to dislocate this system, preferring to listen in. They must have been caused some annoyance by the Royal Rifles officers, most of whom were bilingual and who therefore deliberately spoke French on the telephone.

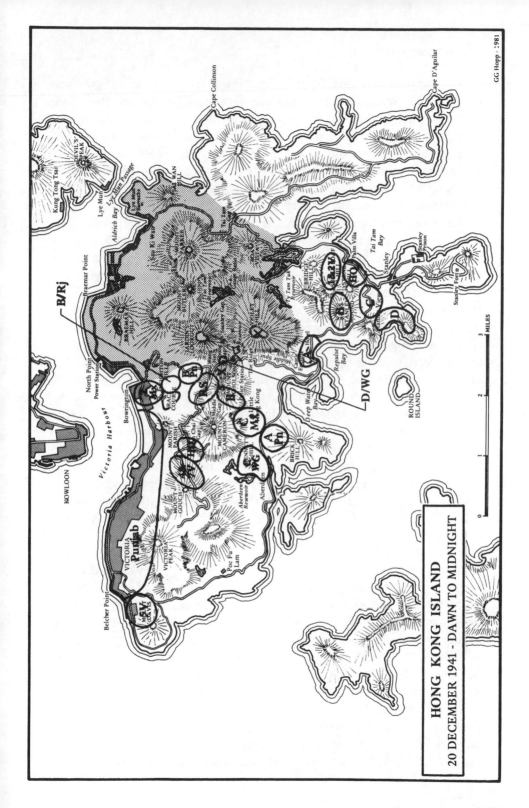

HONG KONG ISLAND
20 DECEMBER 1941 - DAWN TO MIDNIGHT

GG Hopp · :981

cover every time a distant shot or a burst from a machine-gun was heard . . ."[1] When Wallis went on a reconnaissance of the road, however, just before D Company was to move off, he found it was more than a matter of distant shots and bursts—he spent several long minutes in a roadside ditch with Lieutenant Colonel Home and Major Parker under enemy fire. He therefore decided to send D Company to Wong Nei Chong Gap via the east side of Violet Hill, the highest hill feature between the Stanley area and the Gap. It does not seem to have occurred to Wallis that if the enemy were at Repulse Bay, they must of a certainty have already occupied Violet Hill directly behind it. Nevertheless, D Company moved off at 11am through exceedingly rough country. They were totally unfamiliar with the terrain and had absolutely no idea what they might encounter, as "Brigadier Wallis' information about enemy strength and positions was negligible."[2] The company spent the day moving through the hills and along the concrete water catchments. One platoon surprised an artillery pack train and inflicted heavy casualties, and another climbed high enough to fire on the Japanese artillery positions in Gauge Basin, though at least one of these guns began to return the fire. Lieutenant Power, commanding the platoon, noted that the way forward beyond Violet Hill to the Gap was open country and an unobserved approach would be impossible. The company was coming under increasingly intense fire from Violet Hill, and, finding its position was untenable, withdrew. During the withdrawal the mortar section attached to the company was forced to destroy the mortar they had manhandled up the hill and jettison the ammunition. D Company arrived back at Stanley View at 11pm, exhausted.

B Company, like A Company the previous day, was to have a particularly frustrating experience. In the morning they were ordered to take up a defensive position behind A Company, half-way between Stanley View and Repulse Bay. The company quickly carried out the order, marching from Sugarloaf Mountain to Stanley Mound and taking up positions on and around the Mound. At 4pm B Company was ordered to advance along the road (despite the fact that it had been judged unsafe for D Company that morning), pass through A Company at Repulse Bay, and continue to the curve in the road west of Eucliffe. The company moved off but at 4:30 was informed that Brigade Headquarters had changed its plan and B Company was now to fall back on Sugarloaf Mountain. The company had retired as far as Stone Hill by 5:30 when it was ordered to turn around again and advance on Repulse Bay. Half an hour later *this* order was rescinded and B Company was directed to return to Sugarloaf Mountain. By the time the company reached Sugarloaf it was dark and raining. One platoon failed to report in that night.

Headquarters Company was also ordered that morning to move up the road to the Repulse Bay area. Between Stone Hill and the Bay they came under artillery fire, and at 10:30am the company was ordered to halt at the outskirts of Repulse Bay. The road there being swept by small-arms fire, the men were forced to get under cover. Headquarters Company stayed there from 10:30am to 5pm, receiving no orders and, despite continuing Japanese fire, no casualties. They were finally ordered back to Palm Villa.

C Company, aside from a temporary move to Palm Villa, spent a comparatively inactive day after their extensive fighting of 19 December. Major Bishop led a patrol in two Volunteer carriers and had a brief clash with the enemy at Tai Tam Reservoir.

The day's operations had left East Brigade back where it started, except for A Company of the Royal Rifles which was holding out at Repulse Bay. There can be no denying that the Rifles had been a little slow at times, though how much this can be attributed to their lack of training and fatigue and how much to command indecision is debatable. Once again, the artillery had let the brigade down badly. No fire support at all had been given the Royal Rifles, because the coast defence guns could not be brought to bear and the few mobile guns available "were only getting in position and sorting equipment and were unable to fire at this time."

West Brigade

By the early morning of 20 December the two West Brigade battalions that had borne the brunt of the fighting were in dire straits. The remaining Royal Scots were positioned on the lower slopes of Mount Nicholson and were just barely hanging on. D Company Headquarters of the Winnipeg Grenadiers was continuing to hold out in Wong Nei Chong Gap. The Grenadiers' B Company was still at Pok Fu Lam and C Company, less one platoon, was at Aberdeen. The other three companies had almost ceased to exist, except for a few small groups of men cut off in the hills, trying to make their way to safety. Z Company of the Middlesex, the surviving Rajput company (B), and B Company of the Punjabs held the line from Leighton Hill to just north of Jardine's Lookout, and were not under attack by the Japanese infantry, although they were under pressure from the Suzukawa Engineering Unit. The rest of the garrison's regular infantry was still approximately in their pre-invasion locations.

Although Brigadier Lawson had been killed in the morning of 19 December, a new Brigade Commander was not appointed until nearly noon the next day. He was Colonel H.B. Rose, the British regular officer who commanded the Volunteers. Rose's plan, or the one that was imposed on him by Maltby, was simply for the remaining Royal Scots and Winnipeg Grenadiers to attack east, clear the Gap, and push through to East Brigade. For some reason, the Royal Scots could not or would not make the attempt, so the sole attack in West Brigade to fall on the Japanese that day was made by B Company of the Grenadiers. At 10am B Company was brought east from Pok Fu Lam to receive their orders. They were to attack Wong Nei Chong Gap from the direction of Wan Chai Gap. The attack was late in getting under way, apparently because B Company was waiting, in vain, to hear the Royal Scots would participate. In actual fact the Royal Scots company on the eastern slopes of Mount Nicholson withdrew that evening. B Company, Grenadiers, finally moved off alone in the pitch blackness and the pouring rain. The company split into two parties which were to circle Mount Nicholson from opposite directions and meet just above the Gap on the far side of the mountain, where they were to spend the night before attacking at dawn.

In the meantime the Japanese were starting to sort things out. Colonel Doi and Colonel Shoji, who according to his own estimate had already lost 800 men in endeavouring to take the Gap, had intended to co-operate in taking Mount Nicholson. But Doi, habitually the most active and aggressive of the Japanese regimental commanders, reverted to his old tricks and, upon noticing the fog and rain, decided to stage an immediate attack. He used his 1st Battalion, with three companies up and one back. As the Royal Scots had withdrawn from the eastern slopes Doi encountered no opposition until the main body of B Company of the Grenadiers came round the mountain. When B Company reached the area where they intended to spend the night they collided with the three Japanese companies and a fierce fight ensued. Eventually the Grenadiers retired to Middle Gap on the west side of Mount Nicholson to wait out the night, having lost two officers, a sergeant, and 20 men in the encounter.

There was little other activity in West Brigade that day. One company of the Punjabs had been moved south to Aberdeen. Also at about this time the Middlesex machine-gunners not directly engaged were withdrawn from the coastal pillboxes. For the most part, however, they were not thrown into the battle, but were concentrated at Little Hong Kong and Pok Fu Lam in the locations the Grenadiers had formerly held before being committed to the fighting.

The Island

—21 December

21 December was to see the last offensive efforts designed to make headway against the Japanese and rejoin the two brigades. It also marked the last day in which the Royal Navy was able to take any offensive action whatsoever.

After her successful operation on 14/15 December, HMS *Thracian* had been damaged by grounding and then run ashore on Round Island off the south coast of Hong Kong. The motor torpedo boats, after a costly attack against the Japanese troop movements between the mainland and Island on 19 December that caused casualties on both sides, no longer attempted to intervene and were instead used to ferry ammunition and other vital supplies to Stanley. The river gunboat, HMS *Cicala*, which had bombarded the enemy on 20 and 21 December from Deep Water Bay, was bombed and sunk on the 21st. Surviving Royal Navy personnel were to serve as infantry, and all fought bravely until the capitulation.

East Brigade

The activities of the East Brigade on 21 December fell into two parts. The earliest and major effort was the attempt to break out to the West Brigade area. Instead of trying the Repulse Bay route again, the Royal Rifles and a Volunteer company were ordered to drive due north to Tai Tam Tuk, then turn west and head down a small road to Wong Nei Chong Gap via Gauge Basin. A disadvantage of this route was that enfilade fire could be directed against them not only by infantry, but also by the artillery sited above and to the north of them on Mount Butler and Jardine's Lookout. As well, the Japanese had brought their reserve troops across from the mainland. One of these units, the 1st Battalion, 229th Regiment, was in the hills above the road to Tai Tam, and was to be reinforced by another, the 1st Battalion, 230th Regiment, that same day. The only apparent merit of East Brigade's plan was that it had not yet been tried.

Within 15 minutes of starting out the leading company had met with very strong resistance from the surrounding hills. The Royal Rifles sent out small flank guards to clear Notting and Bridge Hills on one side and Red Hill on the other. Because of the pressure of fire, more and more men were sent off to the flanks, until eventually the whole advance guard was involved. The main guard, D Company of the Royal Rifles, also became caught up in the fighting. When Major MacAuley, commanding the advance guard, asked for reinforcements from the main guard to continue the attack, he was told that D Company was already engaged on his flanks!

By 1pm the firing from Bridge, Notting, and Red Hills had ceased and the attack was able to proceed. A machine-gun post at the crossroads north of Bridge Hill was shelled by the Rifles' 3-inch mortar, then rushed by the advance guard and wiped out. At 5pm the Japanese sent some light tanks (probably armoured cars) down the road. The vehicles caused some casualties, but were forced to retire by a steady stream of fire from all sides. However, at 6pm the advance to Gauge Basin was ordered to halt, and the troops were brought back to their original positions in the Stanley area.

Although, according to Wallis, he had earlier begun to "realize that the Battalion was incapable of real fight," he almost changed his mind that day. Reporting to Maltby he said that "he was very worried over the terrible slowness and lack of training of the Royal Rifles, but that they were really doing their best . . . and fighting gamely."[1] For his part Maltby recorded, incorrectly, that the attack had failed by 10:30am, but he added that the Royal Rifles had made "a great effort".[2]

The pattern of failed counter-attacks was a common one throughout the battle for Hong Kong. In terms of human achievement, however, the one to Gauge Basin was a success. It had cleared the Japanese off the road to Tai Tam, beaten off a light tank or armoured car attack, and driven the Japanese off the flanking hills. But with the troops engaged on the flanks, the small numbers of the Royal Rifles and Volunteers prevented any advance. In the end the offensive thrust had been watered down to such an extent that the advance halted, and the column was ordered back to the Stanley area. It is probably fortunate that they never got any further. If any men had survived running the Gauge Basin artillery and light arms gauntlet, they would still have had to crash through four battalions to get into the West Brigade area.

Meanwhile, at Repulse Bay, A Company of the Royal Rifles was holding out against Japanese fire from the hills above. Early that morning the company had received an order from Fortress Headquarters to advance down the road, clearing the houses as it went along. This command was soon cancelled, but at 1pm two platoons were ordered to move north to a position known as the Ridge where an Ordnance Depot was located, approximately 400 yards south of Wong Nei Chong Gap, clear the road at that area, and wait.

The civilian telephone system was still functioning and the Japanese had not cut the lines leading to the Repulse Bay Hotel. Some of the residents had been in direct contact with Maltby and managed to convince him that things were not going as they should in the area. Maltby immediately ordered a Major Templer of the Royal Artillery to proceed to the Hotel, take command of operations in the area, and make an assault on the Gap. Brigadier Wallis was far from happy with this division of responsibility and the diversion of part of his force. Nevertheless, Templer took two Royal Rifle platoons—one from Headquarters and one from C Company—two Volunteer machine-gun crews, and two trucks and arrived at the Hotel at 3pm. He immediately loaded A Company onto the trucks and they roared off, picking up some of the Ridge force *en route*. They advanced quickly toward the Gap in the gathering darkness, intending to attack the police station. Then, realizing the strength of the Japanese and learning that some of the Brens were jamming, Templer decided not to press the attack and withdrew to the far side of the Ridge.

One possible benefit of this futile exercise was that Templer, who appears to have had Maltby's ear, presumably was able to convince him that the Gap really *was* occupied by large numbers of Japanese and that it would take more than platoon and company attacks to evict them.

Two of A Company's platoons were not destined to spend the night behind the Ridge. They were ordered to occupy a concrete water catchment in the hills in order to prevent the Japanese from using it as a supply route. These platoons started out at 7:30pm,

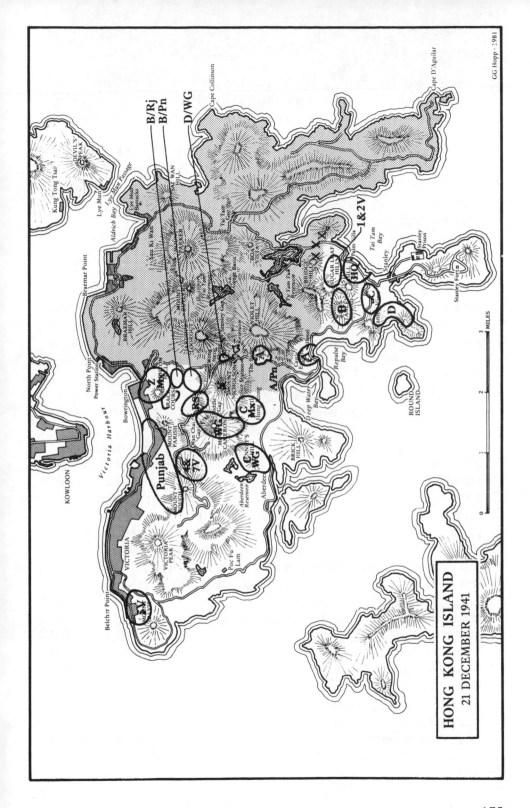

HONG KONG ISLAND
21 DECEMBER 1941

moving into the area occupied by Tanaka's two battalions. Soon after midnight they were ambushed and suffered severe casualties. One platoon made it back to the Hotel, the other took cover in Overbays House, 300 yards south of the Ridge.

The Royal Rifles were forced to stand-to for a period that night due to a false alarm about a possible landing. Apart from that and a few snipers, the battalion front was quiet. The unit diary recorded: "All ranks of the Battalion very tired—no sleep, little food, constant hill-climbing."

West Brigade

If there was one group of men on the Island during the night of 20/21 December who knew what the morrow would bring, it was the men of B Company of the Winnipeg Grenadiers. The Japanese had occupied Mount Nicholson, and at dawn B Company was going to try to take it away from them. The attack went in at 6:45 from both sides of the mountain and over the crest. All the attacking troops were heavily and immediately engaged by the enemy, and, eventually, the overwhelming odds told and the Canadians were forced to withdraw. Of the 98 men that had gone into action, all the officers, the Company Sergeant Major, seven NCO's, and 29 men were casualties. Yet in that grim battle the Grenadiers had made Colonel Doi's 1st Battalion fight for its life. Doi wrote, "At dawn on the 21st, the enemy counter-attacked with about 400 men, but they were repulsed after fierce fighting. In that engagement the unit defending the summit exhausted all its hand grenades and fought by throwing stones. This fighting cost one of the companies about 40% in casualties, including the company commander and platoon leaders."[3]

There was no hope whatsoever now of wresting Mount Nicholson from the Japanese. Therefore, as B Company pulled back, Lieutenant Colonel Sutcliffe informed the Grenadiers' Second-in-Command, Major G. Trist, that the attack had failed and ordered him to form a new line on Mount Cameron, the next hill to the west. Trist mustered 100 all ranks—almost the entire battalion strength available and fit for duty except for most of C Company, still at Aberdeen—and moved to Mount Cameron under continual artillery fire. The new position was very open and no shovels or other entrenching tools were available, though in any case these would have been of little use in the rocky terrain. The line ran along the ridge immediately behind the crest. Throughout the day the Grenadiers were hit by very accurate artillery and mortar fire.

Meanwhile, D Company Headquarters continued to deny Wong Nei Chong Gap to the enemy. Captain Bush, the Staff Captain, recorded that:

> the position was being fired upon from all sides. It might be compared with the lower part of a bowl, the enemy looking down and occupying the rim. The main road running through the position was cluttered for hundreds of feet each way with abandoned trucks and cars. The Japanese were using mortars and hand grenades quite heavily. Casualties were steadily mounting, but at the same time reinforcements were trickling in, in the form of stragglers . . .[4]

Bush and Captain Billings, the C Force Signals Officer, both wounded, had escaped from the Gap on the night of 20 December.

On this day as well, A Company of the Punjabs at Aberdeen was ordered to break through to Repulse Bay. Due to detachments manning pillboxes in the Victoria area, the company had been only 45 strong when it went into action on Caroline Hill on 19 December. By now it was down to 25 all ranks. They moved east, led by the Punjabs' Commanding Officer, Lieutenant Colonel Kidd, and accompanied by a small number of naval personnel. The bulk of Tanaka's two original battalions were still in the Repulse Bay area, but some advanced elements appear to have been on Shouson Hill at the foot of Deep Water Bay. The Punjabs put in a courageous attack against superior numbers and accomplished nothing except the loss of the majority of their force, including Lieutenant Colonel Kidd.

As the day ended, West Brigade was hoping to hold the new line centered on Mount Cameron, despite the day's losses. Shoji's 3rd Battalion was closing in on the shelters in the Gap, and the 2nd must have participated in the morning's battle on Mount Nicholson as it reported the battalion commander wounded and the Adjutant killed in that location. Meanwhile, the 228th Regiment under the energetic Colonel Doi was preparing to follow up its success on Mount Nicholson and assault Mount Cameron.

The Island

—22 December

This was the first day of the battle for the Island that the defenders were unable to exercise any initiative, but were confined to holding their lines or attempting to counter breakthroughs on the part of the enemy. Their task was made the harder by the fact that late the previous day the Japanese had been able to bring their divisional artillery from the mainland and it was now firing in direct support of their operations.

The morale of the defenders may or may not have been uplifted by the following message from Winston Churchill which was being circulated at the time:

> Prime Minister to Governor, Hong Kong   21 Dec 41
>
> We were greatly concerned to hear of the landings on Hong Kong Island which have been effected by the Japanese. We cannot judge from here the conditions which rendered these landings possible or prevented effective counter-attacks upon the intruders. There must however be no thought of surrender. Every part of the island must be fought and the enemy resisted with the utmost stubbornness.
>
> The enemy should be compelled to expend the utmost life and equipment. There must be vigorous fighting in the inner defences, and, if need be, from house to house. Every day that you are able to maintain your resistance you help the Allied cause all over the world, and by a prolonged resistance you and your men can win the lasting honour which we are sure will be your due.[1]

Soul-stirring it may have been, but it did not offer even false hope for Hong Kong.

Not to be outdone, Mackenzie King, too, had sent a message to the Canadian soldiers.

All Canada has been following hour by hour the progress of events at Hong Kong. Our thoughts are of each and every one of you in your brave resistance of the forces that are seeking to destroy the world's freedom. Your bravery is an inspiration to us all. Our Country's name and its honour have never been more splendidly upheld.

More to the point, Ralston, in one of *his* inspirational messages, had asked Lawson to give him as much information as could be passed on. By the time this was received, Lawson and Hennessy were dead and Home, the senior battalion commander, had been cut off. Lieutenant Colonel Sutcliffe answered on 22 December, telling Ralston of the casualties among the senior officers and informing him that the situation was critical, the Canadians were engaged, and casualties were heavy, but "Troops have done magnificent work, spirit excellent."[2]

East Brigade

Whether Brigadier Wallis had any offensive moves in mind for 22 December is not known, however it is certain that the Japanese gave him no opportunity to use them. Tanaka's original two battalions of the 229th were still in the Repulse Bay area, but they were occupied with the siege of the Hotel, had to hold the end of the north-south road, and had been badly mauled in the previous three days' fighting with the Royal Rifles. Two of the three Japanese reserve battalions had been brought across from the mainland the previous day, Tanaka's 1st and Shoji's 1st. These were now deployed in front of East Brigade's main force. There were thus four battalions in the area to face the exhausted remnants of the Royal Rifles and the rest of Wallis' force.

The Japanese attack on East Brigade commenced at noon, when intense and accurate mortar fire started to come down on the Stanley Mound and Sugarloaf positions. B Company of the Rifles now held Stanley Mound, having been directed there after the previous day's abortive advance. When the artillery and mortar bombardment was augmented by machine-gun and rifle fire one platoon from Headquarters Company and two from D Company were brought up to help repel the threatened attack. The enemy fire ceased at 6pm and the two D Company platoons withdrew to Stone Hill. At 9pm the machine-guns and mortars suddenly opened up again and Japanese infantry attacked with grenades and bayonets. They were repulsed several times but when ammunition ran low and all but one of the Brens was out of action, B Company withdrew to the south slope of Stanley Mound.

The noon bombardment was also the preface to an almost immediate assault on Sugarloaf Mountain and Notting Hill. They were no longer held by Canadians, and the Japanese quickly routed the defenders, capturing, in the process, two of the Middlesex machine-guns. The crew of another machine-gun at Palm Villa was wiped out.

C Company of the Royal Rifles was now to show that the courage and efficiency it had shown on 18/19 December was no accident. Captain W.A.B. Royal ran forward under fire, took over the Palm Villa gun, and began to hammer away at the enemy. The two guns on Sugarloaf were recaptured by Sergeants Goodenough and Roberts and Corporal Sannes. Sannes was killed at his new position, but Goodenough, twice wounded, kept one gun in action and drove the enemy to cover, while Roberts went through a mortar barrage to rescue the wounded Major Bishop. Bishop then called for volunteers to take back the Sugarloaf. Three parties were formed, and, with Goodenough's gun forcing the enemy under cover, Sugarloaf was in Canadian hands by nightfall. The already understrength company suffered eleven more casualties that day.

At Repulse Bay, conditions in the Hotel were deteriorating. At 4am Major Young brought forward the remaining platoons of his company to the Ridge, which they occupied at dawn under intermittant fire. At 3pm this party withstood a forceful attack by Japanese infantry, supported by mortars and machine-guns. After three hours of savage fighting the attack was repulsed.

At 2:30 pm the platoon in Overbays House had been ordered by Fortress Headquarters to return to the Hotel. As the position was under fire, Lieutenant Johnston decided to wait until dark. The platoon moved out at 8pm, but still had to fight their way through the Japanese and lost eight of their number killed.

On the Ridge that evening, the British personnel in the Ordnance depot had attempted to surrender but, the Japanese not proving co-operative, had evacuated the area. Major Young, though realizing that his position was untenable and that trying to hold it would serve no useful purpose, determined to stand his ground until nightfall when a withdrawal would be more practical. A Company was moving back to Eucliffe and the Hotel by 11pm.

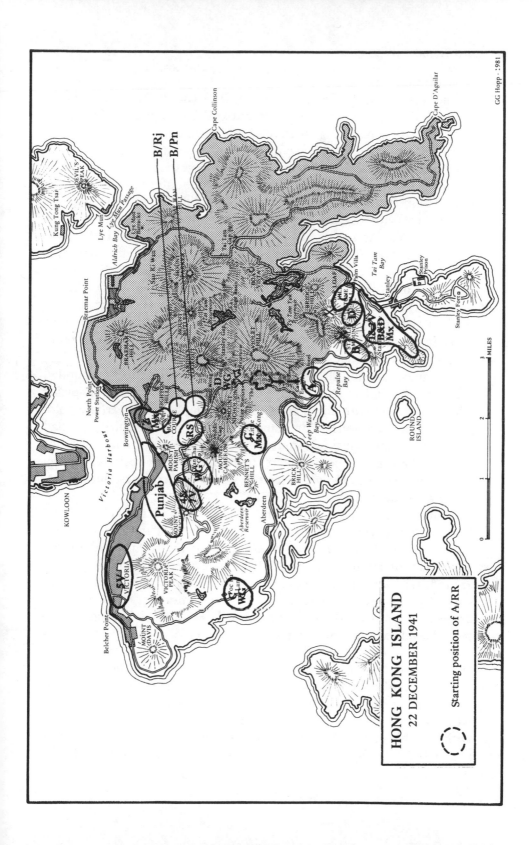

B/Rj

B/Pn

Cape Collinson

Cape D'Aguilar

GG Hopp · 1981

KOWLOON

Kung Tong Tsai

DEVIL'S PEAK

Lye Mun

Aldrich Bay

Lye Mun Passage

Braemar Point

North Point Power Station

Victoria Harbour

Bowrington

Belcher Point

MOUNT DAVIS

VICTORIA

Victoria Peak

Stanley Prison

Stanley

Palm Villa

Tai Tam Bay

Stanley Forts

Repulse Bay

Deep Water Bay

BRICK HILL

ROUND ISLAND

Aberdeen Reservoir

Aberdeen

BENNET'S HILL

Punjab

RS

Tai Ko Shing

MOUNT PARISH

MOUNT CAMERON

Little Mount

D WG

B&D Mx

ST. STEPHEN

WG

WG

MILES

0   1   2   3

HONG KONG ISLAND
22 DECEMBER 1941

Starting position of A/RR

West Brigade

The early morning of 22 December finally saw the end of resistance in Wong Nei Chong Gap. The remnants of D Company had held out for three days, inflicting massive losses on the enemy and denying them the vital area. But D Company had also suffered severe losses. The defenders had been commanded in succession by Captain A.S. Bowman (killed on 19 December during a counter-attack), Captain R.W. Philip (who must have been an incredibly tough individual—he had an eye shot out early in the battle, put it in his pocket, and carried on leading the defence until wounded again), and Lieutenant T.A. Blackwood. Blackwood had been wounded twice, the force was almost out of ammunition, there were 37 wounded men in the shelter, and no more than 12 unwounded. When the Japanese were able to blow in the door of the shelter with a light gun at 5am it became obvious the end was near. Most or all the unwounded men were sent away in two parties to try to creep through the lines. Most of them actually succeeded in escaping; a few were killed.

At 7am all ammunition was finally exhausted and the 37 wounded men were surrendered by Captain U. Laite, one of C Force's chaplains who had stayed with the men. Colonel Shoji, who had earlier apologized to his Divisional Commander for the 800 casualties he had suffered in the fighting around the Gap, termed their resistance "heroic"—no mean compliment from a Japanese officer.[3] Shoji claimed his soldiers looked after the wounded prisoners, but in fact, those who could not walk were killed.

Mount Cameron, which dominated the Wan Chai Gap area, had become the lynchpin of the West Brigade front. The only reinforcement that could be spared for Major Trist and his 100 Grenadiers was a platoon of approximately 30 Royal Engineers. When these men arrived, Trist was instructed to re-organize his force on a two-company basis. Except for the continual artillery and mortar fire the day was uneventful until 8:30pm, when Colonel Doi attacked, using a complete battalion plus one company of another. The enemy attack was concentrated on the Royal Engineer position on the right flank, and after a hard fight the Japanese broke through. They then attacked the main position from the right and rear. Faced with this rapidly deteriorating situation Trist contacted Lieutenant Colonel Sutcliffe, who in turn contacted Acting Brigadier Rose. Trist was ordered to withdraw his men to Wan Chai Gap. The withdrawal was carried out successfully, though under heavy pressure from the enemy and with several casualties. There was some controversy afterward, as Rose was to claim that he had not authorized the withdrawal. Be that as it may, there can be no doubt that the Grenadiers and Engineers did not yield the ground easily. Colonel Doi, who was in a position to know, reported fierce fighting; one of his companies lost all its officers and warrant officers. While Doi's men were on Mounts Nicholson and Cameron they had been continually shelled by one of the big 9.2-inch coastal guns at Stanley. With the proper ammunition this might have exacted a heavy toll, but, according to Doi, the fragments from the armour-piercing shells were so large that only a few men were wounded.

One company of the Grenadiers, C Company under Major Bailie, though now at less than half strength because of detachments, was still in its pre-invasion position covering the emergency naval base at Aberdeen on Bennet's Hill and near the Aberdeen Reservoir. Bailie had a clear view of Mount Cameron, and seeing the signs of battle he contacted Brigade Headquarters. He pointed out that if Mount Cameron were lost his position would be dangerously exposed. Brigade considered that there was no time to reach the Mount Gough position that was to be the main point on the new defensive line, and ordered Bailie back to Aberdeen Village, refusing him written orders when he demanded them. Bailie then took his men plus the remainder of the Aberdeen garrison around to the west in an attempt to reach the Mount Gough position by a circuitous route. They arrived at Pok Fu Lam in the west at first light on 23 December.

Although there was still hard fighting ahead, 22 December had marked the beginning of the end for the defenders. In the east the Japanese had brought up two fresh battalions and had obviously started their drive to push the bulk of East Brigade into the sea. The Repulse Bay position would soon be overrun, freeing Tanaka's two battalions to advance west. The clearing of Wong Nei Chong Gap and the capture of Mount Cameron meant that Colonels Shoji and Doi could now advance northwest against Victoria.

The Island

—23 December

East Brigade

At 1am orders came through for A Company of the Royal Rifles to retire to the main East Brigade area at Stanley. Suggestions were also advanced for the evacuation of the civilians, but these were not implemented, in some cases due to the reluctance of the civilians to take the risk. Two platoons of A Company split into small groups and set out to infiltrate through the enemy lines while Major Young took the remainder of the company, about 100 all ranks, and moved along the coast road as far as Eucliffe Castle, intending to break through to the north. At about 5am Young's party ran into heavy enemy opposition and split into a number of groups which were to try to get through to Stanley independently. Of the men of A Company, a large number succeeded in reaching Stanley, some were captured and killed by the Japanese, and Major Young and 34 other ranks located a boat and made their way to the grounded and abandoned HMS *Thracian* on Round Island. They were forced to remain there for two days before making their way ashore. By that time the Island was in Japanese hands, and as plans to escape to the mainland did not work out, the group eventually surrendered. The civilians and wounded left at the Hotel fell into Japanese hands, but on this occasion the Japanese were guilty of no atrocities.

Although some accounts (mainly from the civilian residents of the Hotel who were not inclined to minimize their personal hardships and who held the standard civilian attitude of 'why doesn't the Army *do* something') do not portray the work of A Company of the Royal

Rifles in a flattering light, a dispassionate look at the facts indicates that the 3½-day siege of Repulse Bay had a significant effect on the Japanese operations. Tanaka's 2nd and 3rd Battalions had been forced to remain in the area for days instead of driving west according to plan. Furthermore, the commanding officer of the 3rd Battalion later reported that he had suffered heavy casualties in the vicinity of Repulse Bay and that his battalion had taken no prisoners. Indeed, the 3rd Battalion had been so badly hurt in the fighting that it stayed at Repulse Bay until the capitulation, taking no further part in the battle for the Island. Most of these casualties had been inflicted by A Company of the Rifles, which did the bulk of the fighting at Repulse Bay.

In the main East Brigade area a high priority was given to recapturing Stanley Mound. The task was given to B Company of the Royal Rifles, the Mound's former occupants. An artillery barrage was laid on and, for once, actually took place. As the attackers went in, covering machine-gun fire was directed on the hill. Unfortunately, this set the grass on the slope on fire, hindering B Company. Almost immediately the company came under a fusillade of bullets from Japanese who had penetrated through sectors not held by the Royal Rifles. This broke up the attack, and Stanley Mound remained in enemy hands.

With the failure of the counter-attack on the Mound and the presence of Japanese to the rear of the Stone Hill/Sugarloaf/Palm Villa area, the Royal Rifles' position had become extremely precarious, especially as the battalion itself was not in good shape. Although men from A Company had started to trickle into the battalion area at 6am, the strength of the Royal Rifles by this time was only 350 men. Casualties among the officers had reached 18 killed, wounded, or missing. All ranks were in a state of exhaustion. By mid-morning it was obvious that the deteriorating situation made it impossible to hold the position with the troops available. Lieutenant Colonel Home had a brief conference with Brigadier Wallis, and it was decided to establish a new line just north of the neck of Stanley Peninsula between Stanley View and Stanley Village. Two secondary lines were to be established further down the peninsula to provide defence in depth. Although this move meant yielding the high ground, Home considered that the narrower front and level terrain offered a better chance for resisting the Japanese than a series of semi-isolated hill positions, against any of which the enemy could concentrate. The

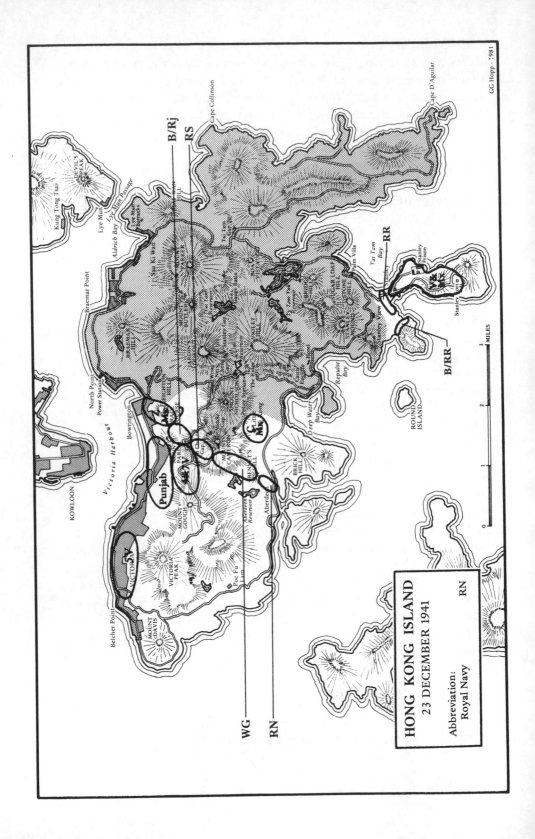

GG Hopp · 1981

HONG KONG ISLAND

23 DECEMBER 1941

Abbreviation:
Royal Navy   RN

Rifles started thinning out their lines at 5pm, and the move was complete by 8pm. C Company covered the withdrawal, keeping up a fierce exchange of fire with the Japanese most of the day. While the bulk of the battalion was to man the main line, B Company was detailed to occupy the small Chung Hum Kok peninsula immediately to the west of Stanley peninsula. Two of the platoons missed the way in the darkness and ended up at Stanley with the remainder of the battalion.

West Brigade

Following the loss of Mount Cameron by the Grenadiers and Royal Engineers the previous night, the Royal Scots took up positions on the mountain's north and west slopes while the Grenadiers re-organized and moved south into new positions north of Aberdeen Reservoir. In the meantime the Grenadiers' C Company had reached Pok Fu Lam. Once there, Major Bailie tried to contact Brigade Headquarters, and failing this spoke directly to General Maltby at Fortress Headquarters. Maltby was annoyed at Bailie's action and ordered him to take C Company back to its original positions, but when Bailie subsequently was able to contact Brigade Headquarters he was told that his move was justified. The company remained at Pok Fu Lam until 3:30, when it moved into line with the rest of the battalion. West Brigade had assumed what was to be its final formation. From south to north the formation was: Royal Navy personnel in line from Aberdeen to the south slopes of Bennet's Hill, the Grenadiers holding Bennet's Hill and on to the southwest slopes of Mount Cameron, the west slopes of Mount Cameron occupied by the Royal Scots, B Company of the Rajputs and a few Punjabs were between Mount Cameron and Leighton Hill, and Z Company of the Middlesex was still holding Leighton Hill. In front of the southern sector of this line an isolated company of the Middlesex was emplaced at Little Hong Kong, protecting the Ordnance Depot there. Two Volunteer and two Punjab companies and some Engineers were also in West Brigade area, but were not put in the front line.

There was bombing and shelling all along the line that day. Several attacks took place between Mount Cameron and Leighton Hill, forcing the Rajputs to withdraw. Z Company of the Middlesex pulled back slightly, but the Leighton Hill position still held and an attack later in the day was repelled.

That night a truck convoy raced through the lines to the Ordnance Depot at Little Hong Kong, loaded up with desperately-needed ammunition, and returned safely. It was obvious that there was little more that could be done before the last stand.

The Island

—24 December

East Brigade

Christmas Eve dawned a fine, bright day. Tanaka's 2nd Battalion had begun moving west, out of the East Brigade area, while the 3rd Battalion was still at Repulse Bay licking its wounds. The two battalions brought over from the mainland, Tanaka's 1st and the 1st Battalion of Shoji's 230th Regiment, were maintaining a heavy pressure on the narrow Stanley front.

The front line had been subjected to continual artillery fire during the night to which only a few pillboxes were able to make a brief, probably futile reply with their machine-guns. At 10am Lieutenant Colonel Home and his Second-in-Command, Major Price, went back to Brigade Headquarters in the Officer's Mess of Stanley Prison, where a heated conference took place with Brigadier Wallis. Home was desperately concerned about the condition of his men: "No R.R.C. personnel had had any rest night or day for five days."[1] Men were not simply falling asleep, they were collapsing with fatigue and exhaustion. The Royal Rifles had done far more marching and fighting than any other component of the brigade, and officers and men were bitterly resentful of other units which they believed were not doing their fair share in the battle. This animosity was also shared by at least one of the Volunteer companies that had participated in several of the Rifles' actions. Resentment was particularly directed toward the Middlesex, two companies of which were now in the peninsula, but most of whom had never been placed in the front line, although they were no longer fighting from pillboxes. The Canadians were later to point out that when East Brigade surrendered, at least 2000 military prisoners of war were marched out by the Japanese. Some of this large number of soldiers could surely have been used during the battle to reinforce the Royal Rifles, who had held the line almost alone. The diary of the Royal Rifles records that Home "insisted that the battalion be relieved otherwise he would not be responsible for what would happen."[2] Maltby was brought into the discussion by telephone, and the end result was an agreement that relief would be sent in that evening for the Rifles, who could then move into Stanley Fort further down the peninsula to rest and re-organize. Orders were issued that afternoon, and by 11pm the Rifles' positions were occupied by men of the Middlesex and Volunteers and the Rifles were in Stanley Fort, where all ranks promptly collapsed.

The exception was B Company which, except for two platoons, was on the adjacent Chung Hum Kok Peninsula. The company had already seen action in its new position, driving off a Japanese patrol. In the early morning the two platoons that had inadvertantly ended up in Stanley tried to reach their company, but were overtaken by daylight before they could cross the main stretch of open ground, now commanded by the enemy, so the attempt was abandoned. That night a Volunteer force was detailed to relieve B Company so it could rejoin the rest of the battalion at Stanley. Unfortunately, the Volunteers were ambushed, so B Company was forced to remain in its isolated position.

West Brigade

Along many sectors of the West Brigade forward line Christmas Eve was uneventful, if this term can possibly be employed to describe a continuous bombardment from Japanese aircraft, mortars, and artillery. The men of the Middlesex Z Company on Leighton Hill were attacked that afternoon by about 200 of the enemy following an unusually heavy bombardment. The Japanese, infiltrating through the buildings, moved in on Leighton Hill from three sides and the defenders were ordered to retreat before they were surrounded. During the withdrawal the company suffered more than 25% casualties. Z Company had held Leighton Hill with their machine-guns for more than five days, resisting both the pressure of the Suzukawa Engineering Unit and the exhausting ordeal of continuous bombardment and shelling from the mainland and the Island. The final assault

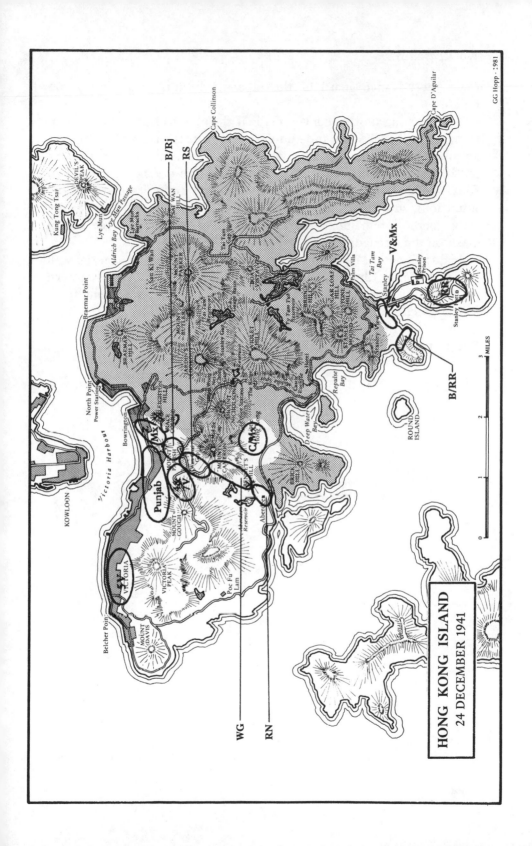

GG Hopp - '981

B/Rj

RS

B/RR

V&Mx

WG

RN

Punjab

M. ...

C/M...

VICTORIA

KOWLOON

Victoria Harbour

Belcher Point

Bracmar Point

North Point Power Station

Bowrington

Kung Tong Tsai

DEVIL'S PEAK

Lye Mun

Aldrich Bay

Lye Mun Passage

MOUNT DAVIS

VICTORIA PEAK

Poc Fu Lam

MOUNT GOUGH

Reservoir

Aberdeen

Hong Kong

WAN HILL

Cape Collinson

Palm Villa

Tai Tam Bay

Stanley

Stanley Prison

Stanley ...

Repulse Bay

Deep Water Bay

ROUND ISLAND

Cape D'Aguilar

HONG KONG ISLAND
24 DECEMBER 1941

0   1   2   3
MILES

from the advance guard of the Japanese infantry was simply too much.

That evening another convoy made it through to Little Hong Kong, bringing in Royal Scots and Middlesex reinforcements and taking out ammunition. There was also considerable patrol activity, particularly in the Grenadier and Royal Scots sectors. The defenders needed to find out as much as possible about enemy activities and possible intentions, and with the loss of the high ground, patrolling was the only method remaining. There was one particularly fierce patrol clash on the Grenadier front at 9:30pm.

Major General Maltby must have seen the handwriting on the wall when at 10pm, Christmas Eve, he received reports from the southern sector of his line that there was "a general move of the enemy from Mount Nicholson/Mount Cameron area northwards towards the Race Course."[3] This was the Japanese main infantry force. Doi's and Shoji's regiments were moving in for the kill.

The Island

—25 December

West Brigade*

Although the primary threat was expected to come from the main Japanese infantry force, it was the 2nd Battalion of Colonel Tanaka's 229th Regiment that was involved in the first serious fighting of Christmas Day. This unit, moving west, had fanned out and occupied Brick Hill *en route*. Then, bypassing Little Hong Kong, it moved northwest to link up with the main force south of Mount Cameron. Elements of all three Japanese regiments were now in line for the final assault.

The advance had brought Tanaka's men up to the Bennet's Hill position, and at about midnight on 24/25 December an assault was made by approximately two companies. The major position held firm, driving the Japanese back with heavy losses, but the lone Grenadier platoon on the feature known as Little Bennet's Hill was pushed back by superior numbers. Major Bailie immediately began to organize a counter-attack.

The approach of the Japanese infantry filled Maltby with apprehension, as the only troops not in the line were two companies of Punjabs in positions covering Government House, Fortress Headquarters, the Royal Navy Yard, and the Military Hospital—what Maltby referred to as "our last stand".[1] All other troops—artillerymen, Service Corps, Ordnance, Signals, and Engineers, all those not

*West Brigade is covered first in this chapter as the fighting ceased earlier in that area.

involved in absolutely essential duties—were fighting as infantrymen. What seemed to make the most impression on Fortress Headquarters and on the defenders in the northern sector and Victoria were the enemy's artillery and mortars. Hitherto they had experienced little more than shelling from the heavy Army artillery firing from the mainland. Now, however, the full weight of fire of the augmented 38th Division Artillery and of the efficient and deadly Japanese mortars, which had previously been used in support of the operations to the south of the Island, was brought to bear. The bombardment had a significant effect on both the defences and the morale of the defenders.

The Japanese had intended to make a general advance on 25 December. They had six battalions in line—one of Tanaka's, two of Shoji's, and three of Doi's, whose third battalion had been brought over from the mainland the previous day. According to Doi, the general advance had been postponed and rescheduled for 26 December. There is nothing in Japanese accounts to indicate that they intended to make a final, decisive attack on 25 December, but they did maintain a steady pressure on the exhausted defenders. By the early hours of the day, the two sides were in contact all along the northern half of the line. The intensity of the fighting was increasing when, at 9am, two civilians who had been residents in the Repulse Bay Hotel came through the Japanese lines under a white flag. They brought a Japanese demand for surrender and the promise of a three-hour truce while the matter was being considered.

The truce took effect almost immediately. One of its results was to halt in its tracks the assault that had been organized by Major Bailie to recapture Little Bennet's Hill, and this assault, which Maltby described as a "promising counter-attack"[2] was never re-initiated. Although some Japanese aerial and military bombardment continued during the truce, a great deal of relief was nevertheless provided for the defenders. Several used the opportunity to destroy secret papers and cyphers. Among these was Captain Bush, the C Force Staff Captain, who ran into some difficulty. The key to the safe holding the Canadian cyphers, which had been kept by Colonel Hennessy, could not now be found. Eventually the safe had to be dumped, unopened, into the harbour.

The two civilians bearing the Japanese message told Maltby and the Governor of the overwhelming Japanese strength they had observed during their trek across the Island. Nevertheless, the Japan-

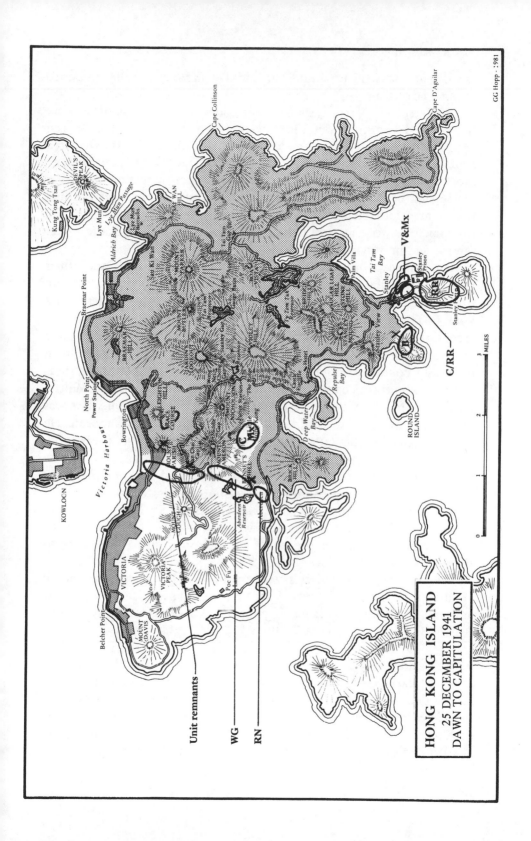

HONG KONG ISLAND
25 DECEMBER 1941
DAWN TO CAPITULATION

Unit remnants

WG

RN

V&Mx

C/RR

GG Hopp · 1981

ese demand was rejected and "at mid-day Japanese artillery opened up on a large scale".[3]

The rejection of the Japanese surrender demand was little more than a final gesture of defiance. Resistance in the west was on its last legs. Not only were the defenders stretched thin and in an exhausted state, but there were only six guns left to the mobile artillery with no more than 160 rounds per gun and no prospect of getting more. Far worse, for both the garrison and the civil inhabitants, was the fact that most of the Island's water reservoirs were in enemy hands and the pipelines to the others had been damaged, so an acute water famine was imminent.

In the three hours after mid-day as the Japanese continued their pressure, the defences began to crumble. Parish Hill was taken and Fortress Headquarters was placed in jeopardy, the Japanese took Wan Chai Gap, the hillsides at Magazine Gap were set on fire by incendiaries and the Gap brought under attack, the defenders near the north shore were pushed back to a second defence line which obviously could not hold long, communications between the various defence sectors became almost impossible, and at 3pm Maltby received a report that Bennet's Hill had surrendered. This last was completely untrue, but could not have improved Maltby's morale. He was led to what he later described as the "inevitable conclusion, namely, that further fighting meant the useless slaughter of the remainder of the garrison, risked severe retaliation on the large civilian population and could not affect the final outcome."[4]

As a result, Maltby informed the Governor at 3:15pm that no further useful military resistance was possible. He then ordered all commanding officers to break off the fighting and to capitulate to the nearest Japanese officer.

The Winnipeg Grenadiers saw the white flag go up, but spasmodic artillery fire continued until 5pm. The Grenadiers destroyed their ammunition dumps with hand grenades and then moved to Mount Austin Barracks, arriving at 7:30pm.

East Brigade

In the early morning, soon after the Royal Rifles had moved out of the line to rest at Stanley Fort, a Japanese attack developed. The Middlesex and Volunteer defenders were pushed out of the positions in Stanley Village that the Rifles had held the previous evening. At 2:30am Brigadier Wallis contacted Lieutenant Colonel Home and ordered him to send one of his companies to establish a line on the high ground north of the fort. C Company was chosen—its men had just enjoyed their first four hours of rest for many days—and was established in its new position by 4am. The rest of the battalion re-organized that morning, and a new A Company and a new Headquarters Company (to operate as a rifle company) were formed.

The situation at Stanley was continuing to deteriorate, and at 10am Wallis ordered Home to mount a company attack to retake the bungalows on the Ridge in Stanley Village. The Brigadier promised Home that artillery support would be provided for the assault, "but as similar promises had been made on previous occasions by him but had not been kept, Lieutenant Colonel Home protested against such [an] attack in daylight as most likely being unproductive of any results but additional Canadian casualties."[5] Wallis insisted that the attack must be made, and D Company under Major Parker was assigned the task.

The company had to move out of its positions and charge down a narrow open peninsula toward the high ground, where the Japanese were strongly established with abundant light artillery, mortars, and machine-guns. D Company began the assault at 1pm, "unsupported by any artillery or additional fire support".[6] They pressed the attack home through withering small-arms fire and a deluge of shells and mortar bombs. D Company's 18 Platoon, commanded by Company Sergeant Major Mcdonnell, penetrated as far as Stanley Village and inflicted heavy losses on the Japanese in the course of stubborn hand-to-hand fighting. The company was eventually forced to fall back to Stanley Fort. During the course of this action, reminiscent of nothing so much as one of the more mindless attacks on the Western Front during the First World War, D Company suffered 104 casualties out of a total strength of 148—almost exactly 70%.

Two reasons were given for the failure of the artillery to support this attack. In the case of the big coastal guns at Stanley, the 6-inch guns could not fire to the right of Stanley Mound and the 9.2-inch guns could not fire further left than Red Hill, and therefore none could hit the Japanese on or near the Rifles' objective. Yet if Wallis had been counting on these weapons to support the assault, surely it would have been simple for him to ascertain in advance if their support was feasible. The mobile artillery—two 3.7-inch howitzers and an 18-pounder—were still being hauled into a safer position to fire when the attack went in. A lack of transport had slowed the movement, and apparently the artillery had been hit during the move. Nevertheless, Wallis had given the artillery their orders at 8:30, and they therefore had 6½ hours to move their guns a few hundred yards. Wallis seems to have made no attempt to ensure that his promise to the Rifles of artillery support could or would be carried out. It is probable that the small weight of fire available would not have been of a great deal of assistance, but even this pitiful support was denied them.

Immediately after the failure of the D Company attack, Wallis ordered another company up the main road on the other side of the peninsula to occupy a line just south of Stanley Village. Once again, the Canadian officers pointed out the inevitable results, Wallis insisted on the advance, and A Company started out. As soon as they moved the Japanese artillery and mortars opened up, and within a matter of minutes 18 men had been killed or wounded. Casualties would have been much heavier but at that moment a car came down the road bearing a white flag and the news that the colony had surrendered.

The officer sent from Fortress Headquarters with the news, Lieu-tenant Colonel Lamb, had not brought written orders for the surren-der, and Wallis considered that "surrender was not warranted by the local situation"[7] (he still had some men and a few acres left). A cease-fire was arranged while Lamb went back for written instructions. Both Japanese and defenders held their ground, waiting for the end. Eventually written confirmation was obtained, and at 45 minutes past midnight on Boxing Day, 1941, the last formal organized resis-tance to the invasion of Hong Kong had ceased.

In the last few hours of the battle, the Royal Rifles had suffered 122 casualties while accomplishing almost nothing. The surviving Rifles were ordered to move back to Stanley. On the way back C Company fell to the side for a brief rest. This company had been steadily bombarded by the Japanese for five days before going into action during the evening of 18 December, and then fought almost non-stop for the next seven. No other unit in East Brigade could say as much. But as Major Bishop, who had led them during those twelve merciless days, came by, every man of the exhausted C Company pulled himself to his feet and cheered.

The Battle for Hong Kong
—analysis and comments

The battle for Hong Kong, while possessing some interesting features, demonstrated few tactical novelties and progressed to an inevitable conclusion.

The Japanese, as is often the situation with the victors, offer little scope for analysis. They deployed a larger force of better-trained and better-equipped troops, exploited their superior mobility, had the capacity to concentrate against weak points in the defence, and so won the battle. Yet there were, indeed, occasions when their talent for flexibility and improvisation seem to have deserted them. The initial slowness in taking advantage of the opening Colonel Doi's initiative had gained for them at the Gin Drinkers Line, and the three days when Shoji's and Doi's men flailed around in the Wong Nei Chong Gap area while Tanaka's men squatted above Repulse Bay, are not examples of supreme military efficiency. Indeed, except for the first day of the Island invasion, when the Japanese exploited their ability and willingness to move over high ground—probably one of the biggest surprises to the defenders—to gain them an overwhelming tactical advantage, the battle was little more than a slogging match until Doi's two, savage, successive blows against Mount Nicholson and Mount Cameron opened the way. After the first few hours of the Island battle it is doubtful whether even a stronger and more skilfully handled garrison could have seriously affected the issue, but there were times when it could have dealt the Japanese some heavy blows and dislocated their plans.

When the defence is considered, it is all too easy for the armchair critic, armed with both hindsight and a view of "both sides of the hill", to condemn the conduct of operations by Major General Maltby and his brigade commanders. Maltby, faced with the execution of a difficult task with inadequate means, unquestionably did his best. To what extent the defence could have been better handled must be left to the reader.

The only possible basis for Maltby's decision to hold the Gin Drinkers Line for a period must have been an inaccurate appreciation of Japanese strength and efficiency. If he had known that he would be attacked by a beefed-up division of experienced and well-trained soldiers, he would hardly have taken the risk of losing half his garrison when the Line was breached. Even though the Japanese were thrown off balance by their rapid penetration of the Line, the fact that the defenders were successfully evacuated is to the credit of all concerned. The decision not to hold Devil's Peak to the last was an unfortunate reversal of original plans.

It is Maltby's dispositions for the defence of the Island that have been subjected to the most severe criticism. Even one of his own senior officers was to state that Maltby, though a newcomer to the Island, embodied in his defence plans strongly-held personal ideas, including one to the effect that the "Japs will not attack over the hills and mountain tops". His decision to adopt a perimeter defence for the Island was against the advice of his brigade commanders, and Wallis believed that during the battle Maltby overestimated his own troops' ability to move over rough terrain as much as he underestimated that of the Japanese.

The lack of provision for a vigorous counter-attack should the perimeter defences be breached is the most obvious fault of Maltby's plan, though it is possible that this lack may be partly blamed on his brigadiers. Despite the increasing indications of the threat to the north coast of the Island, no alterations were made to the defences, and at the moment of the Japanese landing, the only counter-attack force on hand was Lawson's "flying column" of three platoons. A strong case can be made that Maltby should have relied on the powerful south coast defences to delay any attempt to land there and kept the Canadians either near the centre of the Island or, if he had been willing to take the chance, on the rearward portion of the north face. In view of Japanese speed and efficiency and the defenders' lack of transport and Intelligence, whether strong and effective counter-attacks could ever have been made is doubtful, but the siting of the troops made it impossible.

Through a combination of bad positioning, ill fortune during the first day's fighting, command indecision, and faulty information, Maltby's infantry force, which was initially not markedly inferior in numbers to the invaders, was never employed in such a manner as to have any chance of decisively impeding the enemy.

The men of the 5/7 Rajput Regiment cannot be greatly condemned for their dissolution under the impact of many times their number during the invasion of the north shore. The death in this battle of so many of the senior personnel was doubly unfortunate as it meant that the ill-trained and inexperienced men who fled south were never rallied, and only a handful played any further part in the fighting. The effective part played in the battle by the surviving Rajput company (B) showed what this unit might have been capable of under other circumstances.

The 2nd Royal Scots, as Fortress Reserve, was the only battalion that was thrown into the battle on the first day of the invasion with decision, determination, and in almost full strength. Unfortunately, they ran into a succession of bloody ambushes and then were sent into Wong Nei Chong Gap in the same fashion that the Light Brigade went into the valley of Balaclava, and with much the same result. On that day the Royal Scots probably showed more raw courage, suffered more casualties, and achieved less than any other unit. It was reduced to a third of its former strength, and although it stayed in the fighting, it could not be called on to play a major role.

The experience of the 2/14 Punjab Regiment was almost exactly the opposite. It was rarely committed to battle in strength and many of the Punjabs were not heavily engaged until they were used to strengthen the line in the last confused day's fighting before the capitulation. Because so many of its men continued to man pillboxes on the western portion of the north coast or were held in reserve positions in Victoria during the first days of battle, those companies that were sent into the fight had only a fraction of their proper strength. B Company, which held the positions immediately north of Jardine's Lookout, was so weak that it is extremely fortunate Japanese plans did not call for a determined assault on it. When A Company went into the counter-attack on Caroline Hill on the first day it was only 45 strong, and by the time of its final action was down to 25 men. One of the most tragic episodes of the battle was the death of the Punjab's Commanding Officer at the head of this handful of men during the hopeless assault on Shouson Hill. The Punjabs seem to have fought bravely and well when they had the chance and it is a shame that this battalion was not used in a more effective manner.

The 1st Middlesex always fought well. Unfortunately, because of its role as a static defence machine-gun battalion, it was rarely available in strength at any one point. Several days had elapsed before the first troops of this battalion were released to play a more mobile role, and even then their employment and positioning was open to criticism. An exception was Z Company, which was in action from the first day of battle and held Leighton Hill almost to the last. Operating with machine-guns from prepared defensive positions, they withstood the engineers of the Suzukawa Unit for six days. Except for Z Company, the Middlesex were never primarily responsible for holding ground and hence could not be criticized for its loss or for the failure of a counter-attack. For this reason, and because much of their fighting was done under the eyes of senior officers, they were the recipients of a great deal of subsequent praise, which was certainly not undeserved.

The Volunteer companies usually acquitted themselves well, particularly in East Brigade and on Jardine's Lookout, but were not committed to battle in sufficient concentration to permit anything more to be said.

The two Canadian battalions performed the bulk of the fighting for the Island, particularly during the first five days. This may be a sweeping statement, but it is justified by the facts. Comparisons are frequently invidious and sometimes odious, yet inasmuch as some official and private accounts of the battle have been rather derogatory concerning the Canadians, it may be as well to put their activities into perspective.

The Canadians fought "not only under the common disabilities but under additional difficulties arising from lack of transport, lack of fighting vehicles, and the early loss of their two most senior officers."[1] The Canadians were assigned, presumably because of their lack of training, to hold the south coast, but were then immediately ordered to about face and fight the battle almost by themselves. Indeed, with the Rajputs nearly wiped out in the first hours of the battle, the Royal Scots decimated after the first day, the greater part of the Punjabs kept out of battle, and most of the Middlesex immured in their static defences, there was no one to try to hold the Japanese except the Canadians and the handful of gallant Volunteers.

The record speaks for itself. The Royal Rifles executed more counter-attacks at company level or above than the British and Indian battalions combined, and the Winnipeg Grenadiers had the next greatest number. The Royal Rifles certainly moved further on foot during the course of the battle than any other battalion. Of particular importance is the fact that the Canadians, with the exception of the Volunteers on Jardine's Lookout and Engineers on Mount Cameron, carried out the only fighting on the heights of the ridge of mountains running the length of the Island. In a succession of savage battles the Canadians fought for the crests of Mount Parker, Mount Butler, Jardine's Lookout, Mount Nicholson, and Mount Cameron almost single-handedly, to say nothing of such other features as Sai Wan Hill, Violet Hill, the Ridge, Stanley Mound, Sugarloaf Mountain, and Notting, Bridge, Red, and Bennet's Hills, which are minor only by comparison. The other battalions rarely faced the full strength of the Japanese infantry as did C Company of the Rifles in their fight against Tanaka's 2nd Battalion or had the awesome experience of having to withstand the onslaught of one of Doi's formidable battalions as was twice the fate of the Grenadiers. Indeed, the northern half of the West Brigade sector saw little fighting for the first five days except against the Suzukawa engineers who were not intended to take ground but rather apply pressure until the infantry came up.

There is no insinuation that the other units were anything but efficient and courageous. They simply did not have to do the same amount of fighting that the Canadians did and, if the Canadians failed more, it was because they tried to do so much more. A force with the training of C Force and burdened with the handicaps of few vehicles, unfamiliar terrain, and an unfamiliar role could be excused to a great extent if it collapsed when fighting began. The record shows that C Force did not collapse. There was a great deal of muddle and confusion (much at levels beyond the control of the battalion), the troops were often slow in moving, lack of weapon and tactical training cost them lives, but they only halted or withdrew under the most grave circumstances. It is a fact, moreover, that wherever the Japanese ran into problems it was usually the Canadians who were responsible. When the Japanese regimental commanders, whose standards were extremely high, recorded "strong opposition", "fierce fighting", and "heavy casualties" they were almost always referring to fighting against the Canadians. It is a very conservative estimate to say that at least half the Japanese casualties were incurred in battles against Canadian troops.

One of the major handicaps to the defence which had a significant effect on the conduct of operations was the weak intelligence system. Some of the gaps made little difference—Maltby recorded that "the efficiency of the enemy air force was probably the greatest surprise to me," but even if he had known all about it, there was nothing he could have done. On the other hand, as has been noted, if Maltby had credited the reports that the Japanese had large numbers of efficient troops available, rather than choosing to believe those reports that denied this, his plans would undoubtedly have been different.

Lack of information during the battle was seriously detrimental to the direction of the defence. This was particularly important as Maltby was later criticized for trying to run a battle from a concrete box. Major Trist of the Winnipeg Grenadiers wrote, "During the whole period of the Battle for the Island Fortress HQ appeared to have little definite information,"[2] and Brigadier Wallis commented, "It was very noticeable how effectively 'out of the picture' Fortress HQ appeared to be."[3] Possibly one of the reasons was that Fortress Headquarters refused to be put in "the picture". Accounts of the battle abound with incidents where accurate information on Japanese activities and locations was passed on to be ignored or rejected with various "we know better" comments. Wallis had something to say about this as well. "One had an unpleasant feeling that ones reports were not trusted, that a passionate desire to minimize what was obviously a serious situation was responsible for piecemeal attacks being ordered on strongly held difficult positions with resulting failure."[4] Although the last dozen words from Wallis are a blatant case of the pot calling the kettle black, the statement is accurate.

Instead of trusting reports from units in the line, Maltby's staff officers were always out and about to determine the situation for themselves. Because they usually did not have a clue about what was happening they often stumbled into the Japanese. Three of these officers blithely drove into Wong Nei Chong Gap on 19 December and all were promptly killed or wounded. Maltby's staff suffered high casualties during the battle, largely because of this incredible lack of caution.

A Canadian official summary prepared immediately after the war includes a statement to the effect that the confusion revealed by

Fortress Headquarters in official communiqués must have been reflected at Brigade level and below. It seemed mainly to have been engendered by a lack of operational intelligence. Reports from returned prisoners of war portrayed attacks and counter-attacks executed by pathetically inadequate forces, often with little or no covering fire, against an enemy of unknown strength in commanding positions. Information now available does nothing but indicate that this analysis was absolutely accurate.

The lack of operational intelligence and unwillingness to accept information from units in contact with the enemy manifested itself most strongly in a persistent refusal to believe that the Japanese were present in strength. For most of the morning of 19 December, Maltby thought the Japanese had only landed two battalions on the Island.* This led to some ridiculous orders, many of which had tragic repercussions. For example, the Commanding Officer of the Royal Scots was told that the Gap was "lightly held", which must have been partly responsible for the subsequent massacre of the battalion. The orders to Major Hodkinson and his Grenadiers that same day border on the fantastic (see page 162). This attitude continued. When Maltby, on information received from the residents of the Repulse Bay Hotel, became dissatisfied with the activities of A Company of the Royal Rifles (presumably because they had failed to destroy Tanaka's two battalions and then clear the Gap), he sent Major Templer to the area to take over. The episode in which this unquestionably gallant officer dashed off with A Company to the south end of Wong Nei Chong Gap and, on realizing the Japanese strength, straightway retired, would be farcical if the situation had not been so serious.

The Japanese on the other hand had a good knowledge of the fixed defences, due principally to their excellent espionage system, but partially to poor British security. For example, Colonel Doi recorded that on the night of the landing, "an enemy map showing fire positions on Hong Kong Island was captured, and it greatly

*It is strange that the British, knowing they would eventually be reduced to holding the Island, had not organized an intelligence system to inform them of Japanese activities on the mainland. The Japanese could not have policed Kowloon sufficiently to prevent messages being sent by flag or lamp, and, out of nearly a million Chinese, some would surely have been willing to do this. Information as to the number of troops embarked would have been invaluable to Maltby (if he had chosen to believe it).

facilitated our subsequent actions."[5]

The Japanese used psychology and propaganda in an effort to undermine their enemy's morale. They dropped leaflets and set up loudspeakers to play nostalgic music and descriptions of home, et cetera. The British had nothing but contempt for such tactics and claimed they showed "a great ignorance of British and Indian psychology."[6] The Japanese did get some return on their investment. Colonel Shoji noted that on 23 December some 30 Indian troops crossed the Japanese lines with leaflets guaranteeing good treatment, followed by an additional 40 the next day.

The British did try to bolster morale by the announcement of large numbers of Chinese troops advancing to the rescue, which, when nothing happened, led to bitter disappointment. Although the Chinese did make some moves, they were ineffective. It is strange that anything at all was expected. If the Chinese had possessed the capacity they would surely have cleared the rich Canton area of Japanese long before.

The defenders were kept constantly on edge and suffered losses by snipers. The blame was normally laid at the door of Chinese fifth columnists, and some of these were actually caught and executed. However, forward Japanese elements and reconnaissance patrols were usually a day or so ahead of the main forces and, by going across country, operated far behind the defence lines. A large percentage of the shots fired by "fifth column snipers" should have been credited to the Japanese soldiers.

The defence was also handicapped by the communications system, which became increasingly unreliable. Lines were continually being destroyed, and the Signals personnel, both British and Canadian, were constantly on the job, even going behind enemy lines to make repairs. A despatch rider system was organized but because of snipers two men had to go at one time.

In addition to the perfectly genuine reasons for Japanese success, a number of rumours and false assumptions were current at the time, many of which continued to exist post-war. For example, the belief persists that the Japanese were headed by 2000 "storm troops"—in reality the invasion troops belonged to an ordinary Japanese division whose previous activities had been garrison and anti-guerilla duties in South China. The activities of fifth columnists were much exaggerated—one gets the impression that the Japanese were always accompanied by their trusty Chinese guides, whereas the Japanese colonels testified that they made use of none, which, in view of the confusion and control problems they experienced, is probably true. Another rumour was that the Japanese had been sold the demolition plans for the mainland and so were able to cut the lines or have replacements ready. In fact, the rapid Japanese movement of heavy equipment was due partly to hasty demolition and mainly to the efficient Japanese engineers, who could easily deduce what demolitions would be made. A story which gained wide currency was that German officers were the organizers and planners of the expedition, while German pilots were responsible for the accurate bombing. This was too fantastic for Headquarters to give any credence to, but many of the lower ranks believed the tale. This is not surprising—they had been told so often that the Japanese were poorly led, unimaginative, bad flyers, et cetera, that when the battle went so heavily against the defenders, some excuse was necessary.

With the exception of the courage of most of the defenders, there is little that is positive to be gleaned from the defence of Hong Kong. Recognized by informed opinion even before the Japanese attack as futile and wasteful, in the final analysis it remains so, and any claims to the contrary are demonstrably false.

For example, Maltby claimed in his post-war report that two Japanese front-line and one reserve division were tied up at Hong Kong. He must have been putting the widest possible interpretation on "tied up", because when he wrote the report it was known that only one division assaulted Hong Kong. Some of the other units of the 23rd Army had been deployed to protect the 38th Division's rear, but the 23rd Army had been in the South China area for years—it certainly was not sent there for the express purpose of capturing Hong Kong!

There have been claims that, because the battle for Hong Kong lasted almost eighteen days, some inconvenience was caused to the Japanese by delaying their planned deployment of the 38th Division for further conquest in Southeast Asia. All evidence, however, points to the contrary. The Japanese were astounded by the speed with which the mainland fell, therefore it can be assumed that their invasion of the Island was probably ahead of schedule, and, whatever their estimate for taking the Island, it can hardly have been much less than the seven days actually required. The Division sailed for the Netherlands East Indies in January and these also were occupied ahead of schedule. The 38th Division did not meet its fate until more than a year after Hong Kong fell, when it was annihilated after fighting with great courage and tenacity against the Americans at Guadalcanal and the Australians in New Guinea.

The senselessness of the defence was recognized by the Dominions Office when the battle for Hong Kong was nearly over, as a circular telegram to External Affairs states: "The capture by Japanese of Hong Kong would gain them *some* strategical advantages but would not materially alter the strategical situation of China Sea as a whole."[7] This was a somewhat sugar-coated version of what the British were admitting to themselves: resistance at Hong Kong was weakening, and the battle would have no "direct influence in the way of tying up Japanese forces . . ."[8] After the war the British official history made the statement that the battle (and especially the reinforcement by Canadian troops) represented a "lamentable waste of manpower". Since Hong Kong had no strategic importance such a reinforcement was an unnecessary extravagance. Besides, "the extra few days of resistance which were gained by the presence of the two reinforcing battalions sent at the eleventh hour could not, and did not, have any influence on the course of events."[9] To portray the battle, and any consequent upset to the Japanese plans arising from it, as being worth the loss of six, or even two, battalions is therefore nonsense.

In addition to being unable to represent Hong Kong as strategically valuable or its defence as having dislocated the Japanese dispositions or timetable, the defenders could not claim to have inflicted unduly severe losses on the invaders. By that crudest but nevertheless valuable barometer of battlefield results, the body count, the defenders lost again. Their casualties numbered 3,445 killed, missing, and seriously wounded, the first category being somewhat inflated by prisoners murdered by the Japanese. The Japanese official casualty figures are 675 killed and 2,079 wounded, for a total of 2,754. These accord well with the estimates of casualties made by the Japanese colonels. Shoji estimated his at 1000 and Tanaka his at 600. Doi's have been estimated at 800, and the Suzukawa engineers fighting as infantry plus casualties in the other arms would account for the remainder. After the war Maltby estimated Japanese losses as 3,000 killed and 9,000 wounded, almost the strength of the entire 38th Division!

Frequently in warfare, the defence causes more casualties to the attackers than it suffers. This was not the case in Hong Kong, for once the Japanese seized the initiative they forced the defenders to expend much of their strength in a series of unsupported counter-attacks against impossible odds, which were largely responsible for the imbalance in losses. The Japanese casualty figures have never been seriously challenged. They certainly cannot be regarded as light. However, when looked upon as the price for a wealthy seaport and the elimination of more than 14,000 of the enemy who might have posed a serious threat if employed elsewhere, the Japanese had no reason to consider them excessive.

Surrender and Captivity
—the prisoners of war

It is not intended to describe in detail the harrowing ordeal suffered by the survivors of the battle for Hong Kong from Christmas 1941 until the surrender of Japan. During those 44 months when they were totally at the mercy of their captors, they had no alternative but to endure and survive as best they might.

When the white flags went up on 25 and 26 December the fate of members of the garrison varied. Although large bodies of troops were seldom seriously molested by the Japanese, in other situations, particularly in some of the hospitals and dressing stations, there were hideous scenes when wounded soldiers were butchered and nurses raped and murdered. Throughout the battle soldiers who surrendered singly or in small numbers—Canadians cut off from their units after the many battles in rough country, men who fought until their positions or pillboxes were overrun, soldiers who had been wounded and could not be brought off the battlefield—were likely to be killed out of hand by the Japanese. Civilians, both European and Asian, were also the victims of Japanese atrocities immediately after the surrender.

The men of the Royal Rifles, in common with the other members of the East Brigade, were held in the area of Stanley Fort until 31 December, when the prisoners from this area were marched across the Island to North Point Camp. The survivors of the Winnipeg Grenadiers had reached Mount Austin barracks in the evening of 25 December. They spent the nights of 26, 27, and 28 December in Peak Mansion, the lecture rooms of the University of Hong Kong, and Victoria Barracks respectively. At no time during this period did the Japanese issue any rations. Finally, on 30 December, the Grenadiers were moved by a very circuitous route across to Kowloon and into Shamshuipo Camp with the rest of the prisoners taken in the Western sector of the Island. On 23 January 1942 the Grenadiers and Royal Navy were moved to North Point to join the Royal Rifles while the rest of the military prisoners were concentrated at Shamshuipo. At North Point C Force reconstituted itself, and the Japanese permitted the Canadians to administer their own affairs to a certain extent. The naval prisoners were removed in April making North Point an all-Canadian camp.

North Point had originally been built by the British in 1939 to house Chinese refugees. It had been badly damaged in the battle and used by the Japanese to stable their horses and mules. As a result, there were huge piles of garbage and manure outside the wire which the Japanese refused to deal with. Inside the camp conditions were little better with the huts crowded to triple their intended capacity. The departure of the naval personnel eased the crowding somewhat, though the huts still held twice as many men as they were designed to accommodate. No beds or bedding were issued. Flies were "truly amazing in their numbers", and bedbugs, rats, lice, cockroaches, and ants tormented sleeping men.

Rations were at their lowest during the first months of captivity, averaging less than 900 calories daily per man. The food itself was of very poor quality and deficient in many vital respects. Particularly badly affected by this were the prisoners who had been wounded or exhausted during the battle. Such men often died if they were not fortunate enough to be taken to the military hospital at Bowen Road, which had been left in operation by the Japanese, though even there recovery was far from certain due to lack of medical supplies. There was also a hospital in the camp, but it was not the "show piece" that the Japanese considered Bowen Road. The other scourge of the early months was dysentery, caused by poor sanitary conditions and exacerbated by the inadequate diet. Among the fatalities was Lieutenant Colonel Sutcliffe of the Winnipeg Grenadiers, who died in April 1942.

Despite the many problems, the Canadians contrived to keep their morale high and to make the best of conditions. Stern measures taken early eliminated most theft and pilfering. Improvisation and scrounging enabled kitchens and ovens to be built, as well as facilities for cobblers, barbers, and tailors. A library, ration store, and quartermaster's store were also established. Particularly useful was a work-shop with such tools as saws and lathes. As this was illegal, a close watch had to be kept for Japanese whenever it was in operation.

The Japanese paid commissioned officers, who then contributed a substantial portion of their earnings to a fund to purchase amenities for the other ranks, particularly the sick. In addition, the men were put to work by the Japanese, mainly on extending the Kai Tak airfield, and were paid small amounts. At first these work parties were popular, but as sickness increased, even men who were quite ill were forced to participate, with serious consequences.

In spite of illness and other adversities, there were entertainments: music (the Grenadiers established a dance band), handicrafts (there were two all-Canadian handicraft exhibitions held in the summer of 1942), educational classes, and lectures, all of which helped to take the prisoners' minds off their plight.

In the summer of 1942 additional diseases began to make their appearance. Beriberi and pellagra were diagnosed in August, both caused by nutritional deficiencies, and the first cases of a diptheria epidemic appeared in September.

September also marked the move of the Canadians back to Sham-shuipo Camp on the mainland. The move was apparently brought about because that month the Japanese sent their first draft of prisoners to Japan for forced labour. These, numbering more than 1800 men, were drawn from the British troops at Shamshuipo. Almost half their number were drowned when the ship *Lisbon Maru* which was taking them to Japan was torpedoed by an American submarine.

Diptheria raged during the first months of the Canadians' stay at Shamshuipo and 50 of them died from the disease. Only a small quantity of serum was available, some obtained from the Japanese and some purchased on the black market. The medical officers were thus presented with the agonizing dilemma of which patients should receive the serum.

One of the most serious problems faced by the medical officers was the arbitrary manner in which the Japanese determined which prisoners could be hospitalized. By October, the seriousness of the situation forced the Japanese to supply some facilities for the ill. After the war the Japanese Camp Commandant and Medical Officer were both sentenced to death, primarily for this neglect. The sentences were later reduced to prison terms.

The Japanese guards at Shamshuipo were usually arrogant and insensitive rather than actively cruel, although there were some exceptions. One of these was a Canadian-born Japanese, Kinawa Inouye, known to some as the "Kamloops Kid". He was tried and executed after the war for his brutalities.

Between January 1943 and April 1944 a total of 1183 Canadian other ranks and one medical officer were sent to Japan in four separate drafts. There they worked as forced labourers, mainly in coal and iron mines. Very little information is available about these men and their experiences. Conditions varied, but sickness and industrial accidents, including an avalanche at Niigata, caused the deaths of no less than 136 of their number.

For the diminishing band of men remaining at Shamshuipo, conditions did not greatly improve. The Japanese preferred to keep the huts crowded rather than spread the reduced numbers around the camp. Many essential personnel and skilled handymen were taken away on the forced labour drafts, dislocating, at least temporarily, the life of the camp.

Among the things that did improve was the food, largely due to the sporadic arrival of Red Cross food and medical parcels. Despite the pilfering of many by the Japanese, the parcels made a tremendous difference, and the physical condition of the prisoners rose and fell with their availability. Personal parcels started to arrive in 1945, some of which had been despatched in 1942! They, too, had been subjected to theft but were still valuable. Not only were these various parcels worthwhile in themselves, but they also provided articles for trading on the thriving black market, which supplied the prisoners with many necessities. An incalculable boost in morale was given by the arrival of the first large inward mail shipment in March 1943. Others followed erratically, though few letters were ever less than a year old, as the Japanese had first to read and translate them for their own records. There was no consistency in delivery and some Canadians would get scores of letters at a time while others would get none.

All was not quiet submission to the Japanese. Contraband Chinese newspapers were brought into camp, translated, and circulated, so that Japanese propaganda could be counteracted to some degree. Radios were operated clandestinely until April 1943, when penalties became so severe that all radios were disposed of. Some of the prisoners were in contact with British officers in China and with

Chinese Nationalist elements and the Hong Kong Chinese resistance movement. These courageous men were involved in smuggling information and medecine into the camp. Some of these men were arrested by the Japanese and several were executed. One Canadian, Sergeant Routledge of the Royal Canadian Corps of Signals, was sentenced to 15 years imprisonment in a Chinese prison in Canton. Successful escapes were rare, and any escapee who was recaptured was brutally punished or killed. Four Winnipeg Grenadiers, Sergeant J.O. Payne, Lance-Corporal G. Berzenski, and Privates J.H. Adams and P.J. Ellis, escaped from North Point Camp on 20 August. They tried to cross to the mainland in a sampan but it capsized and they were recaptured and shot.

With the departure of the last draft of labourers to Japan, there were approximately 450 Canadians left at Shamshuipo, 150 of whom were in hospital with beriberi and pellagra. These men endured the next year and a half as best they could. In mid-August rumours began to spread about the Russian entry into the war and the A-bomb. By 14 August the C Force diary recorded that there were, "Very few in camp now sceptical." The next few days saw the Japanese depart. The prisoners took over the camp, and conditions immediately started to improve. On 22 August it was announced that a British naval force was on its way to Hong Kong. This rather disappointed the Canadians, who noted, "we feel that if this was a former American possession we would have been out of here days ago; probably the English have to turn back the history pages to find out what the precendent was at Crecy and Ladysmith."

Finally on 30 August the Fleet arrived, including HMCS *Prince Robert.* 31 seriously ill Canadians were transferred to a hospital ship and almost all the remainder embarked on the *Empress of Australia* for Manila. There, on 14 September, they were united with the survivors of the groups who had been sent to Japan. They were to stay at Manila until 18 September, when they embarked on the next stage of their journey home. They left behind them, besides the men who had died in the fighting, 128 who had died in the Hong Kong camps, the four men who had been shot after escaping, and 136 who had died in Japan. In all, of the 1975 Canadians who sailed with C Force, 557 never returned.

Some Questions Have Been Raised...
— events at home

During the 18 days of the battle for Hong Kong, people in both Canada and England were almost completely in the dark about the situation in the colony. The situation reports from Maltby's headquarters were markedly vague. Major events, such as the evacuation to the island and the Japanese landings there, were, of course, identifiable, but there was little more solid information. It was nevertheless apparent within a short time that Hong Kong was going under. Canadian interest in the battle was understandably high—this was the first time the Canadian Army had been in action in the entire war—but even the highest government circles were starved for news. On 19 December the Cabinet War Committee was informed that the situation was very grave, and that no word had as yet been received from Brigadier Lawson.[1]

Almost the only information available to the ordinary man was that published in British newspapers, and these were widely quoted by the Canadian papers. It was in these reports that the Canadian people read for the first time that Hong Kong had always been known to be very exposed to attack. The Canadian government was quite upset over this, and the British High Commissioner was more than a little embarrassed. He therefore sent off a telegram dated 18 December 1941 to the Dominions Office pointing out that United Kingdom newspapers were saying (with perfect accuracy) that Hong Kong was of minor value and its retention had never been seriously counted upon in a war with Japan. He reminded his government that Hong Kong had been represented to Canadians in a very different light when their troops were sent. If it was now publicly announced that Hong Kong was of little importance the Canadians would naturally ask why, in that case, their troops had been senselessly sacrificed.[2] This was a reasonable question, of course, and British government spokesmen soon exchanged their excuses for others even more flimsy, but presumably less offensive to Canadians. They then said that the damage to the American fleet at Pearl Harbor and the sinking of the *Prince of Wales* had upset all their plans. This explanation (also offered by General Stuart before the Royal Commission) is utter nonsense as neither the British nor the American fleets had any intention of sailing for Hong Kong. In the case of the *Prince of Wales* and *Repulse,* even the brief sortie up the Malayan coast and return on which they were sunk was a calculated gamble and the risk they ran was understood. To speak of the United States Fleet, even if it had emerged from Pearl Harbor unscathed, steaming through the teeth of Japanese opposition to the relief of a British colony on the Chinese coast hundreds of miles from any American interest is even more ridiculous.

The unadorned fact is that there was neither the intention nor the capability to rescue Hong Kong in the event of war, and to say otherwise was a downright lie, though perhaps considered justifiable in the interest of wartime morale.

On 21 December 1941 the Director of Military Operations and Plans at the War Office reported to the Chief of the Imperial General Staff that resistance was weakening and would have no "direct influence on operations in the Far East in the way of tying up Japanese forces." As far as Hong Kong was concerned the outpost policy was no longer an abstraction, but a grim reality. Although the function of an outpost (to tie up the enemy forces) had not been fulfilled, the fate of an outpost had to be borne—the garrison was to fight to the last. Not for political benefits, no longer even for military benefits. The only value left in fighting to the end was that the "psychological aspect was of overwhelming importance particularly with an Oriental enemy."[3] The military role of Hong Kong had never been of great magnitude—certainly not worth six battalions—but now men were to continue fighting and dying for the lofty purpose of out-psyching the Japanese!

On 20 December *The Times* of London had spoken up for Canada (perhaps because Canada would not speak up for itself). The loss of Hong Kong, ran its editorial, would be grievously felt. "Its dangerous exposed position was well understood", although recent reports tended to downplay this. *The Times* concluded that "the loss of the Island after so brief, though gallant, a resistance is bound to give fresh impetus to the well-justified demand of the Dominions to be given a more adequate share in determining policy and strategy, especially in those parts of the world in which their vital interests are at stake or in which their forces are engaged."

But was there a renewed demand for a voice in determining policy? Certainly not from Canada. Prime Minister Churchill, in Canada a few days after the fall of Hong Kong, expressed regrets to the War Committee of the Cabinet for the loss of the two battalions. "He spoke feelingly of Hong Kong, saying that he was not sure at first about sending Canadians, on the theory that if war did not come, they would not be needed, and if war did come, it would be a difficult place to hold."[4] After this display of Great Strategy in Action, the War Committee was subdued and appreciative. Churchill also thanked the Canadian government for the lack or recriminations on the United Kingdom's Far East policy. Australia, he hinted, had been rather abusive.[5]

The Dominions Office had done its part toward calming Canadian storms in the unlikely event that any might arise. On 26 December 1941 the Office sent condolences and thanks to Canada for its part in Hong Kong. "The defence of Hong Kong will live in History as yet one more chapter of courage and endurance in the annals of the British Commonwealth."[6] (It will live as representative of other things as well, such as thoughtlessness, crass stupidity, and shortsightedness. "History" is not as malleable as the great men tend to think it is.)

Mackenzie King, for his part, offered the condolences of the Canadian government to the people, especially to the bereaved families. He compared the defenders of the Colony to Dollard des Ormeaux and his men in their stand against the Iroquois at the Long Sault, saving Montreal at the cost of their own lives. He repeated the line about the *Prince of Wales* disaster and Pearl Harbor transforming the defence into a delaying action.[7] King's statement appeared to satisfy the Canadian people for the time being.

Meanwhile, all levels of government concerned themselves with a real effort to gain information on casualties and prisoners of war. Lawson, Hennessy, and Lyndon (the Brigade Major) were known to be dead, but the Department of National Defence had little other information. In the United Kingdom the men of the Hong Kong garrison were simply posted as missing until definite information came in. Canada refused to adopt such a procedure, however, preferring to wait for more exact information via the protecting power (Argentina) and the Red Cross.[8] This was very slow in coming, as the Japanese were most unco-operative. By late 1942 there were still many men unaccounted for, despite very considerable efforts directed by Lieutenant Colonel F.W. Clarke (whose son had been a Captain in the Royal Rifles of Canada). The families of some of the men became very impatient, quite understandably, and one letter writer accused the government of withholding information for political purposes.[9]

This was not an isolated reaction, and soon the whole Hong Kong affair was being used as a political football. In February 1942 a Reverend B.C. Eckert in Welland, Ontario, charged that the King government was deliberately withholding the Hong Kong casualty lists until after the by-elections of 9 February 1942. He claimed: "Ottawa knows them, and more are buried in the blood-stained soil of Hong Kong than are in Japanese prison camps."[10] This was totally untrue, but there were many who were prepared to believe it.

Much of the information that did come in was contradictory and confusing. An example of this was the case of Captain H.S.A. Bush, the Staff Captain. He was originally reported to have been killed along with the other officers at Brigade Headquarters, and his wife was so informed. A message from the British Military Mission in Chungking on 30 January 1942 advised that a full stop should have come after Lyndon in the original telegram, and that Bush was only slightly wounded. Lieutenant General Stuart then "advised Mrs. Bush that we have strong reason to believe that her husband is alive." This was, in fact, the case; Bush had written the original telegram reporting the deaths of the C Force Headquarters officers, and had thrown in his own name as slightly wounded to let his wife know he was still alive. Instead she had grieved over his death for a month.[11]

Earlier in January 1942, the Department of National Defence announced that the Winnipeg Grenadiers and the Royal Rifles of Canada were to be reconstituted. In the case of the Royal Rifles the 2nd Battalion went active, but the Grenadiers did not have a reserve battalion. The new 2nd Battalion, Winnipeg Grenadiers remained a training battalion for the rest of the war, and the 2nd Battalion, Royal Rifles went to England in January 1945 with Lieutenant Colonel Harry Lamb as Commanding Officer and Major Alan Laurie,

Wong Nei Chong Gap from Jardine's Lookout.   (CF PMR 79-166)

Japanese 70mm infantry gun in action in Hong Kong.   (IWM MH536)

Two views of Repulse Bay. In the top photo Eucliffe Castle is on the left and the Hotel in the centre. In the bottom picture, Major General Tanaka is looking directly over the Hotel. The commanding position the Japanese held in the hills is apparent.   (PAC PA114819, CF PMR 79-168)

Lieutenant Colonel W.J. Home, Commanding Officer of the Royal Rifles (seen as a Brigadier in 1946), was the senior Canadian officer to survive the battle. His relationships with his British superiors was often stormy.   (PAC PA116459)

Japanese troops move into Victoria just before the surrender.   (IWM HU2776)

Japanese infantry advance during the last stages of the fighting.   (IWM HU2780)

Naval prisoners of war at Hong Kong moving to a camp.   (IWM HU2779)

Prisoners of war hear the broadcast of the Japanese surrender at Shamshuipo.
(PAC PR480)

North Point Camp just after the Japanese surrender. (PAC PA116796)

George Drew, the principle critic of the government's treatment of the Hong Kong situation. (PAC PA11578)

Sir Lyman Duff, Chief Justice of Canada and the Commissioner appointed to investigate the despatch, training, and equipment of C Force. (PAC PA12813)

HMCS *Prince Robert* and the aircraft carrier HMS *Glory* arrive at Esquimault, British Columbia, carrying Hong Kong prisoners of war.
(PAC PA116787, PA116786)

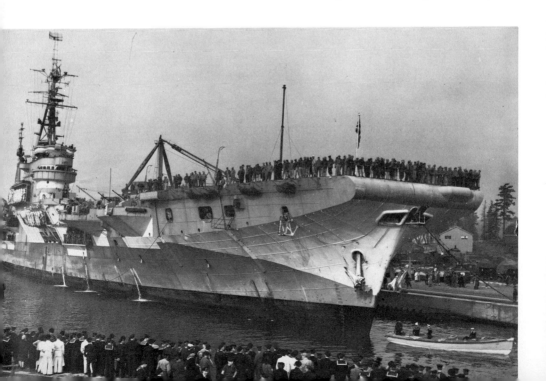

HMCS *Prince Robert*, here shown arriving at Esquimault in 1945 with prisoners of war, carried C Force men both to and from Hong Kong.   (PAC PA116788)

Men of C Force on a CPR vessel at Victoria on the last lap of their long journey home.   (PAC PA116797)

former 1st Battalion Officer, as Second-in-Command. It was disbanded immediately upon arrival to supply reinforcements to other units.[12]

Meanwhile, National Defence personnel were still sorting out C Force's administrative debris. For example, the discovery that sales tax had been included in the price quoted on 52 cases of Pure Marmalade shipped on *Awatea* resulted in a flurry of correspondence between Headquarters and the General Officer Commanding, Pacific Command. The number and weight of boxes of bacon, cheese, and butter were also examined and the information exchanged between the Headquarters in cables marked "Secret".[13]

In January 1942 the British government once again asked Canada for two battalions to garrison an island colony, and the response given illustrated the fact that Canada had at least awakened to the thoughtlessness behind the despatch of the Hong Kong force and was resolved to avoid a similar occurence. These units were requested for the Falkland Islands in the South Atlantic to prevent a possible combined German/Japanese/Argentinian attack(!). The chance of this was exceedingly remote but the British represented it as a pressing threat. It is probable that the main motive was a desire to make a show of strength in the face of a long-standing Argentinian claim on the Falkland Islands, a situation in some ways analogous to Chiang Kai Shek's desire for Hong Kong. The Japanese were bold in January 1942, but it is difficult to see why or how they would want to attack the Falkland Islands.

Norman Robertson wrote a memo to Mackenzie King on the subject dated 16 January 1942 wherein he advised against acceptance:

> The effect on Canadian public opinion of the capture of another two Canadian battalions in an isolated outpost cannot be ignored. . . . The public has taken the loss of the Winnipeg Grenadiers and the Quebec Royal Rifles with a great deal of fortitude, but some questions have been raised as to whether sufficient consideration had been given beforehand to the position in which they would be placed at Hong Kong and to the amount of support which it would be possible to give Hong Kong in case of attack. . . . [If Canada decides to take this on] it might be advisable to insist on having full details beforehand of plans for defence of the Islands and to have the adequacy of these examined. . . . there would be little point in sending in an infantry force as lambs to the slaughter, with no air defence and a very uncertain assurance of naval defence.[14]

If such elementary prudence had been exercised four months earlier it could have prevented the loss of the Royal Rifles and Winnipeg Grenadiers.

The government heeded Robertson's advice and, after some hesitation, refused the British request. As Angus Macdonald, Minister for Naval Services, said: "We have had too many examples of hopeless defences of islands without adequate air support."[15] The government also wished to avoid trouble with the United States, where Franklin Roosevelt and public opinion were both strongly against any signs of "imperialism".

By this time all government hopes for a quick burial of the Hong Kong affair had been dashed, and the public, headed by George Drew, Conservative leader in the Ontario Legislature, was beginning to clamour for more facts. Drew was campaigning in the South York by-election on behalf of Arthur Meighen, the federal Conservative leader who was attempting to win a seat in the House of Commons. In a speech on 12 January 1942, Drew claimed that compulsory military service, for which the Conservatives were pressing, was absolutely necessary—witness Hong Kong. "Let us consider the most terrible example of this shortage of trained men. At the last moment a large number of untrained men were attached to the forces leaving for Hong Kong." Drew went on to say that young men had been shoved into battle without weapon training. In a final, powerful entreaty, he cried, "What a cruel betrayal of public duty it is for anyone who knows the truth to try to convince the Canadian people that the present system of raising men has not failed, and failed miserably."[16] Meighen lost the by-election to the CCF candidate, but not before Drew had unleashed a storm of controversy.

The day after Drew's speech the newspapers (especially the *Globe and Mail,* whose publisher was friendly with Drew) demanded that evidence be provided to rebut Drew's statements, or the government admit their truth. Shortly after Parliament reconvened late in January 1942, Ralston, still Minister of National Defence, in a long speech dealing with C Force, admitted that some men included in the force had not been fully trained. He claimed that the reason had not been lack of men, but lack of time and the need for secrecy. Ralston assured the House that the failure of MT to accompany the force had been investigated and action taken.[17]

This mollified the House for a time, but the members soon scented blood and both major opposition parties called for a parliamentary inquiry. Mackenzie King acceded to this, but later suggested a Royal

Commission instead. Why the Conservatives did not put up more resistance to this old Liberal trick is a puzzle. Even though the Liberals would have outweighed them on Committee, the evidence would have been out in the open. Despite the probability that any censure of the government would be voted down, a parliamentary inquiry would have been much more to the Tories' advantage than a closed Commission. Nevertheless, they made little objection to King's suggestion.

George Drew had already shown a talent for instigating Royal Commissions. He had accused the government in 1938 of irregularities in awarding a Bren gun contract. The appointment of a Royal Commission had damped down that controversy, and the almost indigestible and incredibly dull report extinguished it altogether.

Some squabbling took place in early 1942 before the Commissioner was appointed. The Tories wanted to embarrass the government, but they wanted something else even more—evidence that the army was desperate for men. With this in mind, R.B. Hanson, acting leader of the Opposition, wrote King on 31 January 1942 to express his anxiety that the Commission not be hamstrung by narrow terms of reference. What he wanted were terms "wide enough to enable the Chief Justice to report on the general manpower situation . . ."[18] Hanson had received a draft copy of the Order-in-Council appointing the Commission with the Chief of the Supreme Court, Sir Lyman Duff, as Commissioner. To the terms of reference such as authorization, selection, and composition of the Force, Hanson wanted to add "including the whole question of trained manpower available for the expedition . . ."[19] The government ignored this suggestion and published the order without amendments.

Hanson was annoyed as he had understood from a discussion with King that the Prime Minister was amenable to Hanson's suggested changes. On 13 February he wrote to King to express his disappointment. King replied that the Commissioner would look into manpower in any case, at least insofar as it had touched upon C Force. The inquiry was to deal with Hong Kong, however, and if it became an investigation of manpower, it would be "turning the Chief Justice of Canada into an arbiter on questions involving serious political controversy." The Commission had been appointed "to put it on a plane quite above political considerations". No amendments would therefore be made, but the government would not impinge on the Commissioner's complete freedom to wander where he would.[20]

The Liberals had succeeded in getting their Commission. They also received good publicity by appointing Sir Lyman Duff as the Commissioner. No one could raise a cry of partisanship with the Chief Justice of Canada in the chair. The Liberals pulled off another *coup* by appointing George Campbell, a prominent Conservative lawyer from Montreal, as Counsel for the Government. As the Liberals had taken such a high-minded attitude, Hanson at first hesitated to appoint Drew, who was only too obviously a partisan, as Counsel for the Opposition. But, as Hanson explained to another Tory MP, "Mr. Meighen just insisted on this appointment going to George Drew, and I didn't have much alternative."[21]

The Commission first met on Monday, 2 March 1942 and closed its hearings Tuesday, 31 March 1942. Nearly 300 exhibits were produced and over 60 witnesses called. The Commissioner conducted the hearings fairly in that he put no obstacles in the way of evidence being submitted, but as previously noted, he unfortunately heard (and for the most part believed) testimony from those with an interest in the decision of the Commission. In effect, he treated as expert evidence the testimony of the men who were being investigated, that is, the General Staff and the Office of the Controller of Transport.

Equally unfortunately, the hearings were *in camera.* This was only necessary for a small part of the investigation, when the telegrams between countries were produced or when exact numbers of men were being talked about. Nothing else needed to have been hidden behind a curtain of security, and a public hearing might have resulted in a more realistic finding or a less placid acceptance of the one that was made. There was sufficient evidence presented to justify a censorious finding, and some of this was evidence presented by the General Staff itself. For instance, training manuals and circulars which stressed the importance of good training were ignored by Duff, while the very men who had produced them testified with straight faces about the overriding importance of "character". The Commissioner refused to censure the lack of weapons training of the two battalions and virtually ignored their weakness in tactical training, a weakness that was to prove very costly.

Only the Quartermaster General's Branch received any censure in the final report, and Duff knew quite well that the people involved had already been dealt with. Reproaching this Branch was merely flogging a dead horse, although this would not be evident to the average person reading the report. These men deserved more than just a mild reproof, as the presence of even a few vehicles at Hong Kong would have helped C Force in its desperate battle, but Duff, again ignoring evidence to the contrary, refused to make a finding on whether these vehicles had been needed.

When Duff's report was published in early June 1942 (it was delayed as Drew was unable to present his argument for some time due to illness) the government was happy, the Opposition disappointed, and Drew furious. Round One was over.

Mackenzie King sent a note to Duff, telling the Commissioner that he could not say "how greatly relieved in mind I am at the conclusions reached. I . . . feel that no finer tribute could have been paid my colleagues in the Defence Department. . . . This report will help to give the people of Canada a confidence in their administration which means everything to the country's war effort."[22] And there perhaps lies the rub; Duff, no matter how impartial, could hardly, in mid-1942, have called into question the entire management of the war. Even a mild censure of the government's role in the affair could have had very wide political repercussions. Duff would no doubt have been prepared if necessary to do this in the case of impropriety or illegal activities on the part of government members, but not in judging the management of the war effort. That was the duty of Parliament or, in the final analysis, the electorate. The Liberals felt justifiably secure with a Commission—a few generals might be castigated but the government was safe. As it happened, even the generals escaped unscathed, except for Schmidlin.

For most Tories that was the end of the affair, but Drew stated vehemently that the report was *demonstrably* false and withdrew to prepare notes to prove his case. Hanson accepted Drew's charges: "the Report nauseates me and I cannot believe it reflects the evidence."[23] Most of his caucus, however, were not enthusiastic about pushing the matter. Tempering their desire to cause trouble for the Liberals was the realization that proving the ministers and generals incompetent would seriously hurt the war effort. The Quebec Tories were especially sensitive to this possibility. Drew and his mentor Meighen wished to press on, but finally Hanson decided that he would go along with the majority of the caucus and the matter was officially closed.

Drew had meanwhile been making inflammatory speeches in his most flamboyant style, one of which led to his being charged under the Defence of Canada regulations on the grounds that his speech was prejudicial to recruiting. Meighen, writing Hanson, put forward the theory that Justice Minister St. Laurent went after Drew because he "wants a set-off against his prosecution of Chaloult [an anti-war agitator]. He has had a hard struggle to find one."[24] There may be truth in this theory and Drew would have been a good choice—he was not exactly loved in Quebec.

The Tories once again began to smell blood, but, as Meighen had reported to Drew, acting leader Hanson was getting cold feet. On 11 July 1942 Drew sent Mackenzie King a 32-page letter alleging that the Commissioner's findings were completely at a variance with the evidence and outlining where and why this was so.[25] Copies were sent to the leaders of the three opposition parties and most major newspapers. A public uproar ensued even though the papers had not been allowed to print sections of the letter quoting evidence heard before the Commission *in camera.*

Rejoicing was not universal among the Conservatives, many of whom disliked Drew. One of the latter wrote to Hanson "to express the hope that you will ignore his situation and let him stew in his own fat."[26] Hanson was inclined to agree. If Drew had passed the substance of the letter to the opposition members they could have ambushed the government during the House question period and scored some valuable points. Instead the government had been furnished a plan of the Tories' attack and had promptly sat on the whole affair. King, on the advice of George Campbell, decided not to table the letter on the grounds that it would violate a promise made to the United Kingdom about keeping documents secret.[27] He refused to move from this position and neither the letter nor the Commission evidence was tabled. This was all the more infuriating as all party leaders, most members of parliament, and the editors of most of the major newspapers had read the letter but were not allowed to discuss it publicly.

Hanson accused Drew of disloyalty to the party, as Drew had been appointed as Counsel for the Opposition, and certainly not, as he claimed, counsel for the "public". Drew, for his part, felt that he had been forced to act on his own because the federal Tories had been too frightened to go on.[28] Relations between the two men, never warm, cooled still further.

In the meantime Drew had acquired some strange bedfellows, including CCF Member of Parliament T.C. Douglas. Douglas had given evidence at the Commission as he knew some officers who had been posted to the Winnipeg Grenadiers (see page 60). He wrote to Drew: "I had expected the Report to be whitewash, but I hardly expected the Report to read like the brief for Government Counsel." Douglas believed that Duff had turned his testimony around when including it in the report, giving it the opposite construction to that intended by Douglas.[29] In parliament Douglas called the Report "preposterous", prejudiced", and "amazing", and added that if Duff had treated the rest of the evidence the way he had treated his, it was bound to be inaccurate.

The Liberals had by then decided to drop charges against Drew, but Justice Minister St. Laurent refused in parliament to apologize to Drew for charging him in the first place. The latter had been righteously indignant when he was charged, but now he was angrier still, having been deprived of his chance to stride into court like a modern Socrates and smite the hypocrites hip and thigh. Writing to St. Laurent he said, "Not having apologized for the cowardly course you followed in dropping the charges which you laid against me, at least it might have been expected that you would exercise some caution when you indulged in further slander."[30]

Newspapers began to ask why the charges were dropped. The government announced that according to its legal advisors the matter was before parliament and if it came before the courts it would be *sub judice* and therefore parliament would be unable to discuss it. Yet, the Liberals were clearly on the defensive for a time, and their apprehension can be seen in the notes of some of their meetings. These consist to a large degree of personal attacks on Drew's character and professional conduct.[31] Ralston had some notes prepared to use in the House which contain such references to Drew as, "He wormed his way into the Court Room under the pledge of secrecy" and then proceeded to tell all when the Commission's findings did not agree with his. His use of evidence heard *in camera* was an affront "to the honour of the Bar in this country". The United Kingdom would probably not feel the same confidence as before in passing on secret information.[32] There was probably some truth in this. The High Commissioner to Canada expressed his feelings very plainly in a personal letter to Mackenzie King 21 July 1942. He even gave King advice on how best to muzzle the opposition and the press.[33]

In the end, the Liberals just sat out the storm. They were able to plead diplomatic reasons for not tabling the evidence or Drew's letter, which contained evidence. The Commissioner's report was after all on their side, and no one could actually prove it wrong. The Conservatives themselves were not united on the issue, as some believed that national considerations outweighed political ones. They also did not relish the idea of the Chief Justice of Canada being called in effect a liar or an incompetent, and feared that this would backfire. Thus, the controversy eventually died down.

It is not too cynical, at least in this author's opinion, to say that this whole distasteful episode demonstrates that C Force, having been sent mainly as a political gesture, was having its autopsy used for political reasons as well, even on as low a level as party in-fighting. To the relatives of the men at Hong Kong, it could not have been a pretty sight.

For these people a long and anxious wait was beginning. Atrocity stories had begun circulating, and these were confirmed by Anthony Eden in the British House of Commons on 10 March 1942.[34] When the Japanese had captured Hong Kong, British and Canadian soldiers had been bayoneted, shot, and beheaded after surrendering, Asiatic and European women had been raped, and wounded soldiers murdered in their hospital beds. There was now an increasing amount of evidence to the effect that conditions in the prison camps were deplorable. The British originally wanted to withhold this information, but when confirmation came from escaped British officers they felt they had to publish it. Periodically throughout the war the Allies launched publicity drives concerning the Japanese treatment of prisoners of war in an attempt to get the Japanese to improve conditions, but there were no indications that these had any effect. The Japanese simply reminded the world about British atrocity stories during the First World War (for example, Bloody Boches Bayonet Belgian Babies) and claimed the current stories were a pack of lies. Meanwhile the prisoners went on dying. A total of 264 C Force men died after the surrender.

Except for concern for the prisoners and a very moderate amount of publicity at the time of their return, little more was publicly heard of the matter for a few years. In 1948 the Hong Kong affair was resurrected, but interest quickly petered out. This new eruption had been occasioned by the publication of General Maltby's report on operations in Hong Kong, which, even after deletions made at the request of the Canadian government, seemed to indicate that there was some truth in Drew's contentions. The report created a demand that the Commission evidence now be tabled in the House of Commons and this was done, except that the telegrams between the United Kingdom and Canada were not included. The Conservatives requested King to ask the British for these; King did, and was refused.[35] Drew made a personal appeal to Anthony Eden to use his influence to have the telegrams released, but was rebuffed.[36] The government was loath, in any case, to have the inquiry opened again. Earlier in 1948 the Minister of National Defence had asked the Chief of the General Staff, Lieutenant General Charles Foulkes, for his comments on the Drew letter of 11 July 1942 along with the Duff report. Foulkes' detailed reply (see Appendix C) was probably the first honest analysis the government had seen, and it left no doubt that C Force had been inadequately prepared for its responsibilities. Most of the evidence was now open to the public (with the exception of the Drew letter— King would not stoop to tabling it), but without the high-level telegrams, interest soon waned. This was particularly unfortunate for the Hong Kong veterans, as they were at that time making their first efforts to obtain special treatment. The revelation of the background to their plight might well have generated much-needed public interest and support.

The Canadians Are Being Blamed...

—the scapegoats

"Two important factors have decided me to compile this report without further delay.... The first and most urgent one is the necessity for a very accurate recording of events as they occurred. This would not have been so important but for the fact that it has become very evident that we [the Canadians] are being blamed by the Imperial staff for the early fall of Hong Kong. And while it is not definitely known that the Imperial staff are going to adopt this attitude in their official report every precaution must be taken to ensure that any attempt to make C Force the scape goat is adequately challenged by a submission of the facts while they are still fresh in the memory."[1]

Lt. Col. G. Trist, Winnipeg Grenadiers

Trist, who had taken command of the Winnipeg Grenadiers after Lieutenant Colonel Sutcliffe's death in prison camp, knew whereof he spoke when he wrote these words in the summer of 1942 while the regimental diary for the period of the battle was being compiled. As the immediate post-war Canadian summary (see page 204) commented, the strained relationships and antipathies which resulted from the issuing of orders which were impossible to execute gave rise to mutual distrust and recrimination, with leadership, training, tactics, and even courage called into question. The British were to imply that the Canadians had played a major role in the failure to make a better defence of Hong Kong, and there can be little doubt that they genuinely believed this. Some of the implications did go into the official report, although Canadian protests forced the removal of some of the more blatant ones, and most other accounts either skate politely around them or accept them wholesale. There has never been a great deal of furore on the subject from Canadians, who seem not to realize or to care how their soldiers have been maligned. Nevertheless, as these implications are based almost entirely on either ignorance, misinterpretation, or wilful blindness to the evidence, they should be examined in the light of all the available facts to see how they stand up.

The theme-setter for the British was a Captain P.A. MacMillan, one of Maltby's staff officers who had escaped from Hong Kong when it surrendered. During his debriefing he commented on the Canadians:

> . . . they made the most elementary tactical mistakes. . . . Had we in the morning of December 18 [*sic*] two fully trained battalions capable of carrying out the counterattacks ordered in the difficult country of Hong Kong, we might have localized Jap penetration, prevented further landings and dealt with what was already ashore.[2]

MacMillan's statement does little more than indicate how out of the picture Fortress Headquarters really was. By the morning of 19 December there were six battalions of Japanese ashore and established on the highest ground in the east of the Island. The varibus counter-attacks failed simply because they were ill-conceived, unsupported, and numerically unequal to the task. MacMillan's two hypothetical battalions would have fared little better than the Canadians, even if used in a less piecemeal fashion.

The repetition of the gist of MacMillan's statement is a continuous thread running through most British post-war reports, narratives, and apologia. From the extent to which this theme permeates their writing on the subject, it is obvious that the British, ignoring the lack-lustre performance of the rest of the defence and the fact that the Canadians were more successful than any other component of the garrison whether in attack or defence, siezed upon a very real Canadian weakness, their lack of training, to explain the unsuccessful defence.

Maltby's initial public statement concerning the Canadians was glowingly effusive. During an interview on Formosa just after the Japanese surrender, he declared:

> I am proud that I had the honour of commanding such a gallant body of men. . . . The Canadians had no time to learn the ground they had to fight over.

Their primary task was seaward defence of the Island's southern shores. . . . The odds were 6 to 1 against them but the battle lasted 17 days. A Company of the Winnipeg Grenadiers fought so magnificently the Japs believed the sector was held by two battalions. . . . The Royal Rifles of Canada fought gallantly in heavy gear up the steep hillsides. They fought to exhaustion after suffering heavy casualties. I want all the world to know that those boys, inexperienced as they were, fought gallantly, and those who died died with their faces in the right direction.[3]

Strangely enough, this was more accurate than almost anything Maltby was to say later.

Maltby compiled his official report on the Hong Kong battle in late 1945, submitting it to the War Office on 21 November 1945. As was the custom, it was to be published in the official *London Gazette* shortly afterward, in early 1946. Instead, it was not published until 29 January 1948. One reason for the delay was Canadian protests over part of the contents. Senior Canadian military officers and government members felt they would be in for trouble if the report were published in its original form. As Hume Wrong, the acting Under Secretary for External Affairs, wrote to Lieutenant General Foulkes, Chief of the Canadian General Staff, "Certainly the passages seem to me to be designed very effectively to re-open the Hong Kong controversy in Canada."[4] With the aid of Field Marshal Montgomery some of the offending portions were removed. It seems regrettable that these alterations were made not in order to protect the men of C Force from unfair insinuations, but simply to shield the Canadian government from the possibility of being exposed to the hostile public criticism it so richly deserved.

In the initial draft of his report, Maltby, to do him justice, admitted that the account was compiled mostly from memory and that "memory is a fickle jade". This comment was eliminated from the published version, possibly because it might detract from its authenticity. Throughout the narrative it is obvious that Maltby relied on his own information or that supplied by his staff. He admits in his first draft that he obtained little from other sources, including the Canadians. Information from the Japanese was not yet available at the time he wrote it. It is therefore doubly unfortunate that this report was even allowed to be published, and yet it still stands as the official story on the battle for Hong Kong, being rarely challenged. It is nonetheless valuable as a document illustrating the British impression of the Canadian role in the battle. Maltby's general comments on the Canadians in the final report are accurate as far as they go, though only lukewarm:

(b) *Royal Rifles of Canada and Winnipeg Grenadiers.*—These two battalions proved to be inadequately trained for modern war under the conditions existing in Hong Kong. They had very recently arrived in Hong Kong after a long sea voyage, and such time as was available had been devoted to the completion of the south shore defences and making themselves au fait with and practising the problems of countering a south shore landing. In this role they were never employed and, instead, they found themselves counter-attacking on steep hill sides covered with scrub, over strange country, and as a result they rapidly became exhausted. Many individual acts of gallantry were performed, their stubborn defensive fighting at the Wong Nei Chong Gap and in the area of Mounts Cameron and Nicholson was marked, and the losses they incurred were heavy and deeply regretted.[5]

The version Maltby had originally submitted to the War Office is far more disparaging. The first portion reads:

These two battalions proved to be inadequately trained for modern war. Though possessing first class material, this lack of training rendered them incapable of fire and movement and consequently when launched in many local counter-attacks (and it was on these counter-attacks that the defence of the island depended) they suffered heavily and accomplished little.

The next portion is the same as the published version, with the added comment: "Ably led, well-trained and with more time available, a very different story might have been recorded. It was unfortunate that troops in this state of training were despatched to an area where a crisis might develop at any moment."[6] Whether these comments were eliminated at Canadian request or not is uncertain, but there is little doubt that they reflected Maltby's true feelings. One cannot but agree with his last sentence. Unfortunately, in this report he omitted what he did mention in his first statement after the war, the enormous odds faced in these counter-attacks and the fact that the Canadians did far better than might have been expected even of well-trained troops. He never noted at any time that responsibility for the fact that the Canadians carried out these ill-conceived counter-attacks lay at Fortress and Brigade level. The implication that they were not "ably led" is no doubt based on the considerable antipathy that developed between senior British and Canadian officers. All the evidence indicates that leadership on the officer and senior NCO level was at least equal and frequently superior to the rest of the garrison.

One of Maltby's first comments on the Canadians in the battle for the Island refers to an unsuccessful counter-attack on Sai Wan Fort "organized and led by an artillery officer". This is the Bumpas episode (see page 152), wherein a staff officer disrupted a prompt and possibly effective attack and substituted another which proved unsuccessful. Maltby might better have described this fiasco as "disorganized and misled by an artillery officer".

The story of the siege of Repulse Bay begins with A Company "cooperating in clearing the Hotel grounds", when in fact they were responsible for relieving the defenders. Several times in his account of the Repulse Bay episode Maltby includes the substance of conversations with a resident of the Hotel, but never anything from Canadian sources, and his account differs in several important respects from the records of the Royal Rifles who were there.

In describing the attack of B Company, Winnipeg Grenadiers on Mount Nicholson, Maltby initially stated that, "Artillery support had been arranged but owing to a late start by this company, nothing was achieved, nor was the preliminary clearing of Mount Nicholson effected." Through Canadian representations the comment about the late start was removed, as the delay had been caused by the wait for co-operation from the Royal Scots. As Doi's battalion had taken Mount Nicholson two hours before the time Maltby had set for the attack, it could hardly have succeeded in any event. Maltby does not mention the battle of that evening or the renewed assault by B Company the next morning, when this understrength company gave a Japanese battalion a very bad time and came within a hairsbreadth of retaking the mountain.

This is one of the most annoying characteristics of Maltby's report. Small and insignificant actions and events executed by other units, especially those witnessed by senior officers, are recounted in great detail, but major Canadian fighting is ignored or given a brief and frequently inaccurate mention.

The sorest point with the British as far as the Winnipeg Grenadiers was concerned was the loss of Mount Cameron. Admittedly, the loss was a most serious blow, as Mount Cameron was the key West Brigade position. Yet there is scarcely any cause for reproach. 100 Grenadiers and 30 Engineers occupied the top of a rocky feature where they could not dig in. They were bombed, shelled, and mortared for two days, and then attacked by a battalion plus a company. They fought fiercely and caused many casualties (both facts confirmed by the

Japanese) before the Engineers' flank gave way, for which they can hardly be blamed. The surviving defenders destroyed their equipment and retired to avoid being surrounded.

In his published despatch Maltby said that Colonel Rose had reported that Mount Cameron had been lost, the troops were coming back in disorder, and an attempt was being made to rally them. There is a definite tone to Maltby's comments on the episode that indicates he thought the withdrawal unnecessary. Fortress Headquarters' ignorance of actual events was illustrated in a post-war letter from Brigadier Peffers, one of Maltby's staff officers:

> Towards the end of the fighting this battalion [Winnipeg Grenadiers] was holding a position [Mount Cameron] covering one of the gaps—Wan Chai Gap—and withdrew from its position somewhat precipitately. What caused the withdrawal I have never been able to find out. It seemed to be one of those inexplicable things which happen in war . . . [7]

Acting Brigadier Rose said, immediately post-war, that he had the impression that a patrol had penetrated the line and somebody had hastily given the order to withdraw. This "patrol" was a far cry from the more than 1000 Japanese that actually made the attack.

There seems to have been an enormous amount of resentment among senior British officers over the loss of Mount Cameron. This can only be laid to their wilful and persistant refusal, then and at other stages of the battle, to believe reports in general and Canadian reports in particular about Japanese strength and the scale of engagements. At least one Canadian officer believed that the reproaches and friction resulting from the loss of Mount Cameron contributed to Lieutenant Colonel Sutcliffe's early death in prison camp. Whether this is true is impossible to determine, but it does give an idea of the dislike and mistrust that existed.

The final straw from Maltby's point of view was probably the report that Bennet's Hill had surrendered on 25 December. This was untrue, but he reported it as fact in his post-war report.

The personality conflict and antipathy were even worse in East Brigade. After the disintegration of the Rajputs in the first hours of the invasion of the Island, Brigadier Wallis, described by one senior British officer as having a weakness for interfering with the disposition of his subordinates, was reduced to a single battalion, the Royal Rifles, on whom the success or failure of his plans was to depend. As the battle progressed, what little mutual confidence had existed between Wallis and Lieutenant Colonel Home rapidly evaporated. Wallis watched each counter-attack fizzle out in failure while Home saw his companies decimated in futile and ill-planned attacks against impossible odds with no support. The resulting antagonism was to end in what is probably the most notorious confrontation of the battle and one which must have done much to prejudice British opinion against the Canadians.

It must be remembered that most Canadian officers in both battalions of the rank of major or above were decorated veterans of the First World War. They had served in the Canadian Corps, probably the most efficient unit of that size on either side and one that was noteworthy, not simply for the courage of its soldiers, but for the skill and high degree of intelligence and planning shown in its operations. All of these officers had a very sound idea of the useful, the possible, and the practical, probably far more so than their British counterparts. After 20 December Home was the senior Canadian officer, responsible not only to his local British superiors but to his men, the Canadian government, and the Canadian people. Available opinion from his officers indicates that he took these responsibilities very seriously. Sutcliffe had contacted Home several days before the surrender to see if the latter could do anything about the way his troops were being employed, and Home, apparently, had spoken to Wallis several times on the subject.

The crisis came on the morning of 24 December. Wallis was later to state that Home, in the interview that led to the relief of the Royal Rifles in the line, demanded to speak to the Governor, saying that further resistance was useless. Wallis claimed to have then told Home that Maltby could not be ignored in that way, and gave him the choice of fighting on or marching out under a white flag. Home decided to adopt neither course, talked to Maltby, and the relief was arranged.[8]

Wallis' version is flatly denied by the Canadians at Stanley, who state that capitulation or a separate withdrawal was never discussed, but only the subject of relief for the exhausted Rifles. Bitter protests were made to Maltby during captivity when the Wallis story became known. When it is considered that Home agreed to put one of his companies in the line again after four hours' rest and committed another, albeit after protest, to a suicidal attack in which he had no confidence on the afternoon of 25 December, it appears far more likely, to this author at least, that the Canadian version of the story is the accurate one. Wallis was under tremendous strain and may well, in retrospect, have interpreted Home's request as desire to surrender, particularly if he knew Home's opinion of operations to date.

Whatever the truth of the matter, Wallis' version received wide credence and poisoned still further the relations between British and Canadians. In its most exaggerated form, British prejudice against the Canadians led to the assertion that their lack of training and low morale made them a liability in battle, was directly responsible for several major debacles, and led to the early fall of the Island. The equivalent Canadian opinion was that the British were incompetent, expected the Canadians to do most of their fighting for them, and, when they failed to do the impossible, used them as scapegoats.

Expressing the British opinion in its most virulent form is one Tim Carew, many of whose statements anent the Canadians in his two books *The Fall of Hong Kong* and *Hostages to Fortune*[9] are sufficient to bring every man of C Force to his feet shouting, "It's a damned lie!" For example:

> The Winnipeg Grenadiers and Royal Rifles of Canada were not called upon to put their valour to the test in a counter-attack role because the Canadian contingent as a whole had ceased to exist as a cohesive force—leaderless, dispirited, demoralized and exhausted, they had scattered to the four corners of the island: some sought solace in sleep, others in looted liquor. Others, again, were fastened upon avidly by unit commanders and were coerced and cajoled, sometimes at gun point, into fighting again.

This is as of 20 December 1941, when both Canadian battalions had been involved in, and would continue to be almost wholly responsible for, the major counter-attacks of the campaign. Writing of the prisoner-of-war period, Carew portrays the British as stoical, cheerful soldiers, while the Canadians skulk around, paralized by their own lethargy. Space precludes the otherwise simple task of making a point-by-point refutation of Carew's comments. The only reason for not treating them with the contempt they deserve by ignoring them completely is that both books have had a wide distribution and have therefore been responsible for the sole knowledge many people have of the Canadians at Hong Kong.

It is unlikely that the British tendency to fix a large portion of the responsibility for the early fall of the Island of Hong Kong on the lack of fighting ability and spirit of the Canadians is a deliberate Machiavellian ploy to excuse their own shortcomings, such as is so often attributed to the minions of "perfidious Albion" by a sizable school of historical authors. However, it is no less worthy of refutation simply because its origin and basis lie in ignorance rather than dishonesty. Fortunately, the total available evidence is more than sufficient to do so.

Must They Fight Twice...
—the Hong Kong veterans

Those men of C Force who had survived not only the battle but also the four year ordeal of life as prisoners of the Japanese found that their troubles continued long after their release. Their sufferings had affected all of them physically and many emotionally, and re-adjustment to civilian life was not easy. Some never succeeded, despite valiant efforts. The most widespread of the problems facing the Canadian survivors of Hong Kong was poor health. The years of malnutrition as prisoners of war and the exposure to tropical diseases combined to retard the healing process. It was some time before the survivors were able to return to the normality of the life they had left behind. Even then they still had to suffer the humiliating ingratitude of their country, which, for an agonizing length of time, failed to admit that their experiences were unique and that the permanent effects were such as to warrant adequate compensation and assistance. It was almost thirty years before full justice was rather belatedly done.

The C Force survivors returned to Canada in various stages, and by various means. Those few who appeared reasonably healthy were airlifted home as soon as possible. Many of the remainder were transferred to hospitals in Manila where they were given vitamin-supplemented diets to prepare them for the long trip home.[1] All who were not fortunate enough to fly back returned by sea, often on hospital ships. Ironically, one of the repatriation ships was HMCS *Prince Robert,* which had helped to transport C Force to Hong Kong in 1941.

The men were eventually disembarked at Victoria and went on to treatment centres for three or four weeks depending on their physical condition. One man wrote: "Apparently this was so that we could present ourselves to our families in a reasonable manner when we got back home."[2] The veterans were understandably anxious to get through the treatment centres as quickly as possible in order to return to civilian life. Unfortunately, despite the good intentions of the doctors in charge, many of them had no idea how these men should be cared for, and so provided little treatment beyond ensuring a maximum intake of food and vitamins. The medical authorities' lack of experience in treating tropical parasitic diseases drastically reduced the quality of treatment available. For example, many of the veterans had returned with undetected dysentery, and as there was only one doctor in Canada with experience in diagnosing the disease, these cases were neither identified nor treated. One of the more unfortunate results of this was the contraction of dysentery by wives and medical personnel who had come in contact with the infected men, some of whom suffer to this day from the effects of the disease because of the earlier neglect.[3] One veteran remarked that upon leaving Japan he weighed a scant 79 pounds.[4] His first meal consisted of six fried eggs, three pork steaks, a stack of toast, and a bowl of porridge. On the ship to Canada he kept to no proper diet, and by the time he stepped off the train in Winnipeg he weighed 179 pounds. His condition pleased the doctors of the Department of·Veterans Affairs, but it turned out that he had a severe case of beriberi. Diseases such as this were not readily apparent once the veterans regained their lost weight, and therefore their discharge papers were often stamped "Discharged on Demobilization" (the war is over—you are no longer needed) with no mention of their medical problems. This later created difficulties for Hong Kong veterans who sought disability pensions for their wartime service.

After a few weeks in the treatment centres, the soldiers were given ten days with their families before being sent back to hospitals for rehabilitation that could last months, years, and, in some instances, a lifetime. Some men were simply put on exercise programs, others were admitted to a nerve hospital for psychiatric care. Some of the veterans at the nerve hospital received insulin injections to help them regain their lost weight.[5] Checkups were not carried out annually, although the progressive nature of many of the diseases they suffered from should have made it compulsory. Veterans developed an understandably negative attitude toward doctors as a result, and many flatly refused to seek medical attention in the future: "We are not proud people, and in my own experience I took great exception to young, inexperienced, in my opinion, interns who had never been outside a textbook trying to convince me that there was nothing wrong with me and that I did not have the condition which I claimed I had."[6]

In April of 1947, Dr. T.H. Williams, a pathologist at the Deer Lodge Hospital in Winnipeg, published an article entitled "Intestinal Para-sites—A Survey of Repatriated Hong Kong Prisoners of War" in the *Department of Veterans Affairs Treatment Services Bulletin.* In his examination of 553 Winnipeg Grenadiers, the rate of infestation with intestinal parasites was 72%. All of the men who flew directly home or who had hitch-hiked without being held for examination and treatment at centres *en route* were found to harbour some form of parasite. Of the men surveyed only 28.5% showed no signs of infesta-tion. In comparison, 56% of personnel who had returned from RCAF service in India, Ceylon, and Burma were free of parasites, while 74% of the patients back from service in North West Europe showed no infestation. The most common parasitic ailments were whipworm, hookworm, and threadworm, and multiple infestation was the rule rather than the exception. It was ten months to a year after the return to Canada before infestation was eliminated in all cases.

Nutritional deficiencies were directly responsible for avitaminosis, which afflicted every soldier returning from Hong Kong. Avitaminosis was a blanket term covering all symptoms of vitamin-related illnesses. Paraesthesia (numbness) of the extremities, especially of the feet and the legs, was one of the results of the nutritional deprivation suffered in the Japanese camps.[7] Varying degrees of permanent and non-progressive optic atrophy were detected in 15% of the men, and other disabilities such as undue fatigue and various gastro-intestinal, cardio-vascular, neurological, and psychiatric problems abounded. There was a high incidence of sudden, unexpected death among Hong Kong veterans, and their life expectancy was calculated to be ten to fifteen years below the national average.

In 1948 the Hong Kong Veterans Association was formed. Its members had initially envisioned a social club that would enable survivors to maintain their ties with one another. They soon dis-covered, however, that they were expressing common complaints and experiencing identical problems. It was not long before the Association evolved into an organization primarily concerned with obtaining from the government the benefits and compensation to which its members felt entitled. The constant flow of information which they directed toward the Department of Veterans Affairs[8] and the Parliamentary Standing Committee on Veterans Affairs won them sympathizers who were to aid them in their fight for fair treatment.

Even before the Standing Committee or the Association were established, a fight had begun to get the Hong Kong veterans the bonuses which had already been given other soldiers. In September of 1945 M.J. Coldwell, the leader of the CCF, requested in the House of Commons that the government reconsider its plan to award an additional allowance to the Canadian soldiers who had volunteered for service in the Pacific but never fought there due to the end of the war. Under the terms of the plan as it stood, the Hong Kong veterans were ineligible for this "Pacific Pay". Coldwell stated:

> ... the least we can do is to make them eligible for all special payments provided for the service in the Pacific from the day they embarked on their ill-fated expedition. The dependants of any who perished should be entitled to the payments the soldier would have received had he survived. This seems to me to be simple justice.[9]

For the next three years opposition members tried without success to persuade Mackenzie King's Liberal government to award Pacific Pay to the survivors of C Force. The Hon. John Bracken, Leader of the Opposition, also tried to obtain the award of a special decoration to these men, and the Minister of National Defence, the Hon. Douglas Abbot, promised that he would review the matter at some future time. For the moment, however, he was content to wait to see what other Commonwealth countries would do.[10] In February 1948 MP J.A. Ross revived the subject of Pacific Pay and the government at least showed some reaction, negative though it may have been. The new Minister of National Defence, the Hon. Brooke Claxton, told the House: "In view of the fact that the Pacific rate of pay was made applicable only to members of the Pacific force, it is felt that it would not be justifiable to extend it to those who served in that theatre of war under quite different conditions and at an earlier date."[11] The Minister apparently did not believe that the ordeal suffered by the men of C Force warranted any amendment or addition to the legislation. When Ross pursued the question once again six days later, Claxton side-stepped the issue by attacking the opposition:

It would be hard to find any better reflection of the war effort of Canada and on the war-time administration of this government than to appreciate the fact that now, after the war is over, and six years after Hong Kong, the members of the opposition revive this question as the only serious blot charged against the record of a fine country and a great people doing everything they could to play their part in defeating the enemy.[12]

It did not seem to occur to Claxton that the victims of this "only serious blot" were all the more deserving of government assistance. In June 1948 the *Vancouver Daily Province* ran an editorial titled "Must they Fight Twice for Their Pay?".[13] "Canadians," it stated, "are ashamed of their country's failure to recognize fully the sacrifices made at Hong Kong—sacrifices that dollars can never compensate." The editorial concluded that it was "blood money we owe these veterans and they should not have to fight twice for it."[14]

The Veterans Association appreciated these efforts on their behalf, but were more concerned about long-term protection, and were pushing for medical studies to improve the current methods of treatment for their problems. In 1950 a research project was initiated to study the disabilities of these men. At that time there were 1,415 survivors. Over 1,000 of these were pension recipients and approximately 200 more were entitled to treatment for disability.[15] As their diseases progressed and formerly dormant afflictions re-awakened, the need for medical attention increased. In addition, many men suffered psychological disorders as a tragic result of their wartime experiences. Compensation and assistance were available only when these disorders were recognized as service-related. Yet many of the Hong Kong men had made a tremendous effort to re-adapt to civilian life and had grappled with their problems with the same grim determination they had shown at Wong Nei Chong Gap and Stanley Peninsula. When, years later, they were forced to admit defeat, their disorders were often not recognized as the result of their services. Therefore the Association contended that any question of the relation of psychological or emotional disturbances to wartime experience should be resolved in the veteran's favour.[16]

In March of 1951, the Department of Veterans Affairs decided that all Hong Kong veterans with pension entitlement for avitaminosis would be admitted to the Department's hospitals for diagnosis and treatment of any illness until such time as the Chief of Services or a clinical official designated by him stated that it was not service-related. Thereafter treatment could be carried out only under another section of the pension act. No other class of veterans had previously been given this privilege. It marked the first victory in the Hong Kong survivors' battle to be considered unique.

Once this first step had been taken, other benefits followed. In October 1952 the first war claims payments were granted to Hong Kong soldiers. An Order-in-Council[17] awarded them one dollar per day of imprisonment as compensation for maltreatment.* (In 1958 they were awarded an additional .50 per day.) In July of 1954 all Veterans Affairs districts were instructed to establish an annual personal "after care" service which included welfare counselling, vocational guidance, training or retraining, job placement, and welfare planning. Rehabilitation programs were to be followed up to ensure each veteran's progressive adaptation to civilian life. The service was maintained for three years after which time another complete review of the situation was carried out, and the decision was made to offer this counselling only to those who had an acknowledged need for further assistance.

Through the 1950's and 1960's the Hong Kong Veterans Association continued to fight for what they considered their rights. Appearing before the Standing Committee on Veterans Affairs in May 1960, Lionel Hurd, President of the Quebec Branch of the Association, outlined the group's plan to initiate and review legislation:

> One time I was having an interview with a very high official of the Pension Commission and he said that we could never get what we needed without legislation. So that is why we appeal to honourable members of the House of Commons now to see what they can do. I think that it will have to be legislation.[18]

In a brief submitted to the Standing Committee in May 1961, the Association presented a claim for additional war claim payments of one dollar per day of imprisonment for slave labour. This would place the Canadian veterans payments on a par with the awards received by the American prisoners of war, Japanese Theatre. The Canadians had first requested these payments in December of 1959, but were informed by the Minister of Veterans Affairs of the Diefen-

---

*Following the recommendation of Judge Ilsley of the War Claims Commission, the Hong Kong Veterans Association only asked for maltreatment compensation. When the monies became available, they were advised to pressure for forced labour claims.

baker Progressive Conservative government that the War Claims Commission had been dissolved and the money in the fund largely depleted.[19] When their request for a breakdown of all claims paid was ignored, they sought information from the Minister of Finance through NDP member, H.W. Herridge. In March 1960 the Association was informed that the final report of the War Claims Commissioner had not yet been completed and that the information requested was not available at that time. Responding to a question by Liberal MP Paul Hellyer (for a change of pace, it was the Conservatives who were now under the gun concerning the Hong Kong veterans) the Finance Minister stated publicly that the War Claims Commission had *not* been dissolved, and went on to contradict the statement that the war claims fund had been depleted. The government subsequently granted the veterans' claim for slave labour compensation.

In 1963 representatives of the Hong Kong Veterans Association appeared once again before the Standing Committee. Before presenting their requests and recommendations they recounted, in considerable detail, their miseries as prisoners of war and a history of earlier attempts to improve their lot after the war. Following this justification, they asked for a review of the pensions currently being received by all Hong Kong veterans, the revival of the 1950 disability survey, annual medical checkups, and free dental and optical care. They also requested that studies be made of the effects of avitaminosis, pelagra, beriberi, and dysentery to determine the exact connection between these ailments and the present condition of many of the members. The main objective of this multi-barrelled request was to build up a sufficient amount of evidence to entitle all Canadian survivors of Japanese prisoner of war camps to an automatic pension for 50% disability, based on the residual effects of avitaminosis. The magic of the 50% figure was that this was the level at which the widows of veterans were granted widows' benefits. As a result of the Association's representations the Committee ordered a study of the problems of the Canadian Hong Kong veterans to be conducted by Dr. H.J. Richardson on behalf of the Canada Pension Commission.

David Groos, the Liberal Member of Parliament for Victoria, had become a vocal supporter of the Hong Kong veterans. As vice-chairman of the Standing Committee on Veterans Affairs, he initiated a survey within his constituency to substantiate their claims.[20] In June 1964 he moved to have the Standing Committee empowered to deal with the circumstances of the Hong Kong veterans and reported the opinions of the survivors on special measures that could be undertaken to alleviate the disabilities resulting from their internment. Speaking on this motion Groos said:

> I am a veteran and I take the view—I think it is shared by a great many other veterans—that a man has little claim on his country because of what might have happened to him in uniform, but I do earnestly believe that the nation owes at the very least a decent life to veterans who did suffer lasting damage as a result of service in their country's cause.
>
> I believe we owe it to these men to pass the motion now before the House in order that we may establish the facts in order that we may show these men [Hong Kong veterans] that we are interested in their difficulties and are prepared to grapple with their problems. [21]

The motion was debated but no vote was taken. It was pointed out in the course of the debate that a study was already in progress, and that Dr. Richardson's report was expected to be tabled shortly.

The findings of both the Groos survey and the Richardson Report, which was submitted in 1965, supported the claim of the Hong Kong Veterans Association. [22] As Dr. Richardson quoted in his report:

> The psychological stresses to which the Hong Kong veterans were subjected during their period of imprisonment were severe and long continued. Four years of rough treatment, beatings, and constant threat of torture in many forms, stress of undernourishment, inadequate clothing along with forced labour under intolerable conditions have left hidden personality scars which continue to lower the veterans ability to adjust to normal civilian life. Even cursory observation of many of these veterans today will verify the permanent damage that was suffered under deplorable conditions experienced by no other prisoner of war. [23]

Dr. Richardson found that the death rate of the Hong Kong survivors was 23% higher than that of veterans who had served in other theatres. One in nineteen Hong Kong veterans had gone blind since returning to Canada, and one in five suffered from heart disease and hypertension. Three quarters of those who received pensions had been assessed at less than 48% disability, and their dependents were therefore ineligible for benefits. Many of these men were unemployed because of their inability to compete on the job market, and although they had not offered their services to Canada for monetary reward, they had assumed that if the effects of their service prevented their earning a living their dependents would be provided for. [24] Problems were not only physical, however, and imprisonment had left a permanent mark on the minds of many of the survivors. One man still saved scraps of bread as he had in prison camp, even though his monthly income exceeded $400.

Dr. Richardson's report to the Pension Commission concluded:

Twenty years after the liberation of these men from 44 months captivity, there is conclusive evidence in medical literature and/or in this report of the nature and course of some of the disabilities, such as optic atrophy, neurological, muscular, and minor circulatory defects of the feet and legs, inferior dental health, and an abnormally high death rate from coronary artery (A.S.H.D.) disease. There is impressive evidence though not conclusive in the statistical sense of widespread gastro-intestinal, neuro-muscular, cardiovascular and nervous symptoms, and fatigue disproportionate [to] identifiable physical factors. The extent to which such symptoms are due to organic diseases cannot be determined but the reality of the symptoms and of a disability of greater or lesser degree is not in doubt.

While further study of some of these problems will undoubtedly be required in the future, the public responsibility under existing legislation can, in my view, be adequately discharged only by a sympathetic and generous policy based on the information now available. To wait any longer would be to wait too long.[25]

The report recommended the review of individual disability assessments as soon as possible, as well as an effective date for a pension rate increase over and above anything awarded because of reassessment. The request for a minimum pension level was supported by Dr. Richardson; it was not up to the Committee to initiate legislation that would encompass the recommendations. There was still a period of waiting ahead for the veterans.

One of the 148 recommendations contained in a report submitted in 1969 by a committee established to survey the work and organization of the Canadian Pension Commission (the Woods Report) concerned the pension request of the Hong Kong veterans. Its recommendation, based on the Richardson report, was that any Hong Kong veterans who demonstrated any disability whatsoever should be awarded a 50% disability pension. What the report proposed, in essence, was that service in Hong Kong should automatically entitle the veterans to be treated as disabled. They had endured four years as prisoners in exceptionally arduous circumstances and should be regarded as deserving of a pension under the cited conditions as a matter of right.[26]

Finally, by January 1971, the government was willing to acknowledge the special service of Hong Kong veterans who had died prior to the effective date of the pension act. Their deaths were to be automatically attributed to their service, thereby making their widows and dependents eligible for pensions. The legislation did not apply solely to the Hong Kong veterans, but to all Canadian servicemen who had been captured by the Japanese and held prisoner for a year or more. The Hong Kong Veterans Association had worked hard for over 25 years to obtain this final adjudication, devoting their time unceasingly to the effort and returning to the struggle despite repeated disappointments. Maurice D'Avignon, President of the Quebec-Maritime Branch of the Hong Kong Veterans Association, expressed the common emotion when he spoke to the Standing Committee the following year:

> Then last year [1971] our dream became a reality when legislation to amend the Pension Act was passed. This in itself was a blessing to our widows, dependents, and orphans not receiving war pension and to our Hong Kong survivors below 50% prior to March 30, 1971.
>
> The ironic twist of fate for these men is that in death they know their families will be provided for—in life this satisfaction is denied them.[27]

In April 1976 the last hurdle was surmounted when the government generously gave Hong Kong veterans with assessed disabilities an additional 30% pension. Each man therefore collected a minimum 80% pension. It was not until after the Hermann Report on Second World War POW's that other veterans who had been taken prisoner, such as those captured at Dieppe, were awarded a minimum 20% addition.

In the immediate post-war years the government exhibited all the defensive reactions of an uneasy conscience as far as the Hong Kong veterans were concerned. The shabby episode of the Pacific Pay entitlement occurred at a time when the government was desperately trying to hold the lid down to prevent the whole Hong Kong issue from boiling over again. Unfortunately, the current status of the C Force men was lumped in with other aspects of the controversy.

It is interesting to speculate as to what might have happened if the government had had the courage and integrity to come straight out and admit their responsibility and had thereafter tried to compensate the Hong Kong veterans for the hardships they endured. Possibly the Hong Kong Veterans Association would have remained a social organization. But admission of error has never been a dominant characteristic of politicians, and it took many years of effort and pressure by the Veterans Association, aided by sympathizers in Parliament and by officials of the Department of Veterans Affairs (who have rarely received the acknowledgment they deserve), before full acknowledgment or compensation for their needs was received.

The Hong Kong Veterans Association still exists. Its members, a diminishing band of aging men, still bear the external and internal scars of their experience. Few would now recognize that these were once the fine young men of the Royal Rifles of Canada and the Winnipeg Grenadiers who were so casually despatched to the doomed outpost of Hong Kong over forty years ago.

Conclusion

The introduction described this book as an attempt to create a coherent account of the entire Canadian involvement in the defence of Hong Kong. To what degree this attempt has succeeded must be left to the reader. Its creation was commenced with few pre-conceived opinions, and most of these were demolished as the research results took shape. It would be pointless to recapitulate the answers obtained to the questions posed in the introduction except to say that they were arrived at after as objective an analysis of the available evidence as possible. The compilation of this evidence was done thoroughly and conscientiously.

As the work of preparing the book progressed, the emotion that made itself felt with increasing intensity, even overshadowing that of irritation at political and military ineptitude, was a combination of admiration and sympathy for the men of C Force. No Canadian soldiers before or since got such a dirty deal or deserved it less. They were, quite literally, dropped into it. Casually sent to a death trap long before they could be considered ready for battle, they nevertheless put up a courageous and astonishingly effective fight against overwhelming odds, endured almost four years of squalid and brutal captivity, and then emerged, often physically and mentally marked by their ordeal, to be rewarded by the sneers of their allies and the neglect of their government.

Canada is not a militaristic nation and Canadians are an unmilitary people. Even successful military episodes are considered a little embarrassing and the glorification of failures and heroic last stands is almost unheard of. Whether this is a virtue or not is difficult to say. For the men of C Force it is, in one way, a pity, as the battle they fought deserves to stand beside the most famous exploits of the Canadian army or any other. They were not all heroes, they certainly were ill-trained for their role, but, if the Japanese can be believed, those men from the city and suburbs of Winnipeg and the big farm boys from Quebec must have fought like tigers.

It was never the intention of this book to include graphic battle descriptions. The roar of the automatic weapons as C Company of the Royal Rifles stops Tanaka's 2nd Battalion, the sight of A Company of the Grenadiers moving up into the mist on Mount Butler never to return, the stagnant air reeking of cordite as the little band of defenders holds out in the Gap shelters, the dry-mouthed tension as the men on the rocky summit of Mount Cameron huddle behind their stone barricades under a hail of explosives waiting for the shock of the Japanese assault, the sickening feeling of finality as the men of D Company pull themselves to their feet for the final counter-attack on that bloody Christmas afternoon—all these and many others await an author who can embody the saga of C Force in the prose it deserves. Unfortunately, neither that author nor any other will be able to detail the reason why these men should be in Hong Kong in the first place.

There *was* no reason why.

Carl Vincent

Appendices

Appendix A

Canadian Hong Kong Casualties

	Total			C Force HQ			Royal Rifles			Grenadiers		
	OFF	OR	All	OFF	OR	All	OFF	OR	All	OFF	OR	All
Fatal Battle Casualties												
Presumed killed in action	3	71	74		3	3	1	36	37	2	32	34
Killed in action	18	166	184	4	10	14	6	73	79	8	83	91
Died of wounds	1	18	19	1	2	3		11	11		5	5
TOTAL	22	255	277	5	15	20	7	120	127	10	120	130
Fatal Battle Casualties While POW												
Killed by enemy after capture		4	4		1	1					4	4
Died of wounds received at time of capture	1	8	9					3	3	1	4	5
TOTAL	1	12	13		1	1		3	3	1	8	9
TOTAL Fatal Battle Casualties	23	267	290	5	16	21	7	123	130	11	128	139
Fatal Ordinary Casualties												
Died of disease proceeding to H.K.		1	1					1	1			
Died of disease in Japan after release*		1	1								1	1
Died of disease returning after release*		1	1								1	1
TOTAL		3	3					1	1		2	2

	Total			HQ			Royal Rifles of Canada			Winnipeg Grenadiers		
	OFF	OR	All	OFF	OR	All	OFF	OR	All	OFF	OR	All
Fatal Ordinary Casualties While POW												
Accidentally killed		8	8					6	6		2	2
Died of injuries		3	3		1	1					2	2
Died of disease	4	249	253		12	12		123	123	4	114	118
TOTAL	4	260	264		13	13		129	129	4	118	122
TOTAL Fatal Ordinary Casualties	4	263	267		13	13		130	130	4	120	124
TOTAL Fatal Casualties	27	530	557	5	29	34	7	253	260	15	248	263
Non-Fatal Battle Casualties**												
Wounded prior to capture***	13	278	291		4	4	7	111	118	6	163	169
Wounded—remained with unit		1	1								1	1
Battle injury prior to capture	1	7	8					3	3	1	4	5
TOTAL Non-Fatal Battle Casualties	14	286	300		4	4	7	114	121	7	168	175
Repatriated POW'S												
Wounded at time of capture	8	61	69	3	12	15	2	36	38	3	13	16
Unwounded at time of capture	59	1288	1347	3	42	45	33	632	665	23	614	637
TOTAL Repatriated POW's	67	1349	1418	6	54	60	35	668	703	26	627	653

NOTE: The 2 nursing sisters are not included in the above chart. Unwounded at time of capture, they were repatriated under the regulations of the Geneva Convention.

*2 Grenadiers who died after release are included in Repatriated Prisoners of War.

**Figures for wounded are taken from official documents on file with War Service Records. Wounded prior to capture are included in Repatriated POW's.

***The 4 other ranks wounded prior to capture are included in Repatriated POW's.

Abbreviations: C Force HQ—Headquarters, C Force; Total includes HQ, Royal Rifles of Canada, and Winnipeg Grenadiers; OFF—Officers; OR—Other Ranks; All—All Ranks.

Appendix B

Honours and Awards

Victoria Cross

John Robert OSBORN, Warrant Officer Class II

At Hong Kong on the morning of 19th December 1941 a company of the Winnipeg Grenadiers to which Company Sergeant-Major Osborn belonged became divided during an attack on Mount Butler, a hill rising steeply above sea level. A part of the company led by Company Sergeant-Major Osborn captured the hill at the point of the bayonet and held it for three hours when, owing to the superior numbers of the enemy and to fire from an unprotected flank, the position became untenable. Company Sergeant-Major Osborn and a small group covered the withdrawal and when their turn came to fall back, Osborn single-handed engaged the enemy while the remainder successfully rejoined the company. Company Sergeant-Major Osborn had to run the gauntlet of heavy rifle and machine-gun fire. With no consideration for his own safety he assisted and directed stragglers to the new company position exposing himself to heavy enemy fire to cover their retirement. Wherever danger threatened he was there to encourage his men.

During the afternoon the company was cut off from the Battalion and completely surrounded by the enemy who were able to approach to within grenade-throwing distance of the slight depression which the company were holding. Several enemy grenades were thrown which Company Sergeant-Major Osborn picked up and threw back. The enemy threw a grenade which landed in a position where it was impossible to pick it up and return it in time. Shouting a warning to his comrades this gallant Warrant Officer threw himself on the grenade which exploded killing him instantly. His self sacrifice undoubtedly saved the lives of many others.

Company Sergeant-Major Osborn was an inspiring example to all throughout the defence which he assisted so magnificently in maintaining against an overwhelming enemy force for over eight and a half hours and in his death he displayed the highest quality of heroism and self-sacrifice.

Distinguished Service Order

Wells Arnold BISHOP, E.D., Major

Major Bishop commanded "C" Company, the Royal Rifles of Canada at Hong Kong in December 1941. At about 1930 hours, 18 December, the Japanese landed at Sau Ki Wan, Hong Kong, where positions were held by the 5/7 Rajput Regiment on the left flank of "C" Company positions in Lye Mun Gap. The enemy quickly infiltrated through this line and attempted in considerable force to penetrate through Lye Mun Gap towards Brigade and Battalion Headquarters at Tai Tam Gap. Major

Bishop, with great skill, so manoeuvred his force that, although heavily outnumbered and forced to retire slowly, he was able to prevent the enemy penetrating into Tai Tam Gap and saved the situation from turning into a complete disaster. During this action Major Bishop personally covered the retirement of his force, and his courage, skill and devoition to duty so inspired his men that they were able to cope with enormously superior forces until reinforcements became available to assist him. During the entire period of battle this officer continued to display conspicuous qualities of bravery and leadership and to inspire not only his own men but all ranks in the East Brigade sector and contributed greatly to the maintenance of the high morale necessary to sustain a continuous defence against increasingly overwhelming odds in an obviously hopeless situation. During captivity Major Bishop continued to display outstanding qualities of unselfishness, resolution and fortitude. He participated in all activities essential to the maintenance of health and morale, and contributed in a conspicuous manner in every way. This officer acted continuously in such a manner as to uphold the highest traditions of the service.

Ernest HODKINSON, Major

Major Hodkinson commanded Headquarters Company, the Winnipeg Grenadiers at Hong Kong in December 1941. On 19 December his commanding officer ordered him to take a composite company consisting of three platoons to relieve "D" Company at Wong Nei Chong, clear the area of enemy and attack Wong Nei Chong police station, a Japanese strong point. After overcoming enemy resistance, Major Hodkinson succeeded in reaching "D" Company Headquarters, and after reorganizing the company, proceeded with a patrol through the Japanese lines on a reconnaissance of the police station. Enroute, Major Hodkinson and his patrol successfully annihilated a Japanese section controlling a road block and removed it. Returning, he prepared his plan of attack on the police station which provided for a frontal assault in which he was to take part with a small patrol. This was to precede a major flanking attack by the remainder of the company. This plan was then put into effect, but was defeated by a superior enemy force estimated at one battalion. While unsuccessful in dislodging the enemy from the police station, Major Hodkinson and his patrol were successful in drawing the enemy's attention which permitted the remainder of his company to advance to its limit line. During this assault, Major Hodkinson was seriously wounded and all the members of his patrol were casualties. By this daring and well planned attack Major Hodkinson succeeded in a portion of his task by moving his company into a useful vantage point, inflicting many casualties and demoralized the enemy. Only greatly superior numbers prevented this attack being a complete success.

Military Cross

Frederick Temple ATKINSON, Captain

During the defence of Hong Kong in December 1941 Captain Atkinson was Adjutant of the Royal Rifles of Canada. From 5 to 25 December 1941, and particularly between the date of the Japanese landing on the Island of Hong Kong (the night of 18/19 December) up to the conclusion of hostilities, this officer displayed great energy, initiative and courage. In the early hours of 19 December Captain Atkinson went forward from Battalion Headquarters to select a position for "C"

Company which was being heavily pressed and gradually enveloped by the Japanese attackers. The situation on this part of the front was such that definite information could not be obtained until Captain Atkinson, by his initiative and courage contacted the company commander and brought back information that was vital to the defence of the area and to the correct disposition of the battalion. Again, on the morning of 20 December, he went forward on his own initiative with the attacking company, and, after obtaining information about the enemy, returned to Battalion Headquarters. Besides his onerous duties of Adjutant, Captain Atkinson performed many useful and hazardous functions which assisted materially in prolonging the defence.

Uriah LAITE, Honorary Captain

Honorary Captain Laite was Regimental Chaplain to the Winnipeg Grenadiers at Hong Kong in December 1941. On 18 December at Wong Nei Chong Gap he was with a small group of men holding a position which denied the use of the main road across the Island to the Japanese. Early on the morning of 19 December the enemy attacked this area and the position was cut off from all contact. Practically all personnel at Wong Nei Chong were casualties, including officers. Water, food and ammunition were rationed. No medical personnel were present. Due to the strategic value of the position it was constantly under attack, but due to the determination and gallantry of the defenders, held out for three days until 22 December when, with all ammunition, food and water gone, no further resistance was possible. Of a total of approximately forty, thirty-six were wounded. During this long and trying period Honorary Captain Laite tended the wounded night and day without medical supplies, as well as giving spiritual and moral comfort. Undoubtedly his efforts not only saved some lives, but assisted materially in the recovery of health of many of these men. Due to his efforts in interceding with the Japanese after the capitulation of the post, many of the wounded were taken prisoner instead of being murdered on the spot, as the Japanese intended to murder all those who could not walk. The Japanese were so impressed with the good work of Honorary Captain Laite in attending to the wounded that they released him and directed him to return to the Battalion Headquarters. Throughout the term of imprisonment, Honorary Captain Laite worked tirelessly for the benefit of his men, frequently endangering his health by close contact with the many dangerous diseases ravaging the prisoners of war. In every respect this good man possessed the finest qualities of his corps and cannot be too highly commended for his courage and selfless devotion to duty.

Robert William PHILIP, Captain

On the night of 18/19 December 1941, "D" Company the Winnipeg Grenadiers were in their allotted positions at Wong Nei Chong, Hong Kong. A Japanese landing in force cut through this area—the centre of the Island—and isolated "D" Company Headquarters from No. 17 and 18 Platoons. The Japanese assaulted the company headquarters, beginning at 0700 hours the morning of 18 December and secured the medical shelter about seventy-five yards from the headquarters shelter. At approximately 0800 hours the company commander was killed while attempting to dislodge snipers, leaving Captain Philip in command. Captain Philip advised the battalion commander of the situation and was told to hold his position and deny enemy use of the main road crossing the Island. Relief and reinforcements were promised, but due to strong Japanese positions so close to the shelter this promise could not be fulfilled. The strength of Captain Philip's command at this time was approximately forty men of whom twelve were casualties. By 1400 hours Captain Philip was severely wounded by an enemy grenade, losing his right eye and suffering chest and leg wounds from shrapnel. Nine other casualties were also reported. This gallant little band, under constant fire and within grenade throwing distance of an aggressive and merciless enemy, held out for three days, at which time every one of the forty had been wounded, thirty-six severely and the other four slightly. Throughout this long and dangerous battle, Captain Philip, although seriously and painfully wounded retained control of the situation, receiving the reports of his Second-in-Command, Lieutenant Blackwood, and directing him in the defence of the position. So stubborn was the struggle put up by this small and badly battered group that the Japanese used a great number of men in many futile assaults and repeatedly urged them to surrender. On the morning of 22 December, realizing that the situation was hopeless, no ammunition, food or water being left, line communications being cut, and every man a casualty, Captain Philip consulted a Lieutenant-Colonel of the Hong Kong Volunteer Defence Corps who was seriously wounded and present in the shelter at the time and advised him of the situation. The Lieutenant-Colonel instructed Captain Philip to surrender, no other course being open. The action of this gallant group of men denied the use of the Island road to the Japanese and prevented exploitation of their initial success, undoubtedly gaining valuable time for the re-organization of the Island defence. Over two hundred enemy dead were estimated by Captain Philip prior to leaving the position, and unquestionably the overall casualties inflicted by this small body of men must have proved a serious drain on the enemy. Of this action, Major-General Maltby, commander of Hong Kong says: "A company of Winnipeg Grenadiers fought so magnificently the Japs believed the sector was held by two battalions. When it was over, the Nips would not believe they had been opposed there for three days by only one company. They were incredulous and indignant and they showed it by slapping the faces of the Canadian officers of that company when they interrogated them."

Thomas Alexander BLACKWOOD, Lieutenant

Lieutenant Blackwood was attached to "D" Company Headquarters the Winnipeg Grenadiers at Hong Kong, December 1941. On the night of 18/19 December this headquarters was located at Wong Nei Chong where a Japanese landing in force brought it under immediate attack. As this post controlled the main road across the Island orders were received to hold on at any cost. Early in the action the company commander was killed, and the Second-in-Command, Captain Robert W. Philip, was severely wounded. Lieutenant Blackwood displayed great courage and marked skill in carrying out the orders given him by Captain Philip. The fact that this small body of forty men held out for three days, although short of ammunition, food and water, and caused very heavy enemy casualties, is in no small way attributable to Lieutenant Blackwood. The fact that the Japanese were denied the use of the main road across the Island undoubtedly assisted and prolonged the defence of Hong Kong materially. During this time a report was received that an officer who was obviously wounded was lying about sixty yards in advance of the foremost position and was unable to get to shelter due to his wounds and intense enemy small arms fire. Lieutenant Blackwood and H.6132 Private William Morris volunteered to bring the officer in. After considerable difficulty they brought back safely to shelter Lieutenant-Colonel R.D. Walker, OBE, MC, of the Hong Kong Volunteer Defence Corps. Lieutenant-Colonel Walker was found to be suffering from gun shot wounds in both legs. This difficult and dangerous task took place when the Japanese were in complete possession of the area surrounding the post, and located so close to it they could at times crawl within grenade throwing distance. Lieutenant Blackwood's courage and devotion to duty throughout this arduous period were a source of inspiration to all those around him.

Collinson Alexander BLAVER, Lieutenant

During the Hong Kong operation, Lieutenant Blaver commanded No. 9 Platoon of the Royal Rifles of Canada. Throughout the period 8 to 25 December 1941 this officer displayed great courage, dash, coolness and leadership, and particularly on the night of 18/19 December when he was ordered, with a force of forty men, to proceed to Mount Parker and clear the Japanese from it. This necessitated a climb of some fifteen hundred feet of precipitous mountain slopes under great difficulties. On nearing the top of the mountain, the enemy opened up heavy mortar, machine gun and hand grenade fire at very close range. As the attack developed it became evident that the enemy greatly outnumbered the attacking force and were strongly entrenched. The order was given to withdraw and Lieutenant Blaver with two non-commissioned officers remained behind to cover the withdrawal of the men. Both non-commissioned officers were killed and Lieutenant Blaver wounded, but he managed to hold the enemy for a sufficient length of time to allow his men to withdraw to a new position. Lieutenant Blaver's courageous action undoubtedly saved the lives of many of his men and his conduct throughout the operation was consistently in the best traditions of the service.

William Francis NUGENT, Lieutenant

Lieutenant Nugent was a platoon commander of the Winnipeg Grenadiers at Hong Kong. On the night of 24th December 1941 his platoon was in a defensive position on Bennet's Hill when at about 1900 hours the Japanese heavily shelled it with mortar fire for about one hour and then attacked in force, hoping to secure the heights which commanded the only cross Island road left in our hands at this time. His platoon sergeant was seriously wounded as well as two of his remaining non-commissioned officers, and Lieutenant Nugent received a crippling leg wound. In spite of these conditions, he succeeded in driving off the main force of the Japanese attack and, in addition, his platoon inflicted heavy casualties on the enemy. Although the platoons on his flanks were driven back by the fierceness of the enemy attack, Lieutenant Nugent held his position until relieved the next day when he was hospitalized. This officer's bravery, leadership and ability in action denied a vital position to the enemy.

Francis Gavan POWER, Lieutenant

Lieutenant Power commanded No. 17 Platoon "D" Company the Royal Rifles of Canada at Hong Kong in December 1941. He showed conspicuous courage and leadership throughout the entire defensive action from 18 December to 25 December. On 21 December in the face of heavy machine gun fire he led an attack on enemy positions on Bridge Hill which was pressed home with the utmost vigour and daring. By this successful attack, during which many enemy were killed, a general advance on the Bridge Hill main position was made possible, which when completed, relieved the general situation temporarily. During this engagement Lieutenant Power displayed qualities of courage, dash and coolness which were an inspiration to his men and contributed greatly to the successful outcome of the operation. Again on 25 December his platoon took part in an attack on Stanley Village. In the face of heavy enemy fire and without support by artillery or mortars, Lieutenant Power led his platoon with conspicuous success and again displayed outstanding courage and leadership. During this action Lieutenant Power was wounded.

Distinguished Conduct Medal

Colin Alden STANDISH, Company Quartermaster-Sergeant

Standish was Company Quartermaster-Sergeant of "C" Company, Royal Rifles of Canada at HongKong in December 1941. During the night of 18/19 December at Lye Mun Gap he showed conspicuous bravery in maintaining a constant supply of ammunition to the forward positions of this company which were heavily engaged with the enemy. During the course of his duties he came under extremely heavy mortar and rifle fire. His vehicle received a direct hit during the course of the action, but despite this, he made necessary repairs under fire to maintain his supply. In an endeavour to cut the supply line, the enemy had infiltrated behind our lines, submitting supply personnel to heavy and constant sniping fire. This did not stop Standish from travelling back and forth over this dangerous ground to keep forward positions supplied. During intervals of unloading vehicles in the forward area, Standish took an active part in the action. His conduct was an inspiration to all ranks, and due to his gallantry and efforts it was possible to hold this position until the order arrived to withdraw. This non-commissioned officer never relaxed in his duty, and was conspicuous in his bravery during the entire campaign in securing and delivering food, water and other supplies to the outposts under fire and against heavy odds. At times when transport was not available he carried rations on his back, taking time off to hunt snipers who were a constant threat to all personnel. During the whole period as a prisoner of war he carried on with the same spirit of self-sacrifice, and although quite ill, he always saw that his men received all that was available to reduce the misery of Japanese camp life.

Derek Everard RIX, Corporal

Corporal Rix was in command of a section of the Winnipeg Grenadiers at Hong Kong in December 1941. At dawn of 19 December when the Japanese attacked the Wong Nei Chong area, Corporal Rix and his section were cut off from their platoon. They worked their way from their open position on the hillside above the Blue Pool Valley to join a section of the Hong Kong Volunteer Defence Corps who were holding pill box No. 2 on the slope of Jardine's Lookout and cooperated in the defence of the pill box during the remainder of the morning. At about noon a patrol of Japanese succeeded in reaching pill box No. 1 (about fifty yards further up the steep hillside) and heavily engaged the crew, who were soon in a very difficult situation. After an unsuccessful relief attack by some of the crew of pill box No. 2, Corporal Rix with a mixed party of Winnipeg Grenadiers and Hong Kong Volunteers made another attempt. They were under fire from across the valley and had to climb a steep hillside in the face of the enemy, but succeeded in wiping out the surviving Japanese around pill box No. 1, thereby regaining control of both pill boxes for some hours longer. As pill box No. 1 was no longer of use due to the machine guns being damaged, and the loopholes being under continuous close range rifle fire, Corporal Rix took up a very percarious position close to pill box No. 1 until he was wounded in the right hand when he returned to pill box No. 2 for treatment. Later when enemy pressure increased and there was no sign of relief, the Hong Kong Volunteer Defence Corps officer in command gave leave to walking wounded to retire, but Corporal Rix preferred to stay and see the action through to a finish. Corporal Rix proved himself an able and courageous non-commissioned officer and his conduct throughout was a credit to his unit and the Canadian army.

Military Medal

Stanley Walter WRIGHT, Company Quartermaster-Sergeant, Royal Rifles of Canada
Emile BERNARD, Sergeant, Royal Rifles of Canada
Selden Grant STODDARD, Sergeant, Royal Rifles of Canada
Cecil Thomas WHALEN, Sergeant, Winnipeg Grenadiers
Murray Thomas GOODENOUGH, Lance-Sergeant, Royal Rifles of Canada
Lionel Curtis SPELLER, Corporal, Royal Canadian Corps of Signals
Ronald Edward ATKINSON, Lance-Corporal, Winnipeg Grenadiers
Meirion PRICE, Lance-Corporal, Winnipeg Grenadiers
John Leslie VARLEY, Lance-Corporal, Royal Rifles of Canada
Ernest Irwin BENNETT, Rifleman, Royal Rifles of Canada
William MORRIS, Private, Winnipeg Grenadiers
Gordon Edward WILLIAMSON, Private, Winnipeg Grenadiers

Mentioned in Despatches

Henry William HOCK, Major
Malcolm Thomas Gordon MACAULEY, DCM, ED, Major
William Barker BRADLEY, Lieutenant
John Edward DUNDERDALE, Lieutenant
James Forsyth ROSS, Lieutenant (killed in action)
Arthur Beresford SCOTT, Lieutenant
Maurice D'AVIGNON, Sergeant
George Stuart MACDONNELL, Sergeant
Kenneth Edward PORTER, Sergeant
Charles John SHARP, Sergeant, Royal Canadian Corps of Signals (killed in action)
Leslie Robert STICKLES, Sergeant
James Murray THOM, Sergeant
Charles WATSON, Sergeant

John Joseph FITZPATRICK, Corporal (killed in action)
Edwin HARRISON, Corporal (killed in action)
Lorne Rayburn LATIMER, Corporal (killed in action)
Ernest Charles MCFARLAND, Corporal
George William MCRAE, Corporal (killed in action)
Sydney Albert SHEFFER, Corporal
Edwin George SMITH, Lance-Corporal
Frank BROWN, Private
Bernard CASTONGUAY, Rifleman
Robert DAMANT, Rifleman, Royal Canadian Corps of Signals (killed in action)
Morgan Isaac DAVIES, Rifleman
Aubery Peacock FLEGG, Private
Nelson Carlyle GALBRAITH, Private
Norman Charles MATTHEWS, Private
Lloyd Logan ROBLEE, Rifleman
James Austen WALLACE, Rifleman

Appendix C

Report by Lieutenant General Charles Foulkes

Report by Lieutenant General Charles Foulkes, Chief of the General Staff to the Minister of National Defence, 9 February 1948

1. I have had the Drew Report of 11 Jul 42 examined along with the Duff and Maltby Reports. Attached is a detailed examination of the various points raised by Mr. Drew with our comments. It appears to me that there would be no useful purpose in continuing to examine and re-examine either the conditions of training or equipment of this Force. I am of the opinion, and it is shared by Field Marshal Montgomery, that the outcome of the Japanese attack on Hong Kong would not have been changed to any appreciable extent had these two battalions been trained and equipped to the same standard as the divisions which invaded France in 1944.

2. The most regrettable feature arising out of the inadequate training and equipping was the effect on the morale and fighting efficiency of the Canadian troops, which unfortunately was interpreted by their British superiors as a lack of courage, willingness to fight and even in some cases cowardice. On the other hand this had caused in the minds of Canadian troops bitterness, lack of confidence and resentment in their British superiors. However, you will recall that after discussing this whole question with Field Marshal Montgomery he agreed to have these offending paragraphs taken out of the Maltby report. Therefore, unless this case is reopened these regrettable circumstances can remain in oblivion.

3. I would strongly recommend that every effort should be made to avoid reopening this Hong Kong enquiry. Much of the evidence given at the time of the enquiry in respect to quality of training and equipment of these troops was based on the very limited experience of Canadian officers gained in the first two years of war before Canadian troops were actively engaged in operations. A great deal has been learned since then about training and equipment and it is very doubtful if the same officers who gave the evidence at the time of the Duff report would make similar statements in view of the lessons learnt from the last war. I doubt if Home, Price and others would agree now that they considered that these troops were adequately trained for war. There is also some doubt about Home himself, he was removed from Commanding a Company in the R.C.R. in 1939 as unfit to command in war, and later was appointed to the R.R.C.

4. In regard to training of troops I would like to point out that the most damaging evidence is that which appears in a cable from the late Brigadier Lawson of 15 Nov 41:—

"Both units contain excellent material and a number of good instructors. Having been employed most of their time since mobilization on coast defence duties, neither has done much field training even of sub units. Neither had completed its Tests of Elementary Training for infantry weapons since many of these have not previously been available for them."

Tests of Elementary Training are those tests which the soldier is required to carry out before he completes recruit training. This evidence shows conclusively that even the recruit training was not completed. Therefore, it is very difficult, by any stretch of the imagination, to say that a unit which contains men who have not completed their recruit training is fit for battle. We found in training formations for war that even after recruit training, section, platoon, company and battalion exercises had to be carried out. Then battle innoculation using live ammunition and exercises in every phase of operations were necessary. I can say this without fear of contradiction that even after four years of arduous training I found the 2nd Canadian Division just ready for battle when we landed in North West Europe, and even after the first battle it was necessary for me to make several very serious changes in order to win further battles.

5. The training of men for war is like training a race horse for a race. It is necessary to re-train after each battle, eliminating the weak, tired, or battleweary, and correcting the mistakes of the last battle to ensure victory in the next. I would emphasize that General Crerar summed this up in evidence on page 33 of the Duff report:—

"To my best knowledge and experience however no battalion of any Army even if fully equipped has ever completed its training. Training is an unceasing process."

Therefore, I feel that no matter how many experts are produced no finality can be reached on this question.

6. The statements made by Mr. Drew regarding the training on the 2 and 3 inch mortar and the handling of grenades are indefensible. No commander responsible for the success of a battle would ever agree that a mortar platoon can be efficient without the most intensive practise with live ammunition.

7. With regard to the letter of 16 Jul 42, Mr. Drew's case appears to be that the decision to send a force to Hong Kong was based on the facts that garrison troops only were required and that time would be available for the completion of training when they arrived in Hong Kong. He claims that further information was received from the UK in a message of 24 Oct 41 which would indicate a change of circumstances in regard to the role of the Canadian troops to be carried out in Hong Kong. He indicates that the contents of this message was known by the officers of the Department. I have had the files of DMO&P searched and there is no evidence of the receipt of any such message. This is also confirmed by the late General Stuart. Therefore, it would appear that if such a message was received it was not passed to the Department of National Defence.

8. I do not think it is necessary to comment on whether or not the decision to send the Force should have been reconsidered at that time as that would be a matter of higher policy.

9. I am returning copy No. 4 of both letters.

[signed]   Charles Foulkes
Lieutenant-General,
Chief of the General Staff.

CF/3355/fjl

Military Comment

Duff Report
Duff   Drew
p.4   p.2

1. It is apparent that the Department of National Defence was entirely dependent on information provided by the Government of the UK as to whether or not early attack was possible. There is nothing in either the Duff Report or the Appendix to the Report to indicate that the Canadian Army had available to them appreciations and recommendations from a Canadian Joint Intelligence Committee or a Canadian Joint Planning Committee which would enable them to discuss the relative merits of sending a force to Hong Kong.

[Author's comment: This is in response to Drew's charge that the US/Canada Joint Defence Board should have been the vehicle whereby the threat of war with Japan would have been passed to Canada. However the JDB dealt only with matters pertaining to the immediate security of North America.]

4   2

2. From a military point of view it is hard to reconcile the CGS's comment "both" battalions designated "are units of proven efficiency" with the fact that certain personnel had not even completed basic training, little training had been carried out with the 2" mortar, no firing of live ammunition had been done with the 3" mortar, and troops had not been trained in handling live 36 grenades. In addition to individual basic training, there does not appear in the Report to be any indication that either battalion had carried out any form of sub-unit or unit training.

[This comment on Drew's charge concerning lack of training is accurate, except for the fact that both battalions had done a little sub-unit training, though insufficient to affect the main issue.]

8   2

3. It is doubtful whether such vehicles as the water tanks about which there is much controversy would have greatly altered the outcome of the action at Hong Kong. Similarly, it is doubtful whether the provision of "A" vehicles for the battalions would have delayed very greatly the inevitable outcome of the Hong Kong action. Nevertheless, to attempt to carry on an action without the battalion mortar carriers and the company ammunition trucks is almost a hopeless task.

[This comment, while accurate, skirts the issue. The MT would not have altered the outcome, but it is certain that lack of transport and water caused unnecessary hardship to the defenders, a point the Duff Commission was charged specifically to investigate.]

4. From the Report it is quite evident that there was a definite lack of simple army organization in the movement of the vehicles for Force "C" and in the information regarding the movement of these vehicles.

5. It is difficult to understand what the Report means by a "task of considerable difficulty". If the task referred to is that of the despatch of two battalions, presumably for garrison duties, the description of such a task as "considerable difficulty" can only be interpreted as meaning that the organization of the Department of National Defence was woefully lacking. As divisions had previously been despatched "task" cannot be construed as applying to the despatch of the two battalions. On the other hand, if "task" is considered as the operation of assisting to defend Hong Kong, the Duff Report would appear to be inconsistent as in the first part it endeavours to prove that the authorities despatched this force quickly and rapidly merely to bolster a garrison in the light of the fact that they did not expect an early attack by the Japanese.

[Duff meant by "task of considerable difficulty" the selection, equipping, and embarkation of C Force.]

6. This same point has been covered under Serial 1 of the Drew Letter above.

7. It is difficult to comment on the percentage of men who had not undergone 16 weeks' basic military training. From the Report it appears that the 6% refers to the actual overall total strength of the two battalions. 6% of the total strength would represent a much greater proportion of untrained personnel within the actual fighting ranks of the units depending upon how many of these untrained personnel were required for administrative or battle troops. From Section IV of the Report Page 35, 136 men were required to bring both battalions up to war establishment and 300 additional men were required as first reinforcements to both battalions.

[As only four men with under 16 weeks' training went to C Force HQ, the majority of partially-trained personnel went to the two battalions. Whether they went direct to the ranks or as first reinforcements is irrelevant—first reinforcements can expect to go into battle as soon as casualties occur.]

8. It is impossible to condone the remarks of certain senior Canadian officers concerning the fact that these units were of proven efficiency when, in fact, they had not even fired their 3" mortars. The efficient use of the 3" mortar results only from long practice in range and tactical firing. While simple of operation, it is a weapon

whose maximum efficiency can only be obtained through skilled sighting and constant firing.

The remarks referring to the 3" mortar above apply even more so to the 2" mortar which is practically always used by observed fire. To handle efficiently the 2" mortar requires constant practice. It is a most efficient weapon when used by trained personnel; its value as a weapon becomes almost nil in the hands of untrained personnel. As regards the anti-tank rifle, very little additional training is necessary to convert a trained rifleman to an anti-tank rifleman.

[*"Certain senior officers" include, of course, Major General Crerar and most of the General Staff associated with the despatch of C Force. Foulkes could, however, have said in mitigation that as both 3-inch and 2-inch mortars were practically non-existent in Canada at the time, this criterion meant no unit in Canada in 1941 could be considered efficient. The two Indian battalions in Hong Kong were in no better state regarding mortar supply and training.*]

9. The remarks concerning A vehicles as for Serial 3 above maintain here.

10. On the grounds that the CGS expressed his opinion that there was no military objection to the acceptance of the proposal, it would appear that that officer had come to that conclusion as a result of the recommendations of his staff. The Report indicates that all opinion regarding the acceptance of the proposal was made on the communications received from the War Office, some of which are still privileged documents. However, there is nothing in the Report to show that the Department of National Defence had a staff which could work out the pros and cons of accepting this proposal as a calculated risk of war. In other words, the decision was whether or not to despatch troops based on the information available from the UK Government as opposed to whether or not we agreed with the information provided by the UK Government as to whether or not this was a sound military venture.

[*This is perhaps the crux of the issue. The author cannot agree with Lieutenant General Foulkes. If Crerar and his staff could not work out the "pros and cons of accepting this proposal as a calculated risk or war" they had no business calling themselves a General Staff. Most of these men had studied Hong Kong, some bad been there. They had access to all the relevant studies, defence schemes, and military intelligence. The last sentence is pure bureaucratese. One may ask whether or not to buy a car based on the information provided by the salesman as*

8 7

3 8

opposed to whether or not one agrees with the information provided by the salesman as to whether or not that car is a sound purchase. In both cases, one should shop around. None of the General Staff ever asked for a report on Hong Kong at the time. Being responsible for the conduct of Canada's military war effort, they were sold a bill of goods on the strength of one telegram. When the CGS expressed his opinion that there was no military objection to the operation, he was effectively saying, "Although I haven't looked under the hood, I agree with the salesman."]

11. There is nothing to indicate that the Department of National Defence had an organized Joint Planning Committee, Joint Planning Staff, Joint Intelligence Committee and Joint Intelligence Staff. The remarks concerning our dependence on the Government of the UK for information regarding the probability of an attack as stated above apply here.

12. Again, this controversy hinges on the fact that the Canadian authorities were completely dependent on information received from the UK.

13. In the light of experience of World War II it is impractical to consider that all that is required to build a Canadian fighting force is to take the right type of Canadian off the street, put him into uniform and expect him to fight. Granted the right leadership and the right type of men will greatly reduce the time factor in producing an efficient unit, nevertheless there are so many other factors affecting the production of an efficient unit that it is not a justifiable risk to send troops out of the country to an area where there is the slightest possibility of active operations taking place unless the troops are adequately trained for field operations and fit to fight.

[This is in reply to testimony of officers at the Commission that as long as the Commanding Officers picked the men, they could "whack them into shape" in no time, as spirit, initiative, and self-reliance are all-important and can cover a multitude of defects. Foulkes properly labels this a fallacy, but the testimony regarding this was so strong that Duff accepted it. Drew's witnesses, mostly First World War officers with battle experience, gave opposite testimony, but this was discounted. Foulke's last sentence really sums up the whole situation concerning training.]

14. While there is little difficulty in training a soldier who has mastered the rifle to use effectively a light

4   10

4   11

7   14

4,7   15

machine gun or an anti-tank rifle, the soldier cannot be considered to be trained in these weapons until he has actually carried out considerable amount of firing, both at range and battle range targets. As stated above, the effective use of the 2" and 3" mortar requires considerable training in the firing of the weapon and in the observation and correction of fire. It is possible that certain individual training could have been completed, on board ship but to rely on shipboard training as the sole means of bringing individual training up to the standard where troops are fit to enter active operations is not consistent with present day military thinking.

15. It is not possible to reconcile the remarks of the VCGS [Lt. Gen. Stuart] "in my opinion we were generally adequately trained to undertake defensive responsibilities such as those in prospect in Hong Kong" with the Report of Brigadier Lawson that neither of the battalions had completed its tests of elementary training for infantry weapons. It has always been considered that before even the smallest form of sub-unit training could be carried out with any degree of efficiency all tests of elementary training should have been completed.

16. Probably the only time the officers and men of a unit are known to each other on the scale which is ideal is before the unit takes part in its first operation. As a result of operations, units are required to absorb varying percentages of officers and other ranks who on occasions may have to join the unit in the middle of an operation. So long as the reinforce-personnel are adequately trained and know their jobs, mutual understanding within sub-units quickly develops.

[In the case of C Force, neither the reinforcements nor the units were adequately trained.]

17. As stated above, soldiers completely trained and practiced in the rifle and bren gun can be trained to handle effectively the anti-tank rifle and the tommy gun in a comparatively short time. However, it is essential that before a man can be considered to be efficient in the handling of these two weapons, he must have carried out both range and battle range firing.

[No range or battle range firing was carried out with these two weapons.]

18. As stated above, the efficiency in the use of the 2" mortar depends in the most part on the actual amount of firing which is carried out with the weapon.

33 17

43 17

5 18

5 18

7	19	19. These cross references are a repetition of previous comment regarding training on board ship.
31, 27	19	20. The efficient tactical employment of the 3" mortar does require a great deal of handling and firing. A mortar crew cannot be considered to be efficient in the use of their weapons unless they have actually carried out firing.
27, 28	20	21. Although it may be possible to reach a legal conclusion based on the available evidence, it is certainly not a practical consideration to accept the fact that men can use effectively the Mills bomb if they have only practiced with dummy bombs. It is impractical to ask a soldier to use a live weapon for the first time in active operations. *[The last sentence summarizes the situation regarding weapon training.]*
58	20	22. No comment. Any such lack of energy certainly within 1 Cdn Corps would have provided suitable grounds for a field general court martial. *[Re: MT for C Force.]*
60	21-23	23. This is another repetition of the controversy regarding the A echelon vehicles of the battalions. From the Report it would appear that the vehicles hired were of a commercial type and were merely for the purpose of off-loading equipment from the ships. As stated above, the A echelon vehicles of a battalion are most essential to carry out its task. It might well be that the terrain was such that the movement of vehicles was impossible and that, therefore, it could be said that the battalions were not impaired in their task by not having these vehicles. This point could only be ascertained by a detailed study on the ground in question. But apart from this, it is impossible to think of sending a unit into action without its ammunition and weapon-carrying vehicles. *[The transport Lawson hired was only for moving from dock to barracks. As far as the terrain of Hong Kong was concerned, MT would have been useful in the many withdrawals and counterattacks despite (or because of) the hilly nature of the Island.]*

Acknowledgments, Sources, & Notes

The author has had the assistance of a number of people without whose efforts this book would, at the worst, have been totally impossible or, at the best, vastly inferior.

First and foremost, I am indebted to Michael Childs, on whose superlative research the book depends. It incorporates most of his research, many of his ideas, and some of his words. I am also grateful to Anita Burdett for her invaluable work in London and to Eve Elman for the research on the post-war period.

I wish to express my appreciation for the courtesy and assistance of the staffs of the Public Archives of Canada and of the Directorate of History of the Department of National Defence. Their co-operation was up to its usual high standard.

My thanks also to Hugh Halliday for taking time from his vacation in England to select and order photographs when I could not do so due to the postal strike. The interest and enthusiasm of George Hopp in producing the maps and of Don Connolly in creating the cover and end-paper art was a pleasure to see.

My very sincere thanks are due to Heather Ebbs, who carried out the production of this book with skill and patience and whose editorial ability has vastly improved the text. I am grateful as well to Leslie Jones, without whose enthusiasm and adaptability the project would have taken far longer to complete.

Finally there is my wife Elizabeth, without whose unfailing support and assistance I could accomplish little. I am more grateful than I can possibly say.

SOURCES

Department of National Defence, Directorate of History [referred to as DHist]

File Nos.

002.D11   (D3) Supplement to London Gazette 29 Jan 1948 (Maltby Report)

111.13   (D47) Training reports
         (D52) Training reports
         (D56) Training reports
         (D63) Training reports
         (D66) Memoranda by Ralston and Foulkes on Hong Kong inquiries
         (D72) Drew's speech 12 Jan 1942
         (D74) Article in Macleans, July 1968, by Ian Adams

112.3M1009 (D124) Far East Intelligence Summaries

168.009   (D8) Intelligence file—notes on Japanese Army, Aug. 1941

325.009   (D516) Comments on developments in Far East by Col. Mullahy

352.009   (D1) DCGS Miscellaneous file on Hong Kong Expedition Dec. 1941

593.   (D1) "C" Force HQ Diaries
         (D3) War Diary, Royal Rifles of Canada, December 1941
         (D6) Reports on "C" Force
         (D7) Report of conditions affecting Canadian POW's at Hong Kong
         (D8) Notes on atrocities in POW camps
         (D12) Letter, Brig. Andrew Peffers to Brig. W.H.S. Macklin, 22 Sept. 1945
         (D15) Signals Report "C" Force
         (D16) Lawson's diary, Oct.-Dec. 1941
         (D17) Reports of Medical Officers "C" Force
         (D23) Situation Reports from Hong Kong, 8-25 Dec. 1941
         (D24) "C" Force Diary, 10 Aug.-2 Oct. 1945
         (D25) Honours and Awards, "C" Force
         (D27) Report by Maj. R.J.C. Hamilton, trip to Manila, 1945
         (D28) Draft narrative on Canadian participation
         (D33) War Diary, Winnipeg Grenadiers, 8-25 December 1941
         (D35) Interview with Maj. G.B. Puddicimbe, prosecutor in War Crimes Trial,
               11 July 1947
         (D37) Interview with Hong Kong participants
         (D42) Record of action of HKVDC
593.008   (D1) Troopers to Far East
593.010   (D3) "A Medical Officer in Hong Kong" by Brig. J.N.B. Crawford
593.013   (D5) Canadian Reinforcements
         (D7) Statement by Col. Doi
         (D14) Defence requirements Hong Kong
         (D20) Reports on Defence of Hong Kong
         (D21) Hong Kong Policy
         (D22) Situation Reports from Hong Kong, Dec. 1941
593.014   (D2) Hong Kong Defence Scheme
593.018   (D1) Extracts from War Diary, East Brigade, RA
         (D3) Diary of "C" Coy, Royal Rifles
593.023   (D1) Hong Kong, Intelligence Reports 1941

840.013   (D1) Far East Defence 1921-39
         (D2) Defence in Far East 1929-39

951.003   (D23) Defence Policy, Hong Kong 1938
952.001   (D1) History of Army section, Imperial Japanese GHQ

982.011   (D1) Account by Maj. Gen. Tanaka and Maj. Gen. Shoji
         (D2) Account by Lt. Gen. Ito Takeo

982.013   (D1) History of 38th Japanese Division in World War II
                (D4) Hong Kong Operations Japanese Side, Air Force
                (D93) War Cabinet Draft Narrative on Defence in Far East
982.023   (D12) Draft Charge Sheet, Tanaka
                (D13) Draft Charge Sheet, Maj. Gen. Shoji
982.045   (D1) 38th Division Order of Battle of Dec. 1941

Public Archives of Canada

RG2   Orders in Council, PC8020, 1941 and PC4267, 1952
                7C, Cabinet War Committee, reels C4653A, C4654, C4875, and C4876

RG24 DND Vol 2203, file HQ 54-27-70-14 AG-POW files
                2266, file HQ 54-28-1192-1 Expenses for Hong Kong inquiry
                2865, file HQ 58902 miscellaneous file on Hong Kong
                5823, file S-20-6-20 Despatch of "C" Force
                13806, "C" Force Diary
                15229, War Diary, Royal Rifles of Canada
                15291, War Diary, Winnipeg Grenadiers

RG25   Department of External Affairs; files on relations with Japan, Canadians
                at Hong Kong, and on publications of reports on fighting at Hong Kong

RG33/120   Duff Royal Commission; Exhibits, etc.

MG26   J King Papers; subject files, mainly on Japan, and Strategy and Progress of the
                War, and diaries for the relevant period.

MG27, III B11 Ralston Papers
                D22 Hanson Papers

MG30   E157 Crerar Papers
                E328 Diaries of Frank W. Ebdon

MG32   C3 Drew Papers

Great Britain Public Record Office

WO106/   2364 1937 Report of Defences
                2366 July 1938 Notes Maj. Gen. Grasett
                2376 Jan 1939 New Policy, Notes for Col. Eady
                2371 May 1939 Report of Defences Required
                2375 1938-40 Telegrams between GOC Hong Kong and War Office
                2401 and 2401A 8-25 Dec 1941 Operations at Hong Kong
                2409 Policy re Hong Kong
                2412 Sept 1941-Feb 1942 Hong Kong, Canadian Reinforcements
                2424 1942 Telegrams, War Office and Overseas Authorities
                2426 Report to Lt. Col. Lamb, Fortress Engineers
                4872 Visits of Maj.Gen. Macready and Mr. Ralston to England
                4900 Canadian Government Telegrams
                5362 Dec 1941 Hong Kong, Canadian part in defence

Printed Sources

Butler, J.R.M., ed.
Grand Strategy. Vol.1 ("History of the Second World War, United Kingdom Military
Series") London, H.M.S.O., 1956.

Carew, Tim
The Fall of Hong Kong. [London], Anthony Blond, 1961. [referred to as Carew 1]
Hostages to Fortune. London, Hamish Hamilton, 1971. [referred to as Carew 2]

Chan, Lau Kit-Ching
"The Hong Kong Question during the Pacific War (1941-45)" in the *Journal of Imperial and Commonwealth History*, Oct. 1973, pp. 56-78.

Churchill, Winston Spencer
The Grand Alliance. New York, Bantam, 1962.

Ferguson, Ted
Desperate Siege: The Battle of Hong Kong. Toronto, Doubleday, 1980.

House of Commons Debates (*Hansard*)
10-11 Sept. 1945, 20 Feb. 1948, 6 June 1950, 22 June 1964, 3 Aug. 1964, 22 June 1967, 28 Oct. 1969.

House of Commons *Sessional Papers*
Proceedings of the Standing Committee on Veterans Affairs, May 1960, May 1961, Dec. 1963, May 1966, May 1972.

Lindsay, Oliver
The Lasting Honour. London, Hamish Hamilton, 1978.

Penny, A.G.
Royal Rifles of Canada, a Short History. 1962 (100th Anniversary Booklet).

Power, Charles Gavin
A Party Politician: The Memoirs of Chubby Power. Toronto, Macmillan, 1966.

Proulx, Benjamin A.
Underground from Hong Kong. New York, Dutton, 1943.

Richardson, H.J.
Canadian Pension Commission Report of a Study of Disabilities and Problems of Hong Kong Veterans 1964-1965.

Stacey, Charles Perry
Six Years of War. Ottawa, Queen's Printer, 1955.

Vancouver Daily Province. 21 June 1948. *Victoria Daily Times*. 13 June 1964.

REFERENCES

Pg		
6	1	DHist 840.013 (D1)
	2	W0106/2366
7	3	W0106/2364
	4	DHist 840.013 (D1)
	5	W0106/2366
	6	W0106/2365
	7	Lindsay
8	8	DHist 840.013 (D1)
	9	W0106/2370
	10	W0106/2366
9	11	W0106/2371
10	12	Ralston, v.46
	13	King, v.402
	14	DHist 593.013 (D21)
11	15	W0106/2409
	16	DHist 593.013(D21)
	17	W0106/2409
12	18	Ibid
	19	Ibid
	20	Ibid

15	1	RG25, v.1696
16	2	DHist, 840.013(D1)
	3	Ibid
	4	Ralston, v.46
17	5	RG2, 7C
	6	Ibid
18	7	King, v.402
	8	Ibid
	9	Ibid
	10	Ibid
	11	Ibid
19	12	Ibid
	13	RG2, 7C
	14	Ibid
	15	King, v.369
	16	King, v.407
	17	Ibid
20	18	RG2, 7C
	19	Ibid
	20	King, v.407
	21	Ibid

22		RG25, v.1860
23		King, v.369
24		RG2, 7C
21	25	Ralston, v.49
	26	DHist 593.023(D1)
22	27	DHist 325.009(D516)
	28	RG33/120
25	1	Crerar
26	2	W0106/2409
	3	Ibid
	4	Ibid
27	5	Ibid
	6	Ibid
28	7	Ibid
	8	Ibid
29	9	Ibid
31	1	Power
	2	King
32	3	Crerar

33 4 RG33/120
  5 RG2, 7C
  6 RG33/120
  7 Ibid
  8 Ibid
34 9 Ibid
 10 RG2, 7C

36 1 W0106/2409
37 2 Butler
  3 W0106/2409
38 4 RG25
39 5 RG33/120
  6 Ibid
  7 Crerar
40 8 Ibid
41 9 RG33/120
 10 Ibid
 11 Ibid

44 1 RG33/120
  2 Ibid
45 3 Ibid
  4 Ibid
46 5 Ibid
47 6 DHist 111.1009(D2)
  7 King, v.394

49 1 Stacey
50 2 111.13(D66)
52 3 RG33/120

58 1 RG24/15291
59 2 DHist 111.13(D56)
  3 RG33/120
  4 Ibid
60 5 Ibid
  6 Ibid
62 7 RG24/15229
63 8 RG33/120
64 9 Ibid
 10 Ibid
65 11 Ibid
 12 Ibid
 13 Ralston, v.67
66 14 RG33/120

67 1 RG33/120
68 2 Ibid
  3 Ibid
  4 Ibid
  5 Ibid
  6 Ibid
69 7 Ibid
  8 RG2, 7C
  9 RG33/120
 10 Ibid
 11 Ibid
70 12 DHist 593.(D2)
 13 DHist 593.(D16)
 14 RG33/120
72 15 Ibid
73 16 Ibid
 17 Ibid

74 18 DHist 593.(D2)
 19 RG33/120
75 20 Ibid
 21 Ibid
 22 Ibid
76 23 Ibid
 24 Drew, v.172
77 25 Ibid
 26 Crerar
78 27 RG33/120

80 1 RG33/120

87 24 RG33/120
88 25 Ralston, v.69
 26 Ibid, v.70
89 27 Ibid

93 1 Stacey

95 1 DHist 593.(D4)
96 2 RG33/120
97 3 DHist 593.(D1)
  4 DHist 593.(D2)
  5 RG25
98 6 Stacey
  7 Ibid
  8 DHist 593.(D16)
  9 RG25
 10 DHist 593.(D15)
99 11 DHist 593.(D16)
 12 DHist 593.(D4)
 13 DHist 593.018(D3)
 14 DHist 593.(D37)
 15 DHist 593.(D4)
100 16 King, v.394
 17 RG33/120
 18 Ibid
 19 RG25, v.2865
101 20 DHist 593.013(D5)
 21 Ibid
 22 King, v.394
 23 Ibid

102 1 RG33/120
103 2 DHist 352.009(D1)
  3 Ibid
  4 King, v.283
  5 RG2, 7C
  6 DHist 111.13(D74)
104 7 King, v.407
  8 RG33/120
  9 DHist 325.09(D156)
 10 " 314.009(D156)
105 11 Drew
 12 RG25
 13 RG2, 7C
106 14 DHist 593.013(D5)
 15 DHist 593.013(D21)
 16 DHist 593.023(D1)
107 17 DHist 002.11(D31)
 18 DHist 840.013(D2)

108 1 Lindsay
111 2 Ibid
112 3 Stacey
  4 DHist 593(D2)
113 5 W0106/2409

119 1 DHist 593.(D4)
  2 RG2, PC8020
120 3 DHist 593.(D16)
  4 RG25
  5 DHist 593.(D4)
121 6 Ibid
  7 DHist 593.018(D3)
  8 DHist 593.(D4)
122 9 DHist 593.(D2)
 10 DHist 593.(D37)
 11 Ibid
 12 DHist 593.(D14)
 13 W0106/2409
123 14 Ibid
 15 Ibid
 16 Ibid
 17 Ibid
124 18 Ibid
 19 Ibid
 20 Ibid
 21 DHist 002.011(D31)
125 22 Lindsay
 23 DHist 593.(D3)

127 1 Stacey
129 2 DHist 002.011(D31)
  3 Stacey
131 4 DHist 002.011(D31)
  5 DHist 593.013(D7)
132 6 DHist 002.011(D31)
  7 DHist 593.013(D37)
  8 DHist 002.011(D31)
134 9 DHist 982.013(D4)
 10 DHist 593(D12)
135 11 DHist 593(D3)
 12 DHist 593(D4)

136 1 DHist 593(D15)
137 2 DHist 593(D3)
  3 DHist 593(D1)
142 4 Ibid
143 5 DHist 593(D4)
  6 Carew 1 & Ferguson
  7 DHist 593(D17)
144 8 Ibid
  9 DHist 593(D37)
 10 DHist 593(D3)

146 1 DHist 593(D1)
  2 Stacey
  3 Ibid
148 4 DHist 593(D3)
150 5 DHist 593.08(D3)
152 6 DHist 593(D3)
  7 Ibid
155 8 Ibid
  9 Ibid
156 10 Lindsay

157 11 DHist 593(D3)
160 12 DHist 982.011(D1)
161 13 Stacey
163 14 DHist 593(D33)

168 1 Lindsay
    2 DHist 593(D3)

173 1 Lindsay
    2 DHist 002.011(D3)
176 3 DHist 593.013(D7)
177 4 Lindsay

178 1 Churchill
179 2 Stacey
182 3 DHist 982.011(D1)

189 1 DHist 593(D3)
190 2 Ibid
192 3 DHist 002.011(D3)

193 1 DHist 001.011(D3)
194 2 Ibid
196 3 Ibid
    4 Ibid
    5 DHist 593(D3)
    6 Ibid
    7 Lindsay

202 1 DHist 593(D12)
204 2 DHist 593(D33)
    3 Lindsay
    4 Ibid
206 5 DHist 593.013(D7)
    6 DHist 352.009(D1)
208 7 King, v.407
    8 DHist 593.013(D21)
    9 Butler

215 1 RG2, 7C
216 2 DHist 593.013(D21)
    3 Ibid
217 4 King, v.394
    5 RG2, 7C
    6 King, v.394
    7 King, v.369
218 8 RG24/2203
    9 Ibid
    10 Ralston, v.71
    11 RG24/2865
219 12 Penny
    13 RG24/5823
    14 King, v.371
220 15 RG2, 7C
    16 DHist 111.12(D72)
    17 Ralston, v.90
221 18 King, v.395
    19 Ibid
    20 Ibid
222 21 Hanson, v.83
223 22 King, v.395
    23 Hanson, v.83
224 24 Ibid
    25 DHist 352.009(D1)
    26 Hanson, v.83
    27 King, v.395
    28 Drew, v.166
225 29 Ibid
    30 Ibid
    31 DHist 111.13(D66)
    32 Ralston, v.49
    33 King, v.395
226 34 King, v.394
227 35 RG25
    36 Drew, v.166

228 1 DHist 593(D33)
229 2 DHist 352.009(D1)
230 3 DHist 112.1(D56)
    4 DHist 111.13(D66)
231 5 DHist 002.011(D3)
    6 W0106/2401A
233 7 DHist 593(D12)
234 8 Lindsay
235 9 Carew 1 & 2

237 1 H of C Sess.
238 2 Ibid
    3 Ibid
    4 Ibid
    5 Ibid
239 6 Ibid
    7 Richardson
240 8 Ibid
    9 *Hansard*
    10 *Hansard*
    11 *Hansard*
241 12 Ibid
    13 *Vancouver Province*
    14 Ibid
    15 *Hansard*
    16 *Hansard*
242 17 RG2, PC4267
    18 H of C Sess.
243 19 Ibid
    20 *Victoria Times*
244 21 *Hansard*
    22 Richardson
    23 *Victoria Times*
    24 Richardson
245 25 *Hansard*
    26 *Hansard*
246 27 H of C Sess.

Index

People

Abbot, Hon. Douglas; 240
Adams, Pte J.H.; 214
Arita, (Japanese Foreign Minister); 17, 18
Atkinson, Capt. F.T.; 155

Bailie, Maj; 183, 187, 193, 194
Banfill, Capt. S.M.; 135, 143, 144, 148,
    150, 154, 156
Barron, Gen; 6, 7
Bartholemew, Gen A.W.; 7, 8, 113
Berteau, Col Gerald; 64
Berzenski, L/Cpl G.; 214
Billings, Capt G.M.; 70, 98, 136, 177
Birkett, Lt G.A.; 158-160
Bishop, Maj W.A.; 142, 143, 151-154,
    169, 180, 198
Blackwell, Lt T.A., 160, 162, 182
Blaver, Lt C.A.; 95, 155
Bowman, Capt A.S.; 162, 182
Bracken, Hon. John; 240
Brooke-Popham, Sir Robert; 10, 11, 12,
    36, 113
Browne, Maj-Gen B.W.; 71
Bumpas, (or Bompas), Capt; 152-155, 232
Bush, Capt H.S.A.; 70, 97, 99, 177, 194,
    218

Campbell, George; 222, 224
Campbell, Lt; 163
Chiang Kai Shek; 15, 27-29, 37, 38, 219
Churchill, Winston; 11, 20, 26-28, 37, 98,
    103, 104, 113, 178, 217
Clarke, Capt; 155
Clarke, Col F.W.; 218
Claxton, Hon. Brooke; 240, 241
Clayton, Sgt; 154
Coldwell, M.J.; 240
Collinson, Cmdro; 134
Connor, D.C.; 82-84
Cooke, P.B.; 83, 85, 86
Corrigan, Lt L.B.; 163
Craigie, Sir Robert; 102, 103, 105
Crerar, Maj-Gen H.D.G.; 24, 25, 32, 33,
    39-43, 45, 46, 67, 69, 77, 100

Davies, Capt R.M.; 165
D'Avignon, Maurice; 246
Denison, Lt-Col R.; 75
Dennison, Capt; 95
Dewing, Col; 99
Diefenbaker, John; 242, 243

Dill, Sir John; 26, 36
Doi, Col; 117, 131, 132, 148, 158, 160,
    165, 166, 170, 176, 177, 182, 183, 192,
    194, 199, 203, 205, 208, 232
Douglas, T.C.; 60, 72, 224, 225
Drew, George; 2, 73, 74, 76, 77, 100, 102,
    105, 220-227
Duff, Sir Lyman; 2, 57, 65, 77-81, 85-87,
    90-93, 104, 221-223, 225-227

Earnshaw, Brig Philip; 62, 63
Eckert, Rev. B.C.; 218
Eden, Anthony; 37, 38, 102, 226, 227
Ellis, Pte P.J.; 214

Fearon, Lois; 144
Findlay, Lt; 81, 83
Fleming, Rfln; 75
Foulkes, Gen C.; 50, 92, 227, 230
French, Lt; 158, 159

Gamey, Lt-Col J.C.; 76
Gavey, Capt; 152
Gibson, Col; 39, 68, 69
Gooday, Maj C.; 75
Goodenough, Sgt M.T.; 180
Graham, Lt-Col; 59, 72
Grasett, Maj-Gen A.E.; 8-10, 24-29, 35-37,
    39, 40, 42, 108
Gray, Rfln; 151
Gresham, Maj; 159
Grey, Maj G.E.; 128, 129
Groos, David; 243, 244
Gwynne, Maj; 82, 85, 97, 98

Hanson, R.B.; 74, 221-224
Hart, Adm T.S.; 107
Heeney, A.D.P.; 103
Hellyer, Paul; 243
Henderson, Col; 80
Hennessy Col Pat; 69-72, 74, 75, 96, 165,
    179, 194, 217
Herridge, H.W.; 243
Hirohito, Emperor; 22
Hobbs, Maj A.M.K.; 105
Hodkinson, Maj E.; 162-164, 205
Home, Lt-Col W.J.; 50, 51, 63, 64, 70, 71,
    74, 95-97, 99, 135, 166, 168, 179, 185,
    196, 197, 189, 190, 234, 235
Hull, Cordell; 18, 105
Hurd, Lionel; 242

Units